A Normal Life

A Memoir

Kim Rich

Author of *Johnny's Girl*

ALASKA
NORTHWEST
BOOKS®

Library of Congress Cataloging-in-Publication Data is available.

ISBN 978-1-94-332850-5 (paperback)
ISBN 978-1-94-332851-2 (e-book)
ISBN 978-1-94-332852-9 (hardbound)

Edited by Carol Sturgulewski

Front Cover: background by dikobraziy/Sutterstock.com
Back Cover: author photograph by Karley Nugent

Published by Alaska Northwest Books®
An imprint of

GRAPHIC ARTS
BOOKS®

GraphicArtsBooks.com

Proudly distributed by Ingram Publisher Services.

Graphic Arts Books
Publishing Director: Jennifer Newens
Marketing Manager: Angela Zbornik
Editor: Olivia Ngai
Design & Production: Rachel Lopez Metzger

For Charlotte, Kristan & Mary

Contents

Introduction

This book is for my children. But it is about me and, more important, about my generation. It is about the time when I grew up—the 1960s and 1970s.

My peers and I are not Baby Boomers (though demographers lump us together), nor are we Generation X. We grew up around stay-at-home moms, proud homemakers. We graduated high school expecting to have high-powered, successful careers instead.

I like to think of us as the Transitional Generation, too young to rebel and be hippies but too old to be on the forefront of the digital revolution. Some of us dressed like hippies, but few of my friends actually went off to live on a commune or got on "the bus." But we read about it. Some of us even aspired to it—for a while.

This book also serves another purpose—to pick up where my first memoir left off. My book *Johnny's Girl* captured my unconventional childhood as the only child of a professional gambler, John F. "Johnny" Rich, and my beautiful and doomed mother, Frances "Ginger" Chiaravalle Rich. My parents were both the black sheep of their respective families, and both died tragically and young.

My mother, a sometimes exotic dancer who aspired to be a model, spent most of her life in a state mental institution. I last saw her, briefly, when I was nine; she died of cancer five years later. My father was murdered a year after that, a victim of his life in Anchorage's increasingly ruthless underworld. At age fifteen, I became an orphan.

Looking back, it seems only natural that I would become a journalist and writer. That career choice was determined the day I learned my father was dead. On that day, I promised myself, "Someday I will write about him."

And then I walked away from everything and anyone who had anything to do with him. I was determined to live a normal life—whatever that might be.

After decades of searching for that life, I fulfilled my promise. *Johnny's Girl* was published in 1993. It was reviewed by the *New York Times* and adapted by Hallmark into a TV movie. I can still catch it on cable now and then. The book is still available in paperback.

Johnny's Girl ends not long after my father's death. Many people have asked what happened to me since.

I began this book to answer that question. But then I realized it served a larger purpose.

A friend once described me as a motherless child. Orphaned as a teenager, I have fought a lifelong yearning for something lost. Writing this book, I began to reflect on all the choices I've had to make on my own, all the battles I've fought, all the times I've tried to be there for my children when no one was there for me.

So, girls—Charlotte, Kristan, and Mary—this is about who I am and how I became your mother. This is why your mom acts like a nut sometimes, why I lose my temper on occasion, and mostly why, to your horror, I ask your friends too many questions.

Your mom has always loved a party, a good story, and all three of you.

CHAPTER I

Neverland

Not long ago, I met an old friend from Alaska for coffee in Los Angeles, where I was visiting family. Brent and I knew each other as teens. For what seemed forever, I had an overwhelming and obvious crush on his brother, much to his brother's dismay. I was not the girl everyone wanted to date. With naturally curly brown hair and no hair dryer (and no idea how to use one), I didn't fit the Farrah Fawcett blown-dry, swept-back blonde look popular at the time.

If I had someone to show me how to make my hair look like that, I might have tried. But I was raised by my dad, with intermittent influence from his cocktail-waitress or topless-dancer girlfriends, and one wonderful second wife who lasted less than a year, when my father's explosive rage drove her away. The girlfriends were not much help in the "how to be a girl" department. Go-go boots and fringe and pasties? I don't think so.

In junior high school, I thought Brent was too good-looking for me. He was also a really nice guy, then and now. He is the kind of friend who would race out of his house at nearly the last minute and drive across LA to catch a quick cup of coffee with an old friend. I hadn't seen him in about forty years. Forty years.

I brought two of my young teen daughters with me—a mistake, Brent and I realized as soon as we sat down to reminisce.

The two of us grew up in Anchorage in perhaps one of the toughest eras to be a teen in America, right after the Sixties. The decades—and their pop cultural influences—don't neatly start and end when the calendar turns over. The turbulence and challenges of the late Sixties snowballed into the following decade, picking us up along the way.

"Oh, God, Kimmy, remember all the parties—ah, I mean, ah..."

"Bible group meetings?"

Our conversation drifted into reliving get-togethers—ah, parties... ummm, Bible study sessions—where we would listen to Led Zeppelin.

"Your mom and I never..." Brent said, turning to the girls in the middle of our conversation.

"Oh, God, no," I muttered, shaking my head in case they might have been paying attention. Never fear. Their heads were buried in their smartphone screens.

So, Brent and I took the G-rated journey down memory lane that night. We marveled how we'd both gone to the first concert we had ever been to—Jefferson Airplane. I was twelve, I think, and in seventh grade. I went with a woman friend of my dad's.

At one point, Brent turned to my two daughters and said, "Your mom was a rebel!"

They smiled politely and returned to their smartphones and videos.

I was struck by the label. *Rebel*. Me?

All I ever wanted was a normal life.

THE LAST TIME I had seen Brent, and many of my friends from junior high school, was late summer 1973. That August, my father was kidnapped and murdered.

That was the end of anything resembling a normal teen life.

The police didn't make any arrests of his captors and killers until November. That fall, I lived a life I can only describe as akin to the Lost Boys in J.M. Barrie's *Peter Pan*.

I lived in Neverland.

Before my father's disappearance, he spent most of his time at the living quarters in one of his "massage parlors." I was left at our house—a large, two-story, ugly brown mess of a place at 736 East Twelfth Avenue. It was also known as the 736 Club, the name of the after-hours gambling parlor he operated there when I entered middle school.

Most kids want to live in a candy shop. I got a casino.

I hated the place from the moment we moved in. It was always dark inside. There were few windows, and except for one window in the kitchen, they had all been boarded up by my dad or closed with tight shades. He wanted to keep prying eyes from seeing the illegal activities going on inside.

Even my sole bedroom window was boarded up. To this day, I do not close curtains or blinds during the day in any house where I live. I cannot stand to be shut in. I don't even close up my house after dark.

Even now, I have nightmares about the place. The dreams are always the same: I am back in that house, which is usually remodeled and made to look so different that it's unrecognizable. Unrecognizable to anyone but me, that is. In these dreams, I know what lies under the shiny new furnishings. In these dreams, I wonder at whatever form the house has taken, marvel at how it doesn't look the same, and feel a vague sense of unease, disorientation, and fear that one day I might end up there again.

IN THE EARLY 1970s, Anchorage was a hard-working town of about 147,000 people. Its slapdash post-war, post-earthquake buildings hunkered between the majestic peaks of the Chugach Mountains and the muddy waters of Cook Inlet. The entire state was poised to begin making big money working on the Trans-Alaska Pipeline System. My dad was ready to make big money off the workers.

When I was twelve or thirteen, the 736 Club opened every morning after the bars closed, around 5 a.m. It stayed open until late morning or until everyone left. The illegal gambling club was set up in two connected rooms that made up what must have originally been the home's dining room and living room. My dad hung a colored beaded curtain to divide the two. *Tasteful*, I thought.

In the first room were secondhand couches where patrons sat, drank, and relaxed. The other room had a craps table and large poker table. When not in use, the poker table wore a laminated wood cover my father would slip on to protect the table's expensive padded green surface. In my memory, the rooms are crowded, smoky, noisy.

By the time I was fifteen, the 736 Club was no longer operating. Arguments between my dad and me had grown more frequent, and he became physically violent. I left the house and went to the authorities. I returned when he promised to close the club and seek counseling for his anger issues.

While my dad spent most of his time keeping an eye on business at the massage parlors, he still kept a bedroom at our house. Another bedroom was mine, and my dad's friend, Al, and his girlfriend lived in the third. Al was a longtime friend who parented me perhaps more than my father ever had. He got me up for school. He got me off to my after-school job at the nearby gas station. He cooked dinner every night. Al and I remain close to this day.

But after my father's kidnapping, Al was gone, pushed out by my dad's last wife, Bridget. They had just married that summer, when she was pregnant. Bridget didn't stay long either, perhaps because we did not get along. She was barely seventeen, about a year older than me.

My dad routinely dated gorgeous women—cocktail waitresses and topless dancers and strippers and such. Bridget looked twenty-one or older. She'd been on the streets for years, which probably gave everyone—including my dad—the impression she was old enough. Just barely. Her convoluted life included the baby born after my father disappeared, a child who was believed to be my father's son.

Bridget was my own version of a fairy-tale evil stepmother. Soon after it was clear my father wasn't coming home, Bridget moved in some friends of hers to rent one of the bedrooms. They were a couple. A man and a woman. They were also heroin addicts; he was a pimp, and she worked as a prostitute.

My friends and I called them "the vampires" because they only came out after dark. We managed to avoid them most of the time; thankfully, they weren't interested in socializing with teenagers. When they finally moved out, they left the carpeting littered with bloodied cotton balls and empty syringes.

I started school that fall on my own, but soon Bridget came around and tried to parent me. I would have none of it, because she was also looking for the Social Security checks that came in the mail for me after my mother's death a year earlier.

We would fight, and she would threaten to "call the authorities" and have me picked up and thrown into juvenile detention or foster care. Of course, I had no business living without adult supervision—I'll give her that. But I'd be damned if that supervision came from her.

It wasn't long before she, too, disappeared from my life, as well she should have. She had been a heroin addict before meeting my father and became one again after his disappearance.

So, while everyone who gave it any thought at all probably assumed Johnny's new wife was taking care of Kim, Kim took care of herself.

That winter, other runaway and castaway teens came and went from the house on hearing from one friend or the other that it was an adult-free zone. Some stayed a day or more, some longer. The whole place came to look like an average teenage room—a mess. I'm neat and clean, but somehow the house fell into chaos, with clothes, shoes, even garbage strewn about.

Whenever anyone had some money, we might walk across the street to the grocery store and get some things. A big splurge would be to go over to Mark's Drive-In to buy the "Mark's Special," a hamburger, fries, and milkshake. But mostly our pockets—and the cupboards and refrigerator—were empty.

I have gone hungry twice in my life. The first was when I was about six. I can't remember whether it was for just a morning, a whole day, or longer, but no one seemed to be around to make me anything to eat. My mother was in bed, having fallen into a deep depression and probably a psychosis, as she slowly slipped into schizophrenia. I ate all the frosting off a cake in our fridge. Later I dumped a box of tapioca in a bowl, added water, and ate it.

The second time was that fall of 1973.

I got by somehow on the money I made at my after-school job at the gas station. The utility bills just went unpaid until six months later, when I finally left the house once and for all.

How I hated that house. I would have friends drop me off down the street so no one could see where I lived. I felt depressed about my life, and why not? I was a fifteen-year-old girl, full of angst and self-loathing, with a toilet that had stopped working in the house's only bathroom.

Fortunately, it was the middle of winter, and the temperatures were below freezing. My response to the toilet problem was to scoop the toilet bowl contents into a mop bucket using an old kitchen ladle. Then I'd take the slop to the carport on the side of the house and set the bucket there to freeze. Later, I'd dump it upside down and do it all over again, leaving the frozen and growing blob of sewage to sit there until the spring thaw.

This could have gone for days or weeks. I don't recall. Ironically, I was a clean kid. Before my dad disappeared, I had always kept our house tidy.

SOMEHOW, I MANAGED to get up every day and go to school for my tenth-grade classes at East High School. My bus was full of African-American students from Fairview, Anchorage's largely black neighborhood.

I was scared to death the first time I got on the bus. I had no friends from the neighborhood, never had any. Fairview was full of government housing projects and low-income housing and some modest, working-class homes. Many of my fellow East High students on my bus were streetwise; like me, many were veterans of lousy childhoods.

One day, I mouthed off to the bus driver over something. That drew the attention of one tough black girl who intimidated me. But after that, she decided I was all right, and we sat together from then on.

At school, I kept my head down in class and did my work. I enjoyed art class the most, where a kind teacher named Bonnie, with long, blonde hair and a gentle nature, looked after me.

When home, I did what teens do—I listened to music a lot and talked on the phone. I recall listening over and over again to Neil Young's two albums *Harvest* and *Everybody Knows This Is Nowhere*.

I'd sing along to the former; the latter certainly described life at the new 736 Club, home to wayward teens.

I might not have made it through those months if not for my best friend at the time, Dean.

Dean and I began hanging out in middle school. I was friends with his younger sister, René, and became close to their family: their mom, Sue, her husband, Bernie, and two adorable little brothers, who I would sometimes babysit.

Then and for years after, Sue was like a mom to me; René, a sister; and the younger boys were like my little brothers.

Dean had dark hair worn in a short ponytail. He was handsome, with a little air of mystery, having spent some time in a juvenile facility for some minor behavioral issues.

I initially had a crush on him, as did many girls. But until my late teens, when we went out for a short while, we were always just friends. Good friends.

In 1973, Dean's family moved to Seattle, and he went to Oklahoma to live with an older brother. Dean was half Cherokee Indian on his mother's side. If he graduated from high school in Oklahoma, he could go to college tuition-free, he told me.

But then he learned my father was missing. One day, I heard a knock on the door, and there he stood.

He came back to stay at the house that fall until he couldn't miss any more school and had to go back.

It was a relief to have someone I could rely on in that house.

That Thanksgiving, Dean's mother had a friend stop to check on me and deliver a turkey. I was embarrassed when I let him in. For the first time, I realized how deplorable the place looked. That nice man didn't even blink. He just smiled and gave no indication of the horror he surely must have felt seeing me alone in that house full of debris and neglect.

THERE WERE MOMENTS that winter when a normal life seemed possible. For Christmas, Dean's family bought me a ticket to spend the holiday with them in Seattle. It remains a cherished memory. Sue and Bernie bought René and me a generous number of matching gifts, including clothing and jewelry. It was one the best Christmases I had ever had.

When I turned sixteen in, friends planned a birthday party for me. They created a restaurant-like atmosphere in the living room of the 736 Club, complete with a waiter and a home-cooked meal.

But the real Sweet Sixteen party was the one I planned.

Some of the Lost Boys, as I now call them (some of whom were girls), had moved on from the 736 Club, but I had plenty of friends in high school. Somehow, I got the notion that I would screen the film *Woodstock* for my birthday. This was back before videos were available, but I learned I could rent the actual film (which came in several reels) and a projector from a local company that rented educational films to schools.

Some friends and I hung a white sheet across a wall in the large living room at 736 and then watched in amazement as an overflowing crowd showed up. The living room became a sea of teens from all over town crowded wall-to-wall throughout the two-story house. It was like

Dean "Andy" Mathis, hunting in Oklahoma, mid-1970s. Dean was my best friend my freshman and sophomore year of high school. He and his family were like my own before and after my father's death.

Me and René, Dean's sister and my best friend since seventh grade. This photo was taken in their home in Seattle in 1973, when they brought me down for Christmas. René and I remain close.

any teen party scene held at a teen's home, except in this case the parents weren't merely away; they were never coming back. That cold night in February, we—the youngest of the Woodstock generation—partied like it was 1974.

Despite a huge group of teens doing what teens did at parties like this—play music really loud and drink alcohol—the cops never showed up. That was probably because the house sat in an area partially zoned for commercial development: Al's Body Shop was across the street, the Tesoro gas station where I worked was next door, and Mark's Drive-In was on the corner. There were no neighbors to disturb, no neighbors to watch us—or watch out for me.

CLEARLY, AT SOME POINT, I needed rescuing. Eventually, the cavalry showed up.

One day late in the school year, I was called from class into the counseling office to find a beautiful woman with stylish blonde hair dressed in a fur coat and in no way looking like what she was—a state social worker.

Her name was Michael Giesler and she saved my life that day. She told me my seventeen-year-old stepmother had called their office, saying I was a delinquent. Considering the source, they knew that might not be true, but they did realize at last that no one knew what was happening to this sixteen-year-old orphan.

It wasn't long before I had a court-appointed guardian to help with legal affairs, medical and dental care through the State of Alaska, and a clothing allowance. I was assigned to live at the homes of friends of my choosing.

Aside from the social stigma of my dad's businesses and death, I must have been a pretty good teen. Or they didn't know better. A friend once noted that I was the perfect houseguest: I always picked up after myself, dove in with cleaning, left any room better than I found it. She surmised I learned that after being a guest in so many homes.

I don't think she meant that was a good thing.

I had little oversight, I guess, because unlike many teens in state custody, I didn't get in trouble. I was easy to manage. Beginning the spring of 1974, I had several families whose homes were opened to me, then and forever after: Floyd and Hazel Johnson, Marianne "Mike" and Earl "Red" Dodge, and Rod and Donella Bain.

It wasn't as if things were quiet at their homes. The Dodge and the Johnson families each had six children; the Bains had four. They were solid homes where the dads worked outside the home and the moms were housewives. But the women were, then and now, role models to me. All were smart and adventurous for the times. Hazel Johnson was a World War II army vet (rare for women back then), a member of the League of

Earl "Red" and Marianne "Mike" Dodge. They took me in as a teen despite having six kids of their own.

Donella and Rod Bain, who helped care and house me after my father's death.

Woman Voters, and a community volunteer who read voraciously. Mike Dodge had a bachelor's degree in physics that saw its expression in her oldest son's graduation from the Massachusetts Institute of Technology. Donella Bain was a kind and articulate person who didn't seem concerned when her daughter brought me home one day to stay with them.

Rod Bain was a school teacher and World War II hero, having been a sergeant in Easy Company—the "Band of Brothers" (part of the 506th Parachute Infantry Regiment, 101st Airborne Division) made famous in historian Stephen E. Ambrose's 1993 book and the celebrated miniseries.

Floyd Johnson was a forester who had traveled with his family to Iran at one point for his work on reforestation. Red Dodge was then a captain with Western Airlines. Both these men were also World War II vets, and Dodge had flown dangerous bombing missions in the Pacific.

In addition, the state-appointed guardian was on hand to watch over my "business affairs." He was a friend of a friend, a divorced father of two young children, and one of the most protective and important friends in this period of my life. Walt Morgan came from a longtime Anchorage family. He was an entrepreneur: he ran a bike shop, a janitorial service, a landscaping business, a commercial house painting business, and more. Throughout my teen and college years, I could always find work with Walt and later, whenever I needed it, a home and place to stay.

But more than anything, Walt was a devoted father, sharing custody of his two children with their mother. Some of my first lessons in good parenting came from watching Walt with his son and daughter.

Walt is one of the funniest people I know and a prankster who was always setting up elaborate jokes. When he sold his janitorial business, part of the deal said that he got the buyer's luxury black sedan. As I walked downtown one night, the black sedan pulled up alongside me, the side windows came down, and as if it were a Mob hit, I was pummeled with

Walt Morgan, my court-appointed guardian ad litem and friend who helped take care of me for years.

snowballs.

The Bains, Johnsons, Dodges, and Morgans became my foundation. I couldn't have asked for better homes. No matter how many times I came and went, their doors remained open.

Maybe this, more than anything else, helped me grow up more or less the way I longed for—normal.

ONE RESULT OF THE *Woodstock* party was my introduction to a new group of people. I attended East High, but students from all across Anchorage showed up. One contingent was a group of shaggy-haired, casually dressed kids. They were into the outdoors, hiking, and cross-country skiing. Their parents listened to folk music and the Beatles, were professionals and even politicians.

I felt instantly at home with this group. I was fond of my friends from East High, but with the death of my dad, I wasn't drawn to the normal football game/prom/student government way of life. These new friends would take me in a different direction.

Not long after the *Woodstock* party, Bridget reappeared. I was living with the Johnsons when she called and announced that she had sold everything in my father's house. Walt Morgan and I drove over to Twelfth Street, packed up my belongings, and left. I never saw Bridget after that, and I never again had to deal with the 736 Club.

It was a relief.

CHAPTER 2

Peaceful, Easy Feeling

By summer 1974, at just sixteen, I was ready to leave Alaska and go see America. My destination: Phoenix, Arizona.

I picked Arizona because of a new friend named David Ray.

David was in Anchorage for a brief stay before flying to Phoenix, after working a season at a remote Alaska fish processing plant. A mutual friend introduced us because David needed a place to stay and there was room at my house.

A few years older than me, David took to me like a big brother. Of average build, David had long brown hair he wore down or in a ponytail, was soft-spoken and easygoing, and spoke warmly of his hometown and the American Southwest.

David had heard me talk so much about my dream of going to the Lower 48 that one evening he pulled me aside. He talked about his parents and an older sister and her family who all lived in Phoenix. He said I'd have a place to stay, and more than that—a home with him and his family.

He then did something I've never forgotten—he pulled out a $100 bill.

I was floored. That was a huge amount of money to a teen at the time.

"This is to help you get down there," he said.

I promptly put the money in my bank account and used it later to help pay for my trip.

I WAS ALSO DRAWN TO ARIZONA and the desert by the fact that nearly all of my favorite bands or singers had songs about the area. I wanted to stand on a corner in Winslow, Arizona, as singer/songwriter Jackson Browne had written.

My plan was to hitchhike down the West Coast with a friend named Greg, the older brother of my eighth-grade boyfriend, who had moved to the San Francisco Bay Area with his mom a couple of years earlier.

Greg was going to see his family. Our itinerary called for flying to Seattle then going from there.

We had a big send-off the night we were to catch our red-eye flight. In the handful of grainy-looking color photographs that still exist, we're with the dozen or more friends who showed up to say goodbye. We all looked like hippies, with flowing hair, flannel shirts, blue jeans, and hiking boots.

We all posed for one photo; others show Greg and me preparing to walk down the jetway to board our plane. In still another, I am alone on a padded vinyl bench, writing in my journal. I do not look happy. Perhaps whoever took the photo interrupted my writing, or maybe I had already had the first of many fights with Greg.

Our plan was to fly to Seattle then hitchhike to San Jose, California, where Greg was headed to join his brother and mom. On the way, we stayed at a youth hostel in Eugene, Oregon, where I visited a friend at college.

That first trip emphasized the distance I felt between my Alaska home and the rest of America. Years later, my film director friend John Kent Harrison, a Canadian by birth, quoted a fellow Canadian about growing up above the contiguous forty-eight states: "It was like living in the attic of a house having a party." And boy, what a party. Everything about America fascinated me, and it still does.

Anchorage International Airport, Summer 1974. While waiting to catch a red-eye to Seattle, I took some time out to scribble in the journal I kept at the time.

Greg and I turn around for one last shot before boarding our flight.

That trip introduced me to the vast natural beauty of California, a state I have seen more of than Alaska, in part because most of Alaska is not accessible by road. Over the years, I've driven the coast highway from Oregon to Los Angeles, and I've driven straight through the middle on I-5. I've spent time in Northern California, in the redwoods around Mount Shasta. I've driven to Lake Tahoe, visited a friend's farm in the mountains around Ukiah, gone to the wine country, San Francisco, Silicon Valley, Santa Cruz, Pismo Beach, Santa Barbara, and so on. Sometimes, it all blurs together.

But I have distinct memories of that first trip, including our first night in Northern California. We made it to Redding and got a hotel room. After settling in, I turned on the late-night TV news. The weather announcer reported the temperature was one hundred degrees.

One. Hundred. Degrees. At midnight.

I ran outside and looked up at the stars. Never before had I experienced one hundred degrees. At midnight. I loved it.

I've long joked that my bones are made of permafrost, the part of the Arctic ground that never completely thaws. In Alaska, if it's dark, it's always cold. If it's warm, it's always light. To be warm—even hot—in the middle of the night was an entirely new sensation to me.

Days later, at a party with my old boyfriend and his friends in San

Jose, I stepped outside again to take in the night heat. As I stood there, I could hear Lynyrd Skynyrd's "Free Bird" blasting from inside. In the mid-1970s, that song got played late in the night at every party.

I was an Alaska-raised girl standing in California, where I was born, listening to a rock band from Alabama. The moment was not lost on me. It was one of my first lessons in the power of music as a unifying experience.

Later that trip, Greg and I spent a long, hot day hitchhiking to Santa Cruz to go to the boardwalk and ride the Giant Dipper, the wooden roller coaster. That was all we talked about on the way, but once there, I looked up at the rumbling monster and declared "no way" was I getting on. I repeated this all through the long line, right up until I managed to make myself step aboard.

What happened became a life lesson: I loved it. I loved it so much that when the ride ended, I asked if I could go again.

Ever since, whenever I find myself balking at something—any new adventure, project, or life transition—I tell myself it's like standing in line at the Giant Dipper. It's all fear and anxiety and caution, and then you just do it.

As PLANNED, Greg stayed behind in California and I took a bus the rest of the way to Phoenix.

From the moment I arrived in Arizona by bus from California, I was hooked. I loved the hot desert climate. I would bask, if only momentarily, in the end of summer's excessive heat. In October, a friend called from Anchorage to describe the winter snow and cold. I was still wearing shorts, and it was seventy-plus degrees.

One of the few downsides of the desert was scorpions. I learned to hate them after staying with friends at an old farmhouse on the outskirts of Phoenix. When I arrived and was shown to my room, I noted something odd about the twin bed.

"Why are the legs sitting in glass jars?" I asked.

"So the scorpions can't climb up into the bed," my host said.

I dreamed of giant scorpions every night after that. I slept fitfully, clutching my bedcovers in the fear that they would fall to the ground and the scorpions would find their way up to me.

Soon, I had plenty of other things to distract me. Arizona was the center for much of the New Age/hippie/Eastern mysticism/Eastern religious thinking seeping into American popular culture. In the mid-Seventies, Arizona offered new ideas about everything from what to wear to what to eat, believe, and read.

In just a few months, I was wearing all white: long gauze skirts, white peasant tops, and sandals, almost like a yogi. I tried fasting for days on only apples. I'd never been so miserable, and it was years before I could eat apples again.

I began practicing yoga with *Lilias, Yoga and You*, a TV show on PBS hosted by Lilias Folan. My friends and I hiked in the mountains surrounding Phoenix at night, under a full moon.

It was a time when hippie men began apprenticing in the silver and turquoise jewelry trade as the state's many large and small turquoise mines experienced a boom. I came to appreciate the different kinds of turquoise and Native American culture and arts and crafts. I learned to enjoy desert ecology and nature. I found those in Arizona had the same affinity for wild places that my little hippie-ish (at least in dress) friends and I did in Alaska.

Throughout the remainder of my teens, I traveled between Arizona and Alaska. I slowly developed a style of dress and an attitude that said "hippie." Inside, though, I was still very much your all-American teenager.

My friends and I talked about living on a commune, where we would bake our own bread, make our own pottery and dishes, grow our own food, and milk our own cows. In addition to being essentially a calling for all hippies from that era, to a city kid like me who had never lived a rural lifestyle, this seemed a romantic notion.

When I say "all-American teenager," I mean I didn't fall for the hippie belief in free love. I now like to joke that such a thing was only an excuse for ugly guys to get girls to sleep with them. I still believed in saving myself for that special someone.

I once watched in horror at a party when suddenly someone announced "orgy time," and a bunch of young men and women began taking off their clothes and running around the house naked. I left.

I believed in what other young teens believed in: love, rainbows, and maybe unicorns. In Arizona, that didn't change. It wasn't as if guys were beating down the door to ask me out. I considered myself attractive, but I was never that interested in male attention. I was pretty smart and terrified of the opposite sex. While I had lots of crushes, none went anywhere.

I think my hesitation stemmed from having a father who sold sex. I grew up around women who were victims of the sex trade and nude-dancing business. Although some of them were intelligent and quite nice, and a rare few were college graduates, I knew that most were trapped in a life they hadn't chosen. That wasn't going to happen to me.

I found the hippies and the idea of getting back to nature appealing. It was a trend, but given what I grew up with at home, it made sense. It was my rebellion against my father's lifestyle and the exploitation at the 736 Club. In Arizona, I experienced a personal renaissance. I also discovered *Be Here Now*, the 1971 book on spirituality and meditation by Western-born yogi and Harvard professor Ram Dass.

PHOENIX WAS ALSO the largest city I had ever lived in (aside from Los Angeles when I was an infant). Every major rock or popular music act came through. To a teenager who practically worshipped contemporary music, Phoenix was heaven.

I got a copy of the concert schedule for one of Phoenix's landmark venues, the Celebrity Theatre, a round theater with a revolving stage and intimate setting. Everybody I listened to on the radio seemed to be coming through Phoenix the winter of 1974–75. I decided to stay.

As my original Arizona contact, David, had promised, I found a home in Phoenix. David's older sister had invited me to stay with her, her husband, and their young son. They lived in a small apartment that had only one bedroom, and yet they put me up on their couch that fall.

When that arrangement got to be too much for all of us, I met a beautiful high school sophomore who decided I was to be the sister she never had. In keeping with the times, Donna had changed her name to her chosen yoga name, Anandha Moon. I met her at a George Harrison concert in Tucson, where David took her for their first date. I was dumbstruck when I first saw her—lithe, with hip-length straight brown hair and large almond-shaped eyes, wearing a button-down 1940s-style jacket and long skirt. She was the most beautiful girl I had ever seen.

As if the meeting and the concert weren't enough, that night my two companions and I camped overnight outside Tucson. I had no idea where we were going. We arrived at a campsite way after dark. Somehow, we managed to pitch our tent, unroll our sleeping bags, and fall asleep.

In the morning, when I awoke and stepped outside, I was stunned to see that we were in the middle of Saguaro National Park. All around were towering saguaro cactuses standing like soldiers at attention.

It wasn't long after that meeting that Anandha convinced her family to let me live with them. That fall, I enrolled in the neighboring Maryvale High School. Because I had arrived late, I had to wait a few weeks for the quarter to end before I could begin classes. I went to the school library every day because I was afraid I would fall behind. There, I read magazines, books, whatever caught my interest. And I wrote, one essay after another. I wrote and wrote.

Once in school, I was invited to join the school newspaper—probably because I was new and enthusiastic and one of my teachers who advised the paper liked my work in class. Before long, I was one of its main reporters and writers. I not only did news copy, I wrote poems and essays, including one love poem for the Valentine's Day issue. Looking back, it's pretty embarrassing to read; if nothing else, I had the passionate, overwrought heart of a teen girl.

There, at Maryvale High, with its handsome campus of interconnecting indoor and outdoor halls and walkways, I got to be a carefree teen again. There, I thrived. I developed a couple of crushes—one on a quiet, handsome boy named Buck, and another with curly, shoulder-length hair named Barry. The former I helped get a poem published in the newspaper while the latter talked about finding me "hot." It was hardly the image of myself that I cultivated. I also became friends with the editing staff of the newspaper, and they invited me to their homes. To all at Maryvale High, I was just another teen—no one knew about my dad or what he had done for a living or what had happened to him. I felt free of that yoke, and an amazing thing happened: I earned straight A's in every single class. My English teacher liked one of my essays so much that she even entered it in a state competition representing the school.

My Maryvale High School ID in Phoenix.

Many of my fellow students were bored in school. I was gung-ho simply because I had experienced the absence of school, which was far more boring. I learned then that showing up was everything; just doing the work and showing some enthusiasm impressed the teachers. From the student newspaper advisor to my ceramics teacher, I got nothing but encouragement, support, and a strong belief in myself, at least for a time. I excelled and I thrived.

To the delight of one devoted art teacher, I decided to build a tall rope urn in the shape of a fish. I found a photo of an ancient Egyptian clay work with the most gorgeous turquoise-blue glaze. I was determined that my fish vase be the same color. The teacher must have worked with me for weeks to recreate a color from the time of the pharaohs.

I discovered country rock music and Linda Ronstadt, and thus began a love of singing and the desire to sing professionally.

I began to sense that I would live a life in the arts, though I wasn't sure exactly what I would be doing. Somewhere along the way, I even began to think I might end up living in a utopian society.

Anandha had friends who purchased a large chunk of land in central Arizona. Others, including Anandha, bought into what was simply called "The Land." They held meetings to plan an eco-friendly lifestyle on the wild piece of property, hoping to build homes someday for themselves, their friends, and their families.

I would go with Anandha to The Land meetings. I'd walk home from school in my long, white gauze skirt and peasant blouse, savoring the sun and heat.

That alone was a stark contrast to the life I knew in Alaska.

I should have stayed in Phoenix. But I didn't. Like any teen, I was impulsive. By the spring, I was homesick. I'm not sure how I got the money—possibly from my mother's Social Security benefits that had been coming for me since her death—but one day, on a whim, I flew home to Alaska.

Anandha and her daughter Rhianna at The Land.

CHAPTER 3

The "Hey, Wow, Man" School

I arrived home in the early spring of 1975. I had swapped Arizona's sun and heat for Alaska's gray skies and breakup, when winter's snowfall turns to slush and mud.

I felt disoriented at first; picking up and leaving Phoenix wasn't easy. Back in Anchorage, I had to find a place to live. I had no car—heck, I didn't even know how to drive. I bounced between staying with my guardian, with a friend's parents, and with a group of young people in Mountain View, one of Anchorage's poorer neighborhoods.

The group house seemed like a good idea at first. My friends were all staying together in a broken-down house that was more or less a shack. A couple of the guys living there were in a garage band. They set up their instruments in the living room, where they practiced and played for nearly nightly parties.

The place was small, crowded, and dirty. I hated living there and soon began to become disenchanted with hippies—although it would take a few more years before I abandoned the concept altogether.

Eventually I settled into living with the Dodges or the Johnsons. That fall, I enrolled in Steller Secondary School, Anchorage's alternative public school. Years later, I would refer to Steller as the "Hey, Wow, Man" school. Even so, it wasn't quite as hippie-ish as the so-called Free School some teens had created in Anchorage, where it seemed all they did was drive around together in an old van. Steller was named after eighteenth-century German scientist and explorer Georg Wilhelm Steller, who had extensively mapped Alaska's flora and fauna.

Steller was founded by civic-minded parents and veteran educators who wanted something different—a place where students learned to love learning. The school philosophy emphasized self-learning. Steller was right in line with an educational movement occurring across the country. Parents disenchanted with a traditional education worked to create schools that mirrored the youth-oriented counterculture that had begun a decade earlier. They viewed informal education—or, as they came to call it, "open education"—as an answer to both the American education system's critics and the problems of society. The focus on students learning by doing resonated with those who believed that America's formal, teacher-led classrooms were crushing students' creativity.

At Steller, that meant calling teachers by their first names, forming a student-led government to deal with discipline issues, and letting teachers create any classroom environment they wanted as long as the state-mandated curriculum was covered. Students could come and go from classrooms without hall passes.

The more relaxed atmosphere seemed perfect for me. It was at Steller that I learned to love learning. I constantly discovered new fields of interest and new paths of knowledge to follow.

As much as we really learned, sometimes independent study courses got approval when they probably shouldn't have. For one such independent study program, a girlfriend and I tried to teach ourselves "ground school" in order to learn to fly. Ground school. Two teenagers teaching themselves ground school. This was somehow approved.

My friend and I would meet in the hall, sitting on the floor together, trying to read aloud a textbook on aerodynamics. We used our hands to demonstrate the principles of airflow, air pressure, and lift around an aircraft's wings. It got so hard and so boring that it was all we could do to keep from falling asleep. After a session or two, we dropped the class for something else.

ABOUT 150 MIDDLE and high school students attended Steller. Many came from Anchorage's upper-income homes or families with long histories. They were the sons and daughters of politicians, community leaders, and otherwise civic-minded families.

"We had a school uniform," a friend from Steller quipped. Just about everyone wore hiking boots, belted jeans or corduroy pants, and waffle Henleys or flannel shirts. Back then some students, mostly males, carried buck knives; I used to joke that they were prepared should a wayward moose enter the building during hunting season. Actually, we weren't hunters, or even Eagle Scouts or Girl Scouts ready for a campout. I suppose the knives were for popping open a beer at high school parties.

I took philosophy, music, art, and US government. Once standard high school core classes were covered, students could propose their own course of study. For my government class, my classmate Sigrid and I decided to pursue a project that would explore which agencies owned or managed Alaska's lands. Whoever owned these lands—the federal government, the state, Alaska Native groups, or private owners—was and still is a hot topic in Alaska. Alaska did not achieve statehood until 1959, and when I was in high school, the state was still selecting the lands it was granted through the Statehood Act. Sigrid and I went around interviewing the heads of state parks, those who oversaw federal lands, and directors at the Bureau of Land Management. It was an important topic to us, since most of my classmates were outdoorsy. At Steller, I discovered a life of mountain climbing, cross-country skiing, and all-night bonfires.

My class of 1976 was the school's second graduating class. We had about twenty students. We were, without a doubt, the *Dazed and Confused* generation, like the kids in Richard Linklater's film set on the closing day of the 1976 school year.

We had nothing in common with the Baby Boomer generation that immediately followed World War II. We didn't participate in the rebellion of the 1960s; we didn't march against the Vietnam War; none of my male peers faced being drafted to go to war. By the time we graduated, the Vietnam War was over.

Our cultural rallying cry didn't come so much *against* anything but more *for* something. That something became being outdoors in every fashion and form we could think of: hiking, cross-country skiing, mountain climbing, or getting on the water—usually freezing cold water.

LOOKING BACK, I see many ways I might have died exploring Alaska's vast wilderness. I knew some people who did. Somehow, my friends and I survived, although given some of the risks we took, we were lucky.

One overnight winter camping trip set a group of us—about three or four guys and two girls—on an overnight trip that involved cross-country skiing to Whittier, a small coastal community on the other side of the Chugach Mountains to the east and south of Anchorage.

About sixty miles from the city of Anchorage, Whittier sits on a canal off Prince William Sound. The only land access is via the Alaska Railroad, through a nearly two-and-a-half-mile tunnel.

One of the guys in our group was in a full leg cast.

Our plan involved getting dropped off at Portage Glacier, a popular tourist destination on the highway about two miles away from the tunnel.

Allow me to repeat myself: it was a train tunnel. As in, only a train. In a tunnel. Not a pedestrian walkway, not a road, not a known or encouraged route. It was illegal to walk through the tunnel unless you were an employee of the railroad.

I'm also sure that during the winter months, the train did not keep a regular schedule going in and out of Whittier. In other words, we had no idea if or when a train would come through while we were in the tunnel.

Our trip began well, with an easy ski to the tunnel entrance. Once there, we took off our skis and opened a door meant only for railroad employees. Inside it was pitch black. No lights. We all had flashlights or headlamps, and it was these that guided us down the tracks, with our skis and poles slung over our shoulders.

The walking was perilous. Here and there mounds of ice had formed on the dark tracks where water dripped inside the tunnel.

I don't remember if I had been in on the planning of this trip or if others had meticulously planned the excursion. All I know is that I blindly went along. Once inside the train tunnel, I was terrified that a train might come along.

As I walked, I looked to either side of the track, trying to gauge if there was room for us to stand against the wall and not be hit by the sides of a train. It didn't look like it. In my mind, I practiced splaying my body against the wall, making myself as flat as I could, hoping not to be dragged off.

Fortunately for us, no train came that day, and we reached the other side safely. But our troubles had just begun.

The wind was so strong when we left the tunnel that it knocked us over like matchsticks. We retreated back inside to figure out what to do. The original plan had been for us to ski into Whittier and find a place to camp. But the town was several miles down the tracks, and every time we tried to step outside and put on our skis, the wind would knock us down.

We decided to trek to the side of the tunnel to find a spot to build a snow cave and camp. Leaving our skis and poles in the tunnel, we stumbled along the lower slopes of the mountain, trudging like mountaineers on Everest: Step. Stop. Brace. Step. Stop. Brace.

What we had not prepared for was how deep the snow was around Whittier, which receives an average of nearly 270 inches of snow a year. It snows so much there that walls of snow regularly cover the first-story windows of homes.

Eventually we came to a jagged tree that offered a slim buffer to the winds. There, we set up camp. We didn't have tents, so we dug out under and around the tree and covered the whole contraption with a piece of plastic sheeting.

The Ritz, it was not.

We did have a small propane stove to heat food and drink though. Once inside our makeshift shelter, we were warm enough to take off wet outer layers and hang them on a string tied across the top of the shelter and relax in our long underwear. Our space roomed three comfortably. Maybe four. But five of us? We somehow managed to crisscross our sleeping bags and eventually go to sleep.

The next morning, after thawing clothing that froze on the clothesline overnight, we broke camp and decided to try to get into town again. One of our party, the guy in the leg cast—the least likely to get ahead—struck out on his own. By the time we got to the tunnel to retrieve our skis, he was long gone.

Some of us tried to ski along the snow-covered tracks. Every few feet, the wind would knock us down. Eventually, we took shelter in a small, abandoned wooden building.

There, I cried. My fingers and feet were frozen and hurt. After resting a few minutes, we decided to go back to the tunnel and regroup. Once there, we warmed up. God only knows what we thought we were going to do next.

Then, deep inside the tunnel, we saw a tiny, bright light. As we stared at it, it got bigger and closer. Something was coming down the tracks. Fortunately, it wasn't big enough to be a train.

Like a knight in shining armor upon a white horse, a railroad worker riding a white Polaris snow machine pulled up to us and stopped. He was a young and friendly guy who might have encountered people like us before. He told us to stay put. He went into town, and a short while later, he pulled up outside in a pickup truck.

We loaded our skis and our shivering selves into the back, and he drove us into Whittier. Our rescuer took us to his house, where we camped on his living room floor. Later that night we reunited with our friend in the cast, who had successfully skied all the way into town.

When it was time to go home to Anchorage a day later, we bought tickets on the train.

THAT WAS MY LAST winter camping trip, but not my last attempt at wilderness camping.

One summer in high school, I went with two friends (including one who had been on the ill-advised ski-through-the-tunnel fiasco) to Denali National Park. The park is home to Mount Denali, the tallest mountain in North America at 20,320 feet.

Sigrid, Kim, and I got to the park and picked up our backcountry permit. It would allow us to leave the only road through the nearly ten-thousand-square-mile park and designated wilderness area. That road is ninety-two miles long.

Aside from a fall lottery that allows some lucky motorists to get a pass to drive into the park, most of it is strictly off limits to motorized vehicles of any kind. A yellow school bus, then and now, takes tourists on a long, slow ride through the park all the way to Wonder Lake.

The bus dropped us off at our designated camping area. To assure no disruption of the wildlife in the area—wolves, grizzly bears, and dozens of other types of animals—only so many backcountry passes are issued at any given time.

We felt lucky to get ours the moment we stepped off the bus. Shaggy tundra and bright wildflowers and rippling streams unrolled before us. The mountains we had traveled through on our way to the park suddenly looked like foothills beside massive Denali. There is no view like it on earth.

Our drop-off point was on a high ridge with a gentle slope that went down to a braided river. Carrying heavy backpacks, we easily descended the slope to the bottom of the river valley that runs through the park. We wore our hiking boots but had nothing waterproof for wading through the shallower parts of the river.

We walked up and down, leaping from sandbar to sandbar, as we made our way across. But at one point, there were no more areas we could jump over. We would have to wade across what seemed to be a nonthreatening and slow-flowing branch of the river.

We discussed our options: get our boots and clothes wet or go barefoot and, well, in our underwear. We hadn't brought shorts of any kind, nor perhaps a dry change of pants.

With summer evening temperatures on the cool side, we opted to keep our clothing dry. We stripped off our boots and pants, threw them in our packs, and began to wade through the water.

I discovered, as anyone who has ever crossed rivers and streams in Alaska in summer knows, that the water was freezing cold. Bitterly cold. Painfully cold, as if you are being stabbed with a thousand knives. You feel you can't breathe. You just might die.

Or, in our case, die of embarrassment. As we began our crossing, we turned to see that another park bus was stopped on the road high above us. The bus drivers usually stop to allow tourists to photograph wildlife. Using our binoculars, the three of us realized that the tourists all seemed to be looking in our direction.

We looked around. Could there be something nearby? A moose? A bear?

Nope.

We realized the tourists were looking at three teenage girls in their underwear crossing a small stream of water that turned out to be no higher than our knees.

Oh well, we figured. Not much we could do about it anyway, and besides, it was unlikely there was anybody on that bus who knew who we were. Once on the other side of the stream, we dressed and continued on our way.

We spotted a small hill where we decided to camp. As we approached, we saw something even more alarming than our earlier misadventure. A sign read: PRIME GRIZZLY BEAR RESTRICTED AREA. Or habitat. Or whatnot. The message was clear: our backcountry permit area was right next door to GRIZZLY BEAR HABITAT RESTRICTED AREA.

We knew this meant employing all the bear-deterrent camping rules we had learned from one of the park rangers. We had to prepare, eat, and store our food far from our tent and sleeping area. Somehow, we got the idea that we should also bury our food containers and eating utensils deep in the ground. (We thought this was safe. It didn't seem to occur to us that bears have great noses and big claws for digging.) For extra measure, we decided to leave the clothes we wore that day with the buried food, which meant changing outside. For those who aren't familiar with this kind of terrain, there are few to no trees.

We would have felt clever and prepared had we not forgotten two critical things: matches and, most important, mosquito repellant. The former meant we didn't eat any cooked food that evening. The latter meant that we had to swat mosquitos madly while eating and burying and running to get inside the tent, followed by zipping up the door quickly and then frantically slapping and killing as many mosquitos as we could.

Aside from such moments, our camping spot was perfect. As with all of Denali National Park, the vistas are huge and the landscape epic, like one of those nineteenth-century wall-size paintings of the American West.

That night, as we settled into our sleeping bags, we devised our own bear-deterrent plan. If any of us awoke in the night, we were to peer outside and either yell "Bear!" if we saw one or yell anyway to scare anything in the near vicinity.

We all slept fitfully that night, being near the grizzly bear habitat restricted area. At one point in the middle of the night, I dreamed not of a bear but of a large spider, slowly descending from the top of our tent. I leaped up and slammed my hand down to kill it, yelling loudly.

Immediately, Kim popped up and cried, "Bear!" Then she lay back down and kept sleeping. Sigrid and I, now both awake, just looked at each other. Then we closed our eyes and also went back to sleep, or something like sleep, under the Alaska summer night sky that never gets dark. We hoped the bears next door would stay put.

In the spring of 1976, I graduated high school. At Steller, we made our own graduation gowns in the style of wizards' robes, with hoods and long trumpet sleeves. They were made of beige or white cotton or gauze. We decorated our robes in everything from batik to applique. I tie-dyed mine.

About twenty students were in my class that year. Our graduation

My graduating class at Stellar Alternative School. (Photo courtesy of Alaska Dispatch News)

was held in the gym/cafeteria at Steller. I think we all spoke a few words; I remember saying only, "No more homework!"

A photo of our graduating class, of young men and women in long, flowing hair and long, flowing robes, has always reminded me of a painting of Jesus's apostles.

That, of course, may have been the point. We eschewed all things that were part of conventional and traditional high school life—sports, homecoming, and prom. The girls didn't wear makeup, and the guys didn't get haircuts and, in some cases, didn't shave. I look at photos of me from this period of my life, my hair down to my waist, and think, *Would someone please give that girl some hair care products?!*

In a way, we were like the apostles that spring, minus a leader. Our figurehead was the entire state of Alaska and the outdoors.

The only time I ever engaged in vandalism was after a night of high school partying. A group of us drove out to South Anchorage, to the site of the first-ever overpass/on-/off-ramp constructed along the only highway south of town.

We sneered at this latest development. On the green sign next to the northbound on-ramp, one of our group jumped out and spray painted the word "Los" above the official "Anchorage."

Los Anchorage, as in Los Angeles. One meager on-/off-ramp. Is there a statute of limitations on misdemeanors?

THIS WAS ALSO the era of garage rock bands and the worship of rock band musicians, and I was not immune. If a guy played guitar, had long hair, and even vaguely resembled, say, George Harrison, I was smitten.

For a while, about the time I graduated high school, I had a boyfriend who played bass. The more hippie-ish of my friends and I would go to hear bands in our standard rock concert outfit—long cotton skirts, hiking boots, and peasant blouses.

During those days I met two brothers who had come to Alaska from Rhode Island. One of them dubbed me and my friends "little pioneer women." He once tried to describe what it was like coming to Alaska from the East Coast. At home, his idea of wilderness was the view from a hill above a freeway with nothing but forests or fields as far as the eye could see. But Alaska's wilderness was almost beyond comprehension.

I wasn't sure I understood, but the summer after I graduated high school, I decided to hit the road again to explore the rest of the world.

My bass-playing boyfriend wanted to go to Jamaica because of the growing popularity of Bob Marley and reggae music. I had no such desire. I was willing to go as far as Rhode Island, where I had friends.

We rode the state ferries through Southeast Alaska, flew, hitchhiked, and took buses. From the Pacific Northwest, we went across Wyoming, then into Nebraska, where I still remember the most generous people who opened their homes to us for overnight visits. Iowa was where I began asking, "Is this the Great Plains? Is this?"

At one point, we stopped for lunch at a Howard Johnson's. I picked up something off the table—a condiment, perhaps—and was amazed that it had been manufactured right there, in the town we were passing through. In Alaska, nearly everything comes from somewhere else.

Along the way we reached a small farming town and stopped in a café. The place was filled with regulars—farmers and retirees, old men dressed in coveralls. I felt all eyes on us hippies. I was a little intimidated but more enthralled by what seemed like the all-American scene of middle America.

Later, we hitchhiked amid tall cornfields. A family in a station wagon picked us up—a mom, dad, son, and daughter. I can't recall their names or where they were going, but I was floored by their courage and openness. They were friendly and talkative and kind. I can't imagine anything like this happening today, but in the summer of 1976, it was still possible.

We met a lone female college student who drove us most of the way through the rest of Iowa before we turned north through Minnesota and headed toward my mother's hometown of Ironwood on Michigan's Upper Peninsula.

I ENTERED IRONWOOD with great trepidation. The three years I had spent there between the ages of six and nine were painful at best. My parents had split up, and my mother would spend her few remaining years in and out of mental institutions. But like any place you go back to as an adult, all things that once seemed enormous feel somehow small with time. So, too, were my difficult memories.

I was happy to see my mother's family and felt a sense of belonging, of my roots. I found that my memories of life with my Italian grandmother, once alienating and harsh, were now engaging and quaint. The hill by her house that had been such a long climb was nothing to an eighteen-year-old.

I looked up what childhood friends remained, or their parents. I was struck with how much I liked the place and the people.

I remembered that when I was a little girl in Ironwood, there was one family that had a son, Bobby, who was older than me. My memories of him were not good. He would bully me again and again. He liked to trick me into getting on the bench swings of the old metal swing sets. He'd swing the entire thing so hard and high that it seemed the entire swing set would topple over. I would scream and cry in fear.

Bobby was the boy who wouldn't let me take refuge in his house as a thunderstorm approached one day. In Ironwood, you could see storms approaching on the horizon, all dark, low clouds and menace. I hated thunderstorms and was always fearful my grandmother's house would be struck by lightning.

That day at Bobby's, he had given me no choice but to run all out for my grandmother's house across a large field. I may never forget that day, out in the open in a full-on thunderstorm, getting soaked in the downpour. Terrified.

Now that I was all grown up, I looked forward to confronting that little SOB Bobby.

Bobby's mom was named Stella. She, like the rest of the families that lived in Jessieville just outside Ironwood, had been a friend to my mom and to me.

When I arrived, Stella and Bobby's younger brother greeted me warmly. Then we waited for Bobby to arrive.

"Bobby loved you so much," Stella said. "He still talks about you and always wondered what happened to you."

Huh? Are we talking about the same Bobby here? I couldn't believe what I was hearing. Should I tell her what he had done to me? What my memories were?

I decided against it. Then Bobby walked in the door. He practically had tears in his eyes when we hugged. He was handsome, polite, and soft-spoken.

I don't know if I ever told him of my memories of growing up with him. I might have been too shocked to think of what to say. What would be the use of dragging up bad memories? I just let it go.

During that trip, I visited my mother's gravesite for the first time. She was buried in a downtown plot with her parents, my grandparents Marietta and Paulo Chiaravalle. I suppose that was the right place for her, and I took some comfort in that. But her headstone gave Chiaravalle as her last name, with no mention of Rich.

I thought that someday I would go back and buy a new headstone and include her married name. I have yet to do that.

AFTER MICHIGAN, I headed east to Rhode Island to meet up with the friends I had met in Alaska. My bass-playing boyfriend and I had parted ways, so I continued on alone.

In Rhode Island, I experienced another first. My friend and I took a day trip to Block Island, a popular vacation area. At one point, I stood in the surf for a photo. My friend yelled at me to turn around, and just as I did, I was overcome by a wave of water. For the first time ever, I tasted saltwater.

I had made my way across the entire continent. It was time to go home.

THAT FALL, MANY of my classmates from Steller headed for Ivy League or other storied private colleges in New England. Others chose schools that specialized in arts and crafts, or unique trade school programs, such as a wooden-boat-building school in England.

Initially, I wanted something akin to my experience at Steller, so I found an alternative music program at Western Washington University in Bellingham, Washington. However, my life took another turn.

Someone wrangled me into volunteering at the State Democratic Party headquarters.

It was 1976, the bicentennial of the nation's birth. Jimmy Carter was running for the presidency. Young people were energized by his campaign. I'd been accepted to college, but I deferred my admission as I got swept up in my first and last foray into politics. What I got for my volunteer time was the promise of a job in Juneau as a page in the Alaska House of Representatives.

After Carter's win in November of that year, I packed my bags and moved to Juneau with little money and little idea just how hard such a move would be.

It was the middle of winter. I arrived in a small town that was cut off from the rest of the world except by plane or boat.

I have needed knee-high rubber boots two times in my adult life: in Juneau and in New York City. Both have bitter rain and snow storms. Of all the places I have been, both have the most expensive housing, and people are willing to live in the most God-awful places. And despite the massive size difference between the two—Juneau had about twenty-five thousand residents in the late 1970s, and New York City over seventy million—both seemed to be the center of the universe.

CHAPTER 4

Living Back To Nature Can Be Hazardous To Your Health

To this day, I have dreams about being in Juneau. And nightmares.

Few towns or cities exist in such a spectacular setting. Juneau lies between mountain peaks of the Alaska Coast Range to the east and a handful of channels, bays, and inlets to the west. From Downtown Juneau, one has to walk only a few streets to find the side of a mountain or a wilderness trail along the beach.

Alaska is a land of extremes, and this is certainly true for Juneau. On a sunny day, there is no place more beautiful on earth; during a winter storm, there are few places more miserable. Southeast Alaska is so different in climate and popular culture from the rest of the state that my moving there was in many ways like moving to Arizona. I found myself in a place radically different from any I had known before.

In Arizona and again in Juneau, I fell in love with the place and people. I found a niche and discovered more about myself—even if I had to do it the hard way.

A historic gold mining town with an ancient and rich Native history, the city is located in Alaska's Inside Passage, the lengthy archipelago of islands and waterways along the northern Pacific Coast adjacent to Canada. It's where you or someone you know has been on an Alaska cruise. Alaska is now one of the most popular cruise destinations in the world, but when I moved there, the cruise industry was virtually nonexistent. The town was a mix of isolationism and worldliness, and residents tended to identify more with Seattle and the Pacific Northwest than with Anchorage. In fact, many Juneau residents then and now despise Anchorage. Hate it. It's a feeling not uncommon all across the state toward Alaska's largest city, ostensibly the biggest recipient of state financial resources and attention. With Juneau, it gets personal.

The day I arrived, even my cab driver ranted about hating Anchorage. When I asked if he'd ever been there, he replied, "The airport."

His response was so common that I began telling people I was from Eagle River, a suburb just north of Anchorage.

"Ah, Eagle River," someone might say. "That sounds nice."

Juneauites hate Anchorage because for years legislators from the northern parts of Alaska have tried in vain to move the state capital to the Anchorage area, or at least somewhere on the state's limited highway system. That's where most of the state's population lives—more than half in Anchorage alone. This is because no highway or even rail service connects Juneau to the rest of the state. None. Zero. The only way to get to Juneau is by air or sea—when everything isn't shut down due to a severe storm.

Juneau is also in what is known as a temperate rainforest, with as many as 220 days of rain per year and over 50 inches of rainfall. Most residents wear rubber boots all the time, favoring the brown, steel-toed boots popular with fishermen and those who work outdoors.

It rains so much in Juneau that I was taken aback the first time I saw a fur coat there. The young woman wearing a vintage mink had—of course—just arrived in town that day. Rain gear is de rigueur in Southeast Alaska. I was elated when Gore-Tex was invented.

When I think of my time in Juneau, the weather comes first to mind because I was so often in it. Initially, I had no car, and there was no mass transit where I needed to go, so I ended up walking—a lot.

When I arrived, the city had a lively arts and theater scene, a few good restaurants, and lots of bars to cater to the town's population of blue-collar workers, fishermen, and government bureaucrats.

From a distance, the downtown, with its handful of multistoried concrete and glass office buildings, seems to have the skyline of a large city. Most residents, though, live about ten miles "out the road," accessible via the town's only highway. The Mendenhall Valley is named for the Mendenhall Glacier, a popular attraction and hiking area for locals and tourists alike. Suburban neighborhoods are located along a wide swath of flat terrain created as the glacier retreated to its current location.

The rest of the road services the airport, a shopping mall, and a number of beachfront neighborhoods before coming to an abrupt end about forty miles north of Downtown Juneau.

You'd be surprised how far forty miles can feel when you've got nowhere else to drive.

If my late teens were all about playing in nature, then moving to Juneau put those ideals to the test. For much of the four years I lived off and on there, I did so without running water, electricity, or indoor plumbing.

But my move to Juneau happened to place me in the center of a whirlwind of political and social change that would impact the entire state of Alaska for decades to come.

THE FIRST ORDER of business when I arrived was to find a place to live.

When the Alaska Legislature starts in January, hundreds of people swoop into Juneau, including elected officials and their staffs. Along with this influx come dozens of recent college graduates, lobbyists, and former political volunteers hoping to get jobs.

The annual flood of new people strains Juneau's chronic housing shortage, causing government workers to bunk in apartments and houses like frat brothers. They might seek housing anywhere from cabins to cheap hotels to fishing boats docked in the downtown boat harbor.

In the 1970s, jobseekers longed for the short- or long-term posts with a state employment system known as "the gravy train." This came from the state's then-generous benefits and high pay, attributed to the difficulty in attracting employees when most chose the high-paying jobs linked with construction of the Trans-Alaska Pipeline.

When I first arrived, I stayed with friends in an apartment in the town of Douglas, on Douglas Island across Gastineau Channel from Juneau. Then I learned of a small cabin in the woods I could have if I fixed it up.

The cabin was a small A-frame originally built to be a sauna. It was about the size of your average walk-in closet, with a loft just big enough to sleep in. It came with no windows, no heat source, no running water.

So I did what people who live like the Amish (but are not Amish) do: I organized a work party. About a dozen friends and I descended on my new abode and had ourselves the modern-day equivalent of an old-fashioned barn raising.

Luckily, some of those who showed up were carpenters.

We stapled heavy sheets of clear plastic over the window openings, installed a tin wood-burning stove, built a ladder to the loft, and made the place livable. Sort of.

It was cute. The only downside was I had to live there alone and had to travel a narrow, slippery-when-wet boardwalk through dense scrub brush and evergreens from the road to the front door.

At night, it was pitch dark.

Without streetlights or nearby houses, I had to guide myself using a flashlight. Every time I went home, I feared running into a moose or, worse, a bear. Or any number of other creatures and ghosts and everything my nineteen-year-old mind could conjure. I often ended up bunking on other people's couches.

Once the Legislature went into session in early January, I participated in what was then the tradition of lining up along the second-floor hallway connecting the chambers of the State House at one end and the State Senate at the other. Longtime legislative members and staff recall the spectacle of people lining the halls and passing out their resumes. I've always loved a party, so I did what I always do in such settings: I walked and talked and met a lot of people and made a lot of friends.

I had no idea what I was up against, but I quickly figured out I needed to look more professional in order to compete with all those people on the second floor. I went out and bought a new pair of dress shoes. This was a big deal, as I didn't have much money. I spent some of my last funds on those darn shoes, which I proudly showed off to all my new friends. They were all outraged when I got the news: all the legislative pages had been already hired. I was not one of them.

Then I learned that those hired to be pages had never even appeared in the halls. They were the relatives of political party volunteers, party regulars, and the like, all college age, all great kids, all deserving, no doubt, and all decided upon weeks or months before.

I hadn't had a chance.

Fortunately, I had friends. Many of those I met in the hall that first week of the legislative session got jobs with various representatives and committees. At some point that week, I also made friends with the representatives from Fairbanks. It was that group that sent a sternly worded letter to the House Rules chairman demanding I get hired. He also got an earful from others I had befriended.

I was standing in the hall when the slightly embattled-looking chairman came out of his office and, with a slight grin, handed me a document declaring I was hired.

Normally, there were six House pages. I became the seventh.

THE POSITION OF page was created in part so that young people can learn about how the legislative process works. We didn't do a lot back then. We were strategically placed in tall chairs around the House chambers. From our various vantage points, our job was to snatch notes waved by representatives and deliver them to other representatives, staff members, or people sitting in the visitor's gallery in the back of the room.

When the House was in session, the page's job was usually fairly boring. At times, though, when important pieces of legislation were being debated or voted on, we had a front-row seat to history.

We also had a front-row seat to how adults behaved when isolated in a hard-to-get-to town, away from their spouses and families, where bars are about the only entertainment around.

All of us pages became close friends. One, Libby Roderick, would bring in her acoustic guitar and sing and play during downtimes. (Her gorgeous voice would later build her a career in music.)

I made friends with the staffers who worked for the various legislators, people from all over the state. Despite having what I like to think is an upbeat personality, I must have possessed a less-than-sunny disposition at times. One staff member bought me a *Sesame Street* board book about Oscar the Grouch. On the cover, my name was handwritten over "Oscar." Maybe it was all the coffee. But still, during lengthy debates, it was all I could do not to nod off.

While much of what was voted on did not interest me, several key pieces of legislation did. One was the session where the state created

The other Alaska State House of Representative pages and me at the chief clerk's desk in the House Chambers. With the seven of us sits the Assistant Sargent at Arms Kathleen "Teeny" Metcalfe. From left to right: Paddy McGuire, Spike Dale, Chris Hart, JD Moore, me, Libby Roderick, Teeny, and Lisa Petro. (Photo taken by Kathleen Metcalfe.)

the Alaska Permanent Fund, groundbreaking legislation that basically created a state savings account. Into this account would go a set amount of the money flowing into state coffers from Alaska's share of the oil flowing through the Trans-Alaska Pipeline. Alaska was one of the only states to conserve actively some of its wealth for future generations. Otherwise, no doubt, every penny coming in would have been spent.

The Alaska Permanent Fund would eventually pay out a dividend to every person who had lived in Alaska for at least one year. The program was created in part to ensure Alaska would protect the fund from those interested in raiding the account for short-term gain.

MY OFF-HOURS WERE spent hanging out with a group of young people living in North Douglas at the end of Douglas Island. Then and now, North Douglas is largely wooded and remote. In the 1970s, young people lived in the houses that were either tucked into the deep woods or that lined the shore along Gastineau Channel across from Juneau.

The dense forests of North Douglas, much like all of Southeast Alaska, are filled with towering, almost Sequoia-like evergreen trees, including Sitka spruce, mountain hemlock, and red cedar. The forest of

North Douglas now seems to me like something from a fairy tale. The dense undergrowth is a myriad of different shades of green, from the mossy carpet covering the ground and tree trunks to the huge ferns and skunk cabbage, a large, odorous plant with leaves the size of elephant ears.

Back-to-nature types lived in every kind of housing available: standard wood-frame homes, old shacks, cabins, wall tents, and such. Someone even hollowed out a giant, overturned spruce and turned it into a place to live—or at least camp.

I know because I had to camp there once. I was picked up at the airport by a friend who offered his place to stay for the night. He failed to mention it was a makeshift home like something out of Winne-the-Pooh's Hundred Acre Wood.

However, bunking in my sleeping bag in a damp tree wasn't magical or even remotely endearing. It was ridiculous, and if it hadn't been so late or so far out of town, I would have left. But I did what I could to get through the night and hold up my end of living the "back to nature" movement. That included spurning my friend's sexual advances—but not without hearing a lecture on the concepts of free love and sharing.

I may have heard similar rhetoric before, but when I was in high school, we were normal teens. Normal, fall-in-love, or crush, or whatever teenagers. Sure, there was the occasional sauna (I wore clothes) or drunken party hook-ups (not for me), and later the go-home-together-after-the-bar kind of thing. But I didn't really have a boyfriend until I was eighteen. I honestly don't think I was that attractive to men at that age, or perhaps they were afraid to approach me, given my tough demeanor. I hadn't had a mom or sisters to coach me on dressing, and I didn't wear makeup for a long time.

One of my most significant relationships in Juneau was with a sweet, intelligent man my age. He had arrived in Juneau along with a handful of friends from the upper-middle class and wealthy suburbs of Chicago. Some had started working as loggers, wearing their steel-toed logging boots around town. They all had shaggy, long or long-ish hair, and were a back-to-nature girl's dream guys. Some were from wealthy, established families, the kind of wealth where their last names graced major museums. Others had dads who raced Indy cars for a hobby. One guy described a dining table in his home bigger than the entire house we were standing in.

These young men had something to rebel against. They did so by logging, or learning carpentry or fine woodworking, or becoming commercial fishermen in the small boats that plied Southeast waters.

One of the group was a smart, kind young man who grew up north of Chicago along Lake Michigan. At first, he pursued me. No luck. Then I realized he was a good catch, so I pursued him. For a year, we dated and lived together. That was what young people did back then if things seemed to be going well. You lived together, sometimes almost right away.

His name was Jim, and he was working as a fine carpenter doing kitchen remodels and handcrafting cabinetry. He had long, dark, curly hair, and in a way, we resembled each other. With Jim, I was as secure and stable as I had ever been.

He helped me buy my first car—a forest-green VW Bug. Here's the thing: I bought it before I had my driver's license. I didn't learn to drive until I was nineteen. But when the car was available, and I snatched it up. I did have a learner's permit, and after taking the driver's test twice, I got my license.

One should not learn to drive later in life, if nineteen can be called late. I was afraid to drive. To make matters worse, not everything about the car worked, including the driver's side windshield wiper. In a temperate rainforest. In a place where it rained just about every day, or so it seemed. I did not have a working windshield wiper. On. The. Driver's. Side.

Maybe I wasn't as smart as I thought I was.

But the previous owner had hooked up a nifty string the driver could pull to make the wiper work. And for some reason—a lack of funds or just plain stupidity—that was how I operated that car.

There were other issues, one of which was discovered late one night. I was driving with a drunk friend in the backseat. Suddenly, he began yelling, "I can see the road!"

Turns out the floor had a hole that had been covered up by a piece of plywood under the floor mat. My friend had accidentally dislodged the wood, and his foot almost hit the road whizzing by underneath. I felt as if my cute VW Bug had become one of the cars from *The Flintstones*, where the cars were literally run on foot through holes in the floor.

As if back-to-nature living wasn't appealing enough, after beginning to date Jim, I bought my first home. It was a popular type of Juneau home

My then-boyfriend Jim and me on the float house I bought to live in while going to college at the University of Alaska Southeast, in the late 1970s. We had towed the house by skiff on a high tide to a small creek bed to where it's shown here.

at the time called a "float house."

Like a boat house found in marinas around the globe, a float house was also a structure built on a floating dock. A handful began cropping up around North Douglas, all handcrafted by young men and parked along the upper reaches of streams and small creeks, left to rest tied along the tidal flats. I was told at the time that neither state nor federal authorities had any jurisdiction over the tidelands. I doubt anyone gave much thought to the ecosystem of waterfowl and fish that a haphazardly parked float house might disrupt or even destroy. Eventually, a law change made such encroachments on public or even private lands illegal, but in the late 1970s, a float house was the latest housing trend of North Douglas Island.

I believe the one I had been eyeing might have been the first built in the area. And it was beautiful. But first I had to take possession of it.

When I bought it for a grand total of $1,000, it was sitting on the banks of a large creek in North Douglas. The plan was to wait for a high tide to lift it up off the mud banks. Then my boyfriend and I would tow it out with his skiff to his land a short distance away.

The only problem was severe freezing followed by a heavy winter storm and unusually high tides. The float house froze fast to the mud banks, and when the tide came in, it flooded.

We were finally able to get to it and assess the damage late one afternoon after the high tide receded. The inside looked like one giant slush bucket. At least a foot of crushed ice filled the entire float house.

Undaunted, we brought shovels and slowly hauled out all the ice. Miraculously, there seemed to be little or no damage. We were finally able to move it as planned, and I would stay in it for more than a year.

A TALENTED WOODWORKER and carpenter built my float house using in part building materials gathered from an old church that had been torn down. The floors were solid maple; a small stained glass window was set in the roof under a triangular point. On a clear night, I could lie in bed and see stars and the moon.

The entire structure was about thirty feet long by fifteen feet wide, give or take a few feet. The front featured a door in the middle, tall windows, and window seats below. Inside, there was a small kitchen counter to the left with handmade curtains hiding shelving. An open area to the right held a wood stove. The back half was divided by a wall; to one side was a double bed that could be pulled up like a Murphy bed. On the other side was room for a long dresser and closet. A loft above held storage. It was charming.

I cleaned the entire house before moving in. I painted the exterior in Canada cottage colors, with green exterior walls and white window trim with red touches. The house was adorable and would have made a great getaway cabin.

Of course, there was no running water. A sink drained into a large plastic bucket. There was no bathroom. When I eventually parked the float house on a creek on land Jim owned, I used the same outhouse he built for his wall tent. It was down a narrow boardwalk from Jim's neighbors. All these young people were in their late teens to early twenties, mere babes, as it were, in the woods.

THIS KIND OF LIFESTYLE got me a nickname when I applied during the summer to work for the Municipality of Anchorage Parks and Recreation program.

When the legislative season ended that year, I went back to Anchorage and applied for work at the Summer Playground Program. The city and school district would open about two dozen elementary schools around the city. After a week of training, they'd place two playground leaders onsite to run two recreation programs—one in the morning for little kids, and one in the afternoon for the older ones. The programs were free to Anchorage residents.

That's how rich the State of Alaska was back then. What would now be considered camp cost families about the same as the occasional movie ticket. Needless to say, the program was wildly popular, often maxing out on enrollment. As playground leaders, we led indoor and outdoor games, art projects, and field trips to the movies or zoo.

During my first interview, I met with the head of the program and a supervisor, both longtime veterans of recreation programs. When they asked me what qualified me to do work outdoors with kids, I explained how I lived in the woods without running water, electricity, or indoor plumbing. They thought I was hilarious. I would have too. Thus, I became known as "Grizzly Adams."

This was not exactly the persona I was after.

I THINK I SAW MYSELF as a short Emmylou Harris, the willowy, long-haired, beautiful singer who popularized traditional folk and country music in the 1970s. I don't know if Harris ever had to live off the land. I have read that Dolly Parton grew up without running water—or was that Loretta Lynn? Either way, I was living pretty much as people did in the poorest parts of the Appalachian Mountains. The only difference between me and people living in a "holler" is that I had chosen to do so, and the poorest of the poor would probably choose anything but.

I'm not sure I ever gave it much thought, but over time, I became disillusioned with the whole business of living back to nature. A series of events, including the night in the hollowed-out tree root, led me to conclude that my life wasn't going so well.

It may have been the day I was napping in a friend's cabin with some type of kerosene or propane stove for heat. I awoke with a start, darted for the outdoors, and vomited violently for several minutes. I had been poisoned by a leak in the heater. Thank God it wasn't carbon monoxide, or I'd be dead.

I might have lost faith the day a group of us went to get firewood. We drove out to North Douglas until the guys spotted in the forest what looked like a good tree to take down. In the forest. The US Forest, I believe, as in you-don't-just-chop-down-trees-here federal forest. I could be wrong. Commercial logging has a long and controversial history in Southeast Alaska. Taking down trees for your personal use? Would the forest rangers care? No one knew. But whether or not what we were doing was entirely legal turned out to be the least of our problems.

The tree was high atop a small ridge above the road. Perfect. We could chop down the tree, cut it into rounds, and toss them over the ridge almost right into the back of the pickup truck. We'd hardly have to lift a finger.

The guys went up on the ridge. Cut down the tree. Cut up the tree, then began tossing the rounds down. As they did, the rounds promptly sank into several feet of snow. Somehow, no one had noticed that the snow was deep off to the side of the road. Somehow, our intrepid loggers had managed to get up the ridge without stepping into what was no doubt a roadside ditch deep enough and filled with enough snow to bury large rounds of tree trunk.

I stood there thinking, *This can't be how this is done. Isn't wood supposed to be gathered in the summer? Didn't I read somewhere that it's supposed to dry out or be cured before it burns properly?*

I've never been exactly a stickler for details, but I was wet and freezing and getting sick and tired of being wet and freezing.

AFTER MY FIRST legislative session ended, I got a job as a waitress at one of Juneau's upscale restaurants located on the downtown waterfront.

I had worked in restaurants since I was sixteen. In Anchorage, the places I worked were signs of the times—The Bread Factory and The Cauldron, both emphasizing healthy, natural foods.

The Bread Factory crew made their own bread, and every meal came with thick slices of hearty whole wheat bread. The specials were large tuna melts or frittatas or salads. The Cauldron specialized in homemade soups, bread, and rolls.

In keeping with the egalitarian ideals of the time, all workers at The Cauldron had to do stints at dishwashing. I didn't mind doing the dishes, except that I had plaque psoriasis and sensitive skin, making me allergic to wool and—of course—detergents. For years, I struggled with large rashes that would erupt painfully then dry over, only to reappear again.

For a while, I was roommates with a nursing student at the community college in town. Rona got into an argument with the male co-owner of The Cauldron, telling him I should not have to wash dishes because of my rash. Rubber gloves never worked to keep out the water and detergent.

"She could get a serious infection," my roommate yelled.

My boss was into metaphysics, and I received a rambling lecture about good vibes and mind over matter. I was fairly intimidated by him, as he was known to be highly intelligent, never raised his voice, and—as he told Rona—believed the rash was the result of my negative thinking.

I believe my negative thinking led me to quit that job.

The coffee house scene was still very much alive in those days, so places like The Bread Factory had live music, usually a guitarist singing contemporary ballads. For a long time, a local Episcopal church turned its basement into a weekly coffee house called The Chanting Gull. Full folk bands would play there while the audience sipped "Russian tea" (a blend of Tang and powdered iced tea mix) and danced or sang along.

In Juneau, the restaurant I worked at was nothing like the places I had worked or hung out at in Anchorage. My new job required a uniform of sorts—black pants and a white blouse.

I went out and bought a pair of black pants. I'm also allergic to many synthetic fabrics, so I bought a white cotton peasant blouse to complete my uniform.

My manager did not approve of the top I wore, and somewhere in the middle of our argument, I got fired.

To say I grew up with a chip on my shoulder would be an understatement.

Years ago, a close friend pointed out that I had to learn to fight to survive growing up. The problem was, I fought most of the time over almost everything. Over the years, I've left a trail of angry and exasperated telephone customer service agents. I would fight to the death for an aisle seat on an airline flight reservation. And God help the company whose product broke at my house!

But my tough exterior always came with a price, whether that meant it was time to move on from a bad job or not.

Perhaps because I had been doing it all and raising myself as a teenager, I wasn't enthusiastic about going to college right after high school. But after losing my waitressing job, I vowed to get into college and never to waitress again.

I haven't.

CHAPTER 5

A Warm Hat, a Whale, and a C in Chemistry

*W*hen the 1977 legislative term ended, I returned to Anchorage for the summer. There I worked for my former guardian, Walt Morgan, who was always there for me whether I needed a place to stay, a job, or a good laugh.

With Walt, I learned about hard labor. He was a handyman who also managed some rentals. That summer I did some landscaping work (digging holes in dirt is hard work), a little commercial janitorial work (harder), and even work as a house painter (hardest).

I explored a lot of options as to what I wanted to be when I grew up. My first serious decision was to be a nurse-midwife.

This was a career suggested by Rona in Anchorage, with whom I occasionally roomed when in town. She was a nursing student working as a lay midwife. The natural childbirth movement that took hold in the Sixties was playing out in the Seventies. The idea was to abandon what had become the standard medical practices used in hospitals, such as the use of epidurals or medication for pain relief. Oh, no, none of that. The movement (actually begun decades earlier) preached that birth was natural for women, and we had done without medical intervention for thousands of years. Never mind that even up until modern times, the mortality rate for women in labor was as high as 50 percent in some parts of the world.

This could be another of those times when I should have thought, *What am I thinking? What if a mother died on us? Or the baby?*

I went along as Rona's assistant on eleven home births. I trusted that all would be fine, and it was—until one night it wasn't. During that home birth, the mother had a prolapsed umbilical cord; in other words, the cord dipped below the baby's head and started coming out first, cutting off oxygen to the baby still in the birth canal.

The chance of the baby dying without surgical intervention: 90 percent.

We were in Eagle River, high on the mountain, miles from the nearest hospital, and in the middle of a fierce snowstorm. When Rona realized what was happening, she had me quietly call an ambulance. She then did something her instincts, training, and experience taught her—she put the birthing mother in a position to move the baby back up into the womb, allowing the cord to work free. She then gently pushed the cord back over the baby's head until it fell into its correct place.

I was tense with fear but acted as if everything was fine. We could not cause the laboring woman to panic.

The paramedics arrived looking ashen, no doubt aware of what they were up against. As soon as they realized the midwife had saved the day and the birth was proceeding normally, they were shaking Rona's hand.

After this episode, Rona refused to work with patients who lived more than a few minutes from the nearest hospital; they had to get full prenatal care and could not be high-risk. She eventually went on to become a licensed midwife outside Alaska.

I HEADED BACK to Juneau to enroll at the University of Alaska Southeast. And despite my midwifing scare, I planned to go into nursing—until my first chemistry class.

Despite how much I loved my high school experience at Steller, I seemed to have gotten out of high school without taking algebra. You need algebra to pass chemistry. Fortunately, our algebra professor told his students that if we came to every class, did all the assignments, and took every quiz and test (even if we failed them), then the lowest grade we would make would be a C.

I got a C.

After that algebra class, I knew I was not meant for a life in science. I then decided to major in something I loved—music. Part of this came from my father's appreciation of popular music, which he'd play on high volume in the middle of the night when he'd come home from "working." Imagine Steppenwolf's "Magic Carpet Ride" at 3 a.m. If you're a ten-year-old sound asleep in your bed, it's not fun.

My dad liked it all—pop, rock, even folk. We had the Kingston Trio, Frank Sinatra, The Mamas and the Papas, and that damn Steppenwolf. In the middle of the night. Nevertheless, I was exposed to all kinds of music early on and loved it. I began my studies in music, playing classical guitar and studying voice.

I also took advantage of film classes, including a seminar about the work of famed film director John Ford. I thought I wanted to work in the movies somehow. I also enjoyed the local National Public Radio station in Juneau, KTOO. A lot of people in Juneau knew someone at the station. My boyfriend Jim hosted his own music show once a week, and I would sometimes help out.

Actually, I wanted to be a lot of things during that phase of life between eighteen and twenty. This included, in no particular order, a forest ranger, a carpenter, and even a folk singer.

I did get a job with the US Forest Service. All day, I just sat at a counter doing nothing. I didn't stay long.

Carpentry seemed alternative, right? I decided I'd be a woman carpenter. I had a friend who was accepted into a union apprenticeship program. She advised me to get the textbook, so I did. It was a thick hardback book that I tried reading—but not for long. I decided a life of physical labor wasn't for me, either.

The folk singer phase lasted a little longer. The Alaska Folk Festival held each spring in Juneau was—and still is—a hugely popular event. For years, I had been singing to popular recordings by the likes of Linda Ronstadt as well as taking classical voice lessons at college.

Before I met and dated Jim, I had gone home to Anchorage one summer and fell in love with my last musician. He was a tall guitar player with waist-length hair. Originally from Texas, he played with a band at a local hotel lounge. We met, fell in love, and were together constantly until the gig ended about six weeks later and he returned home. Then I learned what hadn't been made entirely clear before—he had a longtime girlfriend back home. Oh. Here's what you should always ask someone: are you available? He wasn't.

What I got out of the deal was the desire to play the acoustic guitar. I went out and bought a six-string guitar and some songbooks, and taught myself to play. When I enrolled in college, I got a classical guitar for playing classical music. At some point, I decided to perform publicly and signed up for the folk festival.

Solo. What was I thinking?

The event was held at the Alaska State Museum, and it was usually packed. I wore a vintage blue velvet dress that I found at a secondhand store. I chose to perform one song, "Love Me Tender," originally recorded by Elvis Presley and later by Linda Ronstadt.

I have no idea if I was any good or not. I was terrified of making a mistake, and somehow I got through it. But I got enough encouragement to keep performing.

The following year I went back to the festival as part of a band. One of my best friends from Steller, John, had moved to Juneau. John and I linked up with a friend named Cliff to form a trio we named The Maintainers.

Cliff was from upstate New York. He had unkempt shoulder-length blonde hair and played an electric guitar. I adored Cliff, although he hardly fit my back-to-nature philosophy. But that's why John and I hooked up with him. John has always had a wicked sense of humor, and we both loved Cliff. We figured the folk festival needed something besides banjos and fiddles.

We came up with an opening comedy bit that made us a hit with the audience. John, a natural at the microphone, began our set with something like this: "Hi. We're thrilled to be here. We'd like to begin our set with a classic folk song. Feel free to sing along if you know the lyrics. It's called, 'Play That Funky Music (White Boy).'" Then Cliff launched into the opening guitar riff from the 1976 disco hit by Wild Cherry.

The place erupted in laughter. They loved us! The rest of our set—some Crosby, Stills & Nash, and another song or two—went just as well.

The audience loved us so much that the next year, we were given a Saturday night slot, considered the biggest performance night. We had

Alaska State Folk Festival, 1979.

added a violinist and banjo player. A bunch of friends came down from Anchorage, including one who brought satin tour jackets monogrammed with the band's name.

We insisted the emcee introduce us as "live and direct from Anchorage"—our ironic reference to the way Juneau residents felt about our hometown.

Just before going on stage, we had one snag. Someone had left a car running with the doors open right in front of the hall's main door. The emcee made an announcement looking for the driver. *Who would be so dumb?* I wondered, as we waited to go on stage. Then a friend ran up to us.

It was my car.

A friend moved the car, and we were ready to go. We opened with another bit delivered by John.

"We'd like to begin our set with a song we wrote as part of a promotion we did for the Anchorage bus system," he announced. "It's called, 'Another One Rides the Bus.'"

Then Cliff played the opening guitar riff to "Another One Bites the Dust," by Queen.

"Another one rides the bus," we all sang, with the audience singing along, too. "Another one rides the bus."

Again, the house exploded with laughter.

That was The Maintainers' final show. I am still friends with John but have lost touch with Cliff, who I wouldn't mind finding someday. But after that, I stopped performing, aside from school recitals.

EVEN WITH THE relative success of my short-lived musical career and music studies, I was still undecided about what I wanted to do for work. Another career idea: sailor.

I read the book *Dove*, the true story of Robin Lee Graham, who at sixteen sailed his twenty-four-foot sloop around the world. Of course, a part of my newfound passion for sailing was inspired by the handsome, golden-haired Graham.

Hey, I was a girl in college. I tended to get crushes on adorable guys.

I had friends in Juneau with sailboats, so I began hanging around them and learning the terminology of knots and sails and sailboats. I was all gung-ho for this until the day I went out for a sail with a friend. I discovered there is no feeling quite like being under wind power. And there is no feeling quite like being seasick.

That didn't initially stop me. I joined a group of friends on a week-long boat trip planned over the Fourth of July. A friend crocheted me a red, white, and blue hat for the occasion. I loved that hat. I wore it for years after. But whenever I would bemoan Alaska's weather, I would think of that thick, warm hat for the Fourth of July. That's how cold it can get on the water in Southeast Alaska. I was often so bundled up in Juneau, with my hair tucked away and layers of padded clothes on me, that I once complained, "You can't tell whether I'm a boy or a girl!"

There were two boats going out on the Fourth of July trip, a motorboat and a sailboat. I was invited by the owner of the motorboat to go along with several other friends. Our goal was to circumnavigate Chichagof Island in the Alexander Archipelago of Southeast Alaska. At seventy-five miles long and fifty miles wide, the island is the fifth largest in the United States. It is home to four small fishing communities, and it has the highest population of bears per square mile of any place on earth.

I did better on the motorboat than I had on the sailboat, but my stomach was still not prepared to commit to a life at sea.

What I remember best about the trip was the evening a humpback whale spectacularly surfaced nearby, spraying us with a fine mist from his spout. It smelled like the inside of a barn. A few days later, we watched in wonder as a group of orcas, or killer whales, swam in unison like synchronized swimmers.

I'd never explored as much of the natural world as I did when I lived in Juneau.

Once, Jim and I decided to spend the holidays on Chichagof Island in a US Forest Service cabin. We were to cross-country ski from our beach landing site to the cabin, a few miles deep into the Tongass National Forest.

The trail was difficult, twisting, and longer than we had anticipated. We found ourselves skiing well past dark, with headlamps to light our way, in temperatures that dipped far below freezing.

I told myself, *Focus. Ski. Stay positive. Pray we get to the cabin before we freeze to death or stumble over a large grizzly bear and get eaten.*

We eventually made it to the cabin, and our scare ended in front of a cozy fire.

I'm not sure whether this kind of adventure made me scorn the wilderness, appreciate it, or declare, "Never again!" But it was the sort of thing you did when you were a young person living in Alaska in the 1970s.

A FELLOW JOURNALIST once told me that she, too, could never decide what she wanted to do for a profession until she discovered journalism.

"I found I could be anything for a day—a test pilot, a governor, a chef—depending on what story I was doing," she said.

I began approaching that discovery for myself at college in Juneau. My back-to-nature phase ended when a friend contracted hepatitis A in Mexico and shared it at a potluck dinner on his return. My episode with the disease meant I couldn't drink alcohol for a year, which put an end to my college partying. My liver fully recovered and has been fine since, and I have pretty much stopped drinking. (But as I told my friend who gave several of us hepatitis, "A basket would have been fine.")

Then I failed my freshman English placement exam (a fact I like to share with my college students today). I had never written a college paper, my grammar was atrocious, and aside from a *Rolling Stone* magazine or an occasional book on Eastern mysticism, I didn't read.

I had to complete a course in remedial English in order to enroll in freshman composition. This turned out to be a workbook filled with grammar and vocabulary exercises. Thanks a lot, alternative high school!

But by second semester English, I was hooked. In his introductory lecture, my professor introduced himself as a fan of dime-store detective stories and trashy novels. He told us he had avoided college in his early twenties and rarely read at all. Somehow, he discovered good books and decided to pursue a two-year college degree in English. He went on to earn a four-year degree in English, followed by his PhD.

This was someone I could relate to.

Whatever apprehensions I had about college were lost that second semester in English 201. I devoured the reading list and was amazed when my professor analyzed my short story about a girl's trip to the dentist, saying it was a metaphor for rape. Heady stuff for a twenty- year-old who was coming from behind with this writing business.

I never did like writing college papers. For the life of me, I could not understand why I had to pull together a bunch of writing others had done and put it into my paper. Without knowing it, I liked what's called "primary research"—talking to people, learning firsthand about a subject, going out into the field, and reporting on events around me.

Whenever a parent worries about a teen son or daughter who isn't reading, I suggest giving them Hunter S. Thompson's *Fear and Loathing in Las Vegas* or Tom Wolfe's *The Electric Kool-Aid Acid Test*. They'll read. That's what I began reading in earnest. Wolfe and Thompson were both originators of a form of new nonfiction writing labeled "new journalism." The genre blended reporting and the narrative tools of fiction—setting, character, dialogue, and plot—to create true stories as vivid as a novel.

This new form had debuted nearly two decades earlier with the publication of Truman Capote's *In Cold Blood*, the achingly beautiful depiction of the mass murder of a farm family in Kansas by a pair of drifters.

Wolfe wrote about pop culture, or about events and people uniquely American. This mannered Southerner was the quintessential journalist who, like me, was fascinated by everything American.

Thompson developed what became known as "Gonzo journalism," so named because of his propensity to write when he was either stoned or drunk out of his mind. Despite his excesses, he was a brilliant reporter.

He and Wolfe were equally skilled at immersing themselves in their subjects' world.

In my little float house, reading by the light of a kerosene lamp, I devoured every magazine article or book the pair wrote. They seemed passionate about America in the same way I was.

Little did I know that I had found my calling.

CHAPTER 6

A Normal Life, Round One

By the end of my sophomore year in college, I had learned two things: one, I had no desire to play music in smoke-filled bars, and two, the world did not need another mediocre classical guitarist. It was time to choose a new major.

That summer, I moved back to Anchorage. I had run out of courses to take at the Juneau campus, unless I wanted to be a fisheries biologist. Instead, I looked at theater and communications.

I had done a theater practicum class in Juneau and worked with Perseverance Theatre, Alaska's longest-enduring professional regional theater. I absolutely loved it. I did the lighting for a production of a Sherlock Holmes play, little knowing that one day I would return to the same theater to write and help stage the theatrical adaptation of my first memoir.

But in Anchorage, I found the theater department head to be too, well, dramatic. I felt more at home with the primly dressed former corporate affairs officer who was head of the communications department and who seemed to want me in her program. I signed up for the Journalism and Public Communications School at the University of Alaska Anchorage. I chose the broadcast section because I had a strong interest in public broadcasting, having spent lots of time at the public radio station in Juneau.

Another reason I returned to Anchorage was that I had met my future first husband there. Eric was a handsome young man who was once on the US cross-country ski team. Unlike my quasi-hippie high school experience, Eric was a jock, a state champion runner, and even his high school prom king.

We moved into a makeshift nine-hundred-square-foot A-frame home on the hillside behind Anchorage and began the most normal life anyone could imagine.

Upstairs was just large enough for a queen-size bed and an area with two built-in desks overlooking a ground-level wooden deck. It was not uncommon for me to hear a loud *clump clump* and go to the upstairs window to find myself staring at the head of a large bull moose.

Eric and I developed a good credit score by buying a small plaid loveseat and paying it off in time. We had a purebred black lab named Treadwell. We were typical young Alaskans.

Eric had left college to ski and train for the Olympics, so he worked while I finished college. The plan was that after I graduated, he would go back to school to finish his business degree.

I loved my classes, especially communications law. The professor was smart and witty, and he used war analogies to describe defeating opponents in the courtroom by "blowing their ships out of the water!"

With each new class, I discovered a little more about what I wanted to do. I took a film editing class where we had to make our own short video. I loved the creative side of the process but hated hauling the camera and editing. I was lousy with machines of any kind.

For me, finding my way was as much about discovering what I didn't want to do as what I did.

ABOUT THAT TIME, I began to share Eric's love of running. I ran every day: up and down the mountain roads near our home, around the track at the indoor ice rink at school, and on trails at the university. That spring of 1982, I entered the annual Women's Run in Anchorage. Out of a field of several thousand runners, I came in forty-fifth.

In the fall, I worked on campus in the ticket cage at the sports complex. One day, while talking to one of the cross-country ski coaches, I told him about my race. He recruited me on the spot for the UAA women's cross-country running team. Most of my teammates were preparing for the cross-country ski season as well.

We had two to three hours of running practice every afternoon in the fall of 1982. We'd often begin by running from the school down the trails that led to a local golf course and park. There, we'd run laps on a loop with many hills. I'd never worked so hard in my life and never loved something more.

On the weekends, we'd head up to the mountain trails behind Anchorage and run. On one occasion, we ran across a mountain pass then down into another valley. We raced locally and in Fairbanks and Seattle. I was an average competitor, but I know I would have improved with more time.

When winter came, I trained with the cross-country women's ski team. The sport draws the toughest and fittest athletes in the world, and the UAA team was no exception. In no way was I good enough to compete with them. It was physically and mentally demanding—and not just for the students. One Saturday we went into the mountains to ski what seemed to be an unmarked trail. Midway through the day, our coach broke his collarbone in a fall. But he didn't stop. He continued to ski for another hour or so, and we didn't go to the emergency room until we were done for the day.

IN THE SPRING of 1983, I graduated with honors. I walked in the graduation ceremony, robe and all. I had never felt more proud. My parents barely finished high school; I believe I was the first person in my family to graduate from college. No one earns a college degree through luck or through who you know. There are just too many hoops to jump through, too many classes to pass. I had earned this myself every step of the way. My father once told me that an education is the one thing no one can take from you. He was right.

That August, Eric and I were married at the same Episcopal church that housed the Chanting Gull. We had a modest wedding party but a large reception. It was held at the home of Red and Mike Dodge. Red walked me down the aisle. We honeymooned in Hawaii, staying at the Dodges' spacious high-rise condominium near the posh Diamond Head side of Oahu. That's how much the Dodges treated me like family.

I was as happy and stable as I had ever been. This was indeed foreign territory to me. I thrived, and I was about to begin a career—a normal life.

DURING COLLEGE, I did an internship at the local CBS affiliate, which led to my first job after graduation. It was with a new radio news network created by a local commercial radio station. The network was developed by a team of some of Alaska's best and most senior journalists—all men, by the way, except for me and another woman who was also a recent college graduate.

I loved the energy of the newsroom and my colleagues. Almost immediately, I was writing broadcast news and doing my own stories. I soon learned that because newspapers had much larger staffs than our local TV stations, the TV news writers would often rewrite newspaper stories for broadcast. After seeing a few of these, I began to think I wanted to work at the source—a newspaper.

The network produced a half-hour newscast morning and evening, with updates throughout the day. I was the assistant to the morning news anchor, which meant I started work at 4 a.m.

I hated the hours. I mean, really hated the hours. It was summer, and trying to go to bed at eight or nine o'clock in the glaring midnight sun was almost impossible. Then waking at 3 a.m.? I felt like dying. But every morning, I trudged into work while other people were just leaving the bars.

My job was to help put together the morning newscast—and I do mean put together. Before the digital revolution, newsfeeds from the various wire services we subscribed to were recorded on tape. I listened to the newsfeed, physically cut and spliced the taped stories, and recorded them on carts that looked like 1970s-era eight-track tapes, and the anchor would play them as he was doing the newscast. It's hard to imagine now how such a thing worked, but it seemed amazingly high-tech to us.

At this job, I met someone who would become a lifelong mentor: a reporter and editor named Mike Doogan. He was already a veteran newsman of Irish-American descent and from a large Fairbanks family.

University of Alaska Anchorage Spring Commencement, 1983. I'm seated with my fellow graduates in the Department of Journalism and Communications, along with the department chair Sylvia Broady. (Photo © Michael Dinneen/dinneenphoto.com)

Doogan was—and still is—one of Alaska's best journalists. He and his wife, Kathy, had two small children back then. Over the years, both he and Kathy became mentors and some of my closest friends, and Mike would change the course of my career.

Early on at the network, I learned how quickly things come and go in radio news. Within six months, the news network folded and everyone else was laid off. I was kept on to report for the flagship AM radio station news, which consisted of one anchor and myself. But in the next several months, that anchor left, and I was soon anchoring and producing news all by myself. I longed more than ever to work in print.

At that time, Anchorage was lucky to be one of the few towns in the United States to have two newspapers. The *Anchorage Times* was the largest and considered the more conservative paper. The *Anchorage Daily News* was the upstart morning paper looking to unseat the *Times*. The two papers were continually trying to outdo one another, which created an exciting, challenging atmosphere for writers and a wealth of news for readers.

I had heard it was hard to get hired at the *Daily News* if you had no experience. I think Mike Doogan suggested I first get a job at the *Times*, gain some experience, and then apply at the *Daily News*.

So I tried. I applied at the *Anchorage Times* and was called in to meet with an editor. She gave me two freelance stories to report and write. If I did a good job, she said, I would be hired.

One assignment was to cover some guy who was speaking to an elementary school about teaching health habits. At any rate, he had sent out a press release saying so. But when I went to his talk at the school, it wasn't what anyone had expected. He was some sort of strange religious fanatic espousing a lifestyle that stunned at least the adults in attendance. I learned that that often happens in covering a story—the story doesn't always pan out or another story emerges.

I don't remember what the second assignment was, but I do recall that it, too, fell through. That was probably why neither story was assigned to any of the reporters in the *Times* newsroom. They were, as Doogan called them, "dog stories." After much discussion with the editor, there was nothing to be gained by writing about either assignment. I handed in an attempt at a story but never got a call back from the *Times*.

Then I did something I probably should have done to begin with—I applied at the *Daily News*. What got me an interview was a reference letter from Doogan. He gave me a copy. He said I had the potential to be one of Alaska's best journalists.

I thought he was nuts.

The next thing I knew, I was in an interview with one of the *Daily News* editors and feeling really intimidated. Unsure how things were going after a while, I noticed he had an accent.

"Where's your accent from?" I asked.

"Texas."

I had a best friend from junior high whose family was from Texas. I kept probing. The editor explained that he came from a military family and had moved a lot, but he didn't think of himself as Texan. The conversation continued, but suddenly I was asking the questions. And there it was—I had instinctively diverted the focus of the interview away from me and onto him. The unconscious tactic told him I was fearless, curious, and possibly self-destructive—all qualities needed to be a good newspaper reporter.

I got the job.

In the mid-1980s, the *Anchorage Daily News* was known as a writer's newspaper. It was also the place ambitious reporters went to seek their fame and fortune. The paper had seen many of its reporters go on to work for the likes of the *New York Times* or even have successful careers in Hollywood. It was known as the best newspaper in Alaska and one of the best in the country. In 1976, the *Daily News* won the first of what would become two Pulitzer Prizes in community service reporting.

WHEN I STARTED at the *Daily News*, it was going through a growth spurt. The newsroom was on the first floor of a modest building in a nondescript part of Midtown. It had a bank of windows that slanted outward, overlooking a two-lane road. The leaning windows had the double disadvantage of letting in little light and collecting snowfall and dust at the bottom, which left the newsroom feeling dim even in the middle of a long summer day.

The newsroom was thick with cigarette smoke, cramped, messy, and filled with noise and chatter. Throughout the day, you could hear cranky city desk editors—those who managed the daily beat reporters such as "cops" and "courts"—shout reporters' last names to summon them.

"Hey, Rich, get over here!"

Maybe the editors weren't all cranky and cantankerous, but that's how I remember them, and fondly so.

Like many newsrooms that eschew standard office cubicles, the room was wide open, a sea of desks lined up in this direction and that. I shared a desk with another reporter. He was messy. I was neat. Jokingly, I drew a line down the middle of the desk for "his" and "her" sides.

Not only were there not enough desks, there weren't enough computers. After 5 p.m., those of us filing a story for the next day often went over to the classified ads department of the paper and used their cubicles and computers.

It wasn't uncommon for the daily deadlines to keep me there well past dinnertime. Frustration, hurt feelings, and falling short of expectations often brought me to tears. But I couldn't have loved my job more. The *Anchorage Daily News* newsroom in the mid-1980s was the most exciting place I'd ever been.

My first job was as a part-time court reporter, and I wrote freelance for the weekly religion section. While writing about religion is traditionally viewed as the rookie beat, it may have been one of the most intriguing.

I hung out with and wrote about the local Bikers for Christ, an outlaw-looking Christian motorcycle group. They had colors, leathers, long hair, bandanas, and the whole look of the type of folks I usually associated with drugs and criminal activity. And they did charity work.

I visited the local Scientology hall. During my interview, I saw a poster on the wall. It showed a series of steps that rose to describe ascending states of higher consciousness, with an accompanying space describing what one could expect to feel. At the very top, the spaces became blank.

"Why aren't those filled in?" I asked my interviewee.

"Oh, those of us unenlightened cannot comprehend the highest levels of Scientology," he said.

"Huh," I said, looking down and scribbling in my notes. "That's what they tell you guys who are stuck in the Alaska office instead of maybe the Bahamas."

He didn't laugh. I thought it was funny.

But I wasn't kidding when, during another interview, I asked a local Mormon spokeswoman where they kept the golden plates where God had written his commandments to religion founder Joseph Smith. I honestly and naively thought they were in some museum in Utah. But no.

"God took those back," she explained.

"Uh-huh," I said, scribbling in my notepad. *How convenient*, I thought.

In the other half of my job, I was the assistant to the court reporter. There, I was lucky to apprentice under Sheila Toomey, one of the best journalists I'll ever know.

I had originally met Sheila in Juneau, where she was an anchor of KTOO's legislative news show. She has this great, husky voice—devoid of her New York City roots—that's perfect for broadcasting. She was also one of the best writers in the newsroom—or anywhere. She was tough and deeply compassionate. For years after the awful murder of a trio of young teenagers in an Anchorage park, she kept a photo of the teen girl on her desk.

One day I told Sheila how, during an interview with a deeply religious woman, I found myself practically praying with her. Sheila said she would get down on her knees and pray with a source if that's what it took to get the story. It's advice I've never forgotten.

My job for Sheila was to check daily the court docket at the state and federal courthouses. She took me around the buildings, showing me where the court schedules were hung, where the files were kept, and where to attend the 1 p.m. felony arraignments. My job was to look for newsworthy cases or report on the pro forma entering of what was usually a "not guilty" plea by defendants.

I found it fascinating. Defendants arrested the night before would be led in dressed in their prison garb and shackled together. Each would be addressed by the judge, and either a lawyer would be there to represent them or the judge would appoint a public defender. A trial date would be scheduled, other matters brought up by either the district attorney or defense lawyers would be discussed, and bail would be set. Here was the heart and soul of the American justice system.

When I asked Sheila why the arraignments worked the way they did, she explained that it was an opportunity for the judge to see the defendants and to make sure they hadn't been roughed up by the police or others. No college class could teach the lessons I learned just by showing up at the courthouse every workday.

I also checked the daily civil court docket that lists trials or hearings involving civil cases. I was to bring back a copy of each new case if it seemed newsworthy or go to the courtroom to see what was going on.

Everything was on paper in those days. If I needed to get a copy of a charging document against a defendant, I'd have to go to the court clerk's office to request it. Ditto if I needed to look at a file. Often, files would be in a judge's chambers, and I'd have to go upstairs to those offices and ask to look at the files.

Court files are open to the public and only on rare occasions are they sealed or closed. Everyone understood they had to give me what I was requesting, but they didn't have to make it easy. I had to walk a fine line between being assertive and deferential. Judges' secretaries and law clerks could be friendly but wary; judges could be polite or downright hostile. I had to befriend the clerks in the clerk's office. I genuinely liked them, but they were leery of the press. Every day I felt on edge as I negotiated gaining people's trust to do my job.

At first, my job was to let Sheila know if she needed to be in court to cover a specific case. But it wasn't long before she had me stay to cover hearings or even a full day of trial.

Aside from teaching me how to be a reporter, Sheila was one of my writing mentors. She once said no journalism program can truly prepare a student for the job of writing for a newspaper. It's on-the-job training. She was right. The process of writing and being edited on a daily basis was challenging and transforming, whether it was a court brief or summing up a day of trial in twelve inches of news copy. I learned to write even if it meant doing rewrites until midnight.

For the most part, I was intimidated by all my editors that first year or so. At my first annual employee review, I met with Mike Doogan and the night editor, Mark Salgado. Salgado was a hardened newsman from San Francisco. He could also be a teddy bear.

During that review, both Mark and Mike gave me high marks, with some areas they thought I could work on to improve. When it came my turn to speak, I had only one thing to say: I asked Salgado if he could go a little easier on me, as he sometimes made me cry. He was shocked to hear that because I always tried so hard to come across as tough. He felt terrible. After that review, I never had to cry again when I was late on deadline or made a stupid error.

Years later, when Salgado didn't show up to work one day, another reporter was sent to his house to check on him. Sadly, he had died of a heart attack. The entire newsroom was heartbroken.

Maybe all good jobs become like this—a family ready to prop you up in tough times. And journalism has its share of mistakes and insecurities. Even Sheila, the best in the newsroom, once said that every day she expected someone to walk up to her and say, "We're on to you. You don't know what you're doing, and you're no good."

That summed up my feelings nearly every day I went to work. Once a friend asked me this question: if you could be in any room anywhere, where would you wish to be? I don't remember my answer. But I remember his: the *Daily News* newsroom. "Here? Why?" I asked. His response: it was the center of the universe.

I agreed. I loved my job like no other. I still have dreams about working in the newsroom. Sometimes I'm nude, or behind deadline, or full of anxiety over a tough story. But mostly, I miss it. It set me on a future I could never have imagined.

I'm not sure I believe in fate. But what else could explain that, as I worked at my desk each day, the clues to my family's fractured history lay waiting down the hall in the files of the *Daily News*? It was there that I would fulfill a promise I made to myself at the time of my father's death:

"Someday I will write about this."

AFTER TWO YEARS of court reporting, I transferred to the features desk, where I found my calling and an editor who helped pull out the biggest story of my career, one that would change my life.

But first I did what writer John McPhee says writers often do—I circled my intended subject. I began a series of magazine-style pieces on events and people from Anchorage's recent past. Each memorialized the times in which they took place and the era in which we were living.

The first was inspired during a dreaded Saturday shift. Every reporter had to do a Saturday stint. As luck would have it, my editor for a series of Saturdays turned out to be Mike Doogan. We had both grown up in Alaska, so when there was nothing going on in the newsroom, we thought up feature stories.

The first piece we came up with was "The Bun Drive-In." The story took a look back at a drive-in hamburger stand that had waitresses on roller skates (in the summer, at least) and a booth atop the building that broadcast *The Coke Show*, a two-hour radio program that was the first to play rock 'n' roll over the airwaves in Anchorage.

The Bun opened its doors in the early 1960s and closed the summer of 1970. Within that era, it captured the attention of nearly all teens living in Anchorage at the time. They either tuned in nightly or flocked to The Bun in hot rods to hear *The Coke Show's* flamboyant disc jockey, "The Royal Coachman." The RC, Ron Moore, was an actual teen heartthrob.

For the story, I tracked down women who had worked as servers at The Bun, people who hung out there, the owners, and even the Royal Coachman himself.

Mike and I decided I should open the story with the first night Ron Moore aired *The Coke Show* and played rock 'n' roll in Anchorage. Mike had me do a bit of reporting I've used many times since—look up the weather on the day in question. With that information, I was able to recreate that chilly night when Moore had to scrape ice from the inside of the windows of the booth while spinning records on the turntable.

My next story was about a boarding house in a rundown part of Anchorage called Fairview, which did not have much of any view except dilapidated houses and dour public housing. "The Warehouse" began with a bunch of political upstarts and revolutionaries who tried to take over the state Democratic Party in the early 1970s. The building later became home to whatever pop culture had to offer—hippies, punk rockers, Goth kids, and so on.

The inspiration for the story came from reporting on another piece. I'd been sent to cover a concert. While there, I approached a young woman dressed in black, with thick-soled black leather boots. I introduced myself and asked her a few questions. At some point, she said she "hung out" at the Warehouse in a tone that signaled that a square like me wouldn't know what she meant.

I used to hang out at the Warehouse, I thought.

BUT THE REAL PURPOSE of my circling history was to write one thing and one thing only, and that story came about in a way I never saw coming.

My memoir began with working for the new features editor, Gary Nielson. He was of average build and full of high energy. He had a good sense of humor and somehow we nicknamed him—with his approval—"Jitball." I have no idea why.

Nielson and his wife, Jill, were from Connecticut. They had Northeastern accents. Jill hated Alaska. She was not outdoorsy. I didn't blame her.

Back east, Gary had worked with reporters doing stories about real organized crime and the Mob. "My father was kind of a mobster," I told him. Because I knew my dad was from Connecticut—about all I knew at the time—I began to tell Gary stories about my dad. He, in turn, would tell me stories about life on the East Coast and writing about the underworld. Gary was the first person with whom I talked about my dad and my life growing up.

Then in 1987 came the tenth anniversary of the completion of the Trans-Alaska Pipeline System. To commemorate this major milestone in Alaska's history, the *Daily News* planned to have each section of the newspaper produce a story or series of stories related to the pipeline and its impact on Alaska.

I was chosen to write the feature section piece. My assignment was to report on how construction of the pipeline changed crime in Alaska, particularly vice crimes—gambling, prostitution, and drugs. It was as if being the daughter of a professional gambler had somehow made me an expert.

Nonetheless, I went to the newspaper's morgue, the clippings library. (Remember, this was pre-Internet). As I flipped through files from the mid-1970s, I was struck by one thought: the paper had already written the story I had been assigned. What surprised me more was that my senior boss, the executive editor of the newsroom, Howard Weaver, had once been a reporter. Howard had written about my dad and his activities.

A sense of coming full circle took hold of me. Like everyone in the newsroom, I deeply respected Howard. He was the consummate boss. Several times a day, Howard would emerge from his office to meet with staff or visit editors or reporters. Often, when presented with a problem or issue, he had a relevant quote ready, frequently from Winston Churchill. Under other circumstances, this might sound pompous or silly. But Howard was and is a genuine, brilliant newsman who rose through the ranks, learning—as I did—from the bottom up. Like me, he came from working-class roots, the grandson and son of Texas farmers, the working poor. He had a way of making everyone in the newsroom, from star reporter to receptionist, feel important and part of the team. I felt lucky to work for him, and when I saw his byline on stories about my dad, I felt a kinship.

My assignment from Gary was to come up with an angle on the "underworld and the pipeline" story by a certain date. Gary planned a lunch where I would pitch him on my idea. I struggled with this, fearing I'd have nothing because the original concept seemed redundant and uninspiring. Then I had an epiphany.

At some point as Gary and I headed into the restaurant, I took a deep breath and said, "I think I want to write about my dad."

His response was something I will never forget.

"We were hoping you would say that."

For some time, I had been gathering information here and there about my father. I once did a profile of James Vaden, an Alaska State Trooper official going into retirement. I learned he had been the lead investigator into my father's murder. At one point, I asked him if he could help me get a copy of my father's FBI rap sheet. He did.

As a court reporter, I would occasionally look up criminal and civil cases under my dad's name in the index card file while waiting for a clerk to retrieve other paperwork. I would jot down each case number and title on a sheet of yellow legal paper, creating a column nearly two pages long.

When I got the go-ahead to write about my dad, I threw myself into the project. I began making calls to everyone I could think of or to names given to me through referrals. I had a six-week deadline.

Every day, I'd come back to the newsroom with some new story about my father and his activities, or what Anchorage was like during the 1960s and 1970s. I'd share every tale with Gary. He told me to forget the pipeline angle and just keep reporting.

The stories seemed to get better and more revealing about vice in Anchorage. Some old cohorts of my dad would talk to me, but only if I didn't quote them in the story. Others wouldn't talk to me at all. Still others terrified me. Once, I was followed after an interview. Another time, a nightclub owner met me in a parking lot. He was a big man dressed all in black, and I'd been told he'd want to see ID to prove I was Johnny Rich's daughter.

At one introduction, a source said, "Look, it's Johnny Rich's daughter, Kim Rich." The other man, a former associate of my dad's, moved toward me with a big smile on his face, until his friend finished, "She's a reporter with the newspaper now." The other man stopped and politely shook my hand, but the interview was over.

I was given an unprecedented six months—rather than the original six weeks—to research and write whatever it was we were doing; the pipeline assignment was long gone. When I started a draft of my story, I began at the beginning, when my parents first arrived in Alaska when I was a baby. After many rewrites and reviews, the story was finally done in the fall of 1987. It would run in three parts on the Sunday front page for three consecutive weeks.

Gary and I met with several editors to discuss the story. One was the features copy editor, Mark Dent. He was a master of editing and writing headlines. For a story I wrote on rocker Ted Nugent, who came to Alaska for a bow-hunting conference, Mark created what I consider perhaps the best newspaper headline ever: "Rack 'n' Roll." For the series on my life with my father, Mark came up with "Family Secrets."

Good enough, we all thought. *Now what?* Why should any reader, half of whom didn't even live in Alaska back when my tale took place, care to read this story—much less three stories—over three weeks?

So, there we sat, trying to come up with an opening paragraph that would introduce the series and tell readers why we were telling them this story. We were all pretty smart and experienced writers, and none of us could come up with a good answer.

"This is the story of Alaska's rough and tumble days." Nah.

"This is a murder story that resonates to this day." Nope.

"This is the story of how big oil impacted Anchorage." No, no, no.

Finally, in exasperation, I blurted out, "How about: This is the story of my life with my dad."

We all felt it: "Aha! That's it!"

And that's basically what we wrote on top of the first in the series of stories that Sunday in October 1987.

I GOT UP EARLY that first Sunday. It was winter in Alaska and still dark outside. I was the first one stirring. I went out and fetched the newspaper in its usual bundle, dry inside a heavy plastic bag.

I tore it open and spread out the front page on the carpeting. I stared at the artwork done by Peter Dunlap-Shohl, the newspaper's full-time artist and cartoonist. There was also a photo of me standing next to a chain-link fence surrounding the lot where the house at 736 East Twelfth once stood. Inside, on the jump pages—as we say in the newspaper business—were photos from my personal collection.

I sat there for a few minutes just staring at the story. The house was quiet. Everyone else was asleep.

I say "everyone" because I was no longer living in my mountain A-frame. I was no longer living with my husband. For reasons that will always confound me, I had left.

I was twenty-nine that October. There was no other person in either of our lives. We'd had the standard newlywed squabbles about money and careers and who did more housework, though the beauty of a nine-hundred-square-foot house is that housework isn't much of a chore.

We had a big dispute over whether or not to build a more permanent home. I wanted to do more, see more, travel more. I have always been restless—not always a good quality to possess.

Eric wanted to start on a new home; I did not. Without knowing exactly what I was doing and what I was risking, I left and moved in with friends.

Most of the upheaval in my life had been caused by others who were in control. Now, I was fully at the wheel. I know I didn't appreciate how important my next step was, realize the personal chaos I was about to endure and the regrets that would haunt me for a long time.

Maybe going back over my past unearthed my present. That's what I concluded with a counselor I had been seeing. Another possibility was one I explored with a friend whose marriage came apart at about the same time. Unlike me, she came from a stable family. The one thing we both had in common was that we had periods of time away from our spouses. *How much had that contributed?* we wondered.

In my case, Eric worked for several summers at a lodge in Southeast Alaska owned by a group of rich Texas oilmen. I visited there once, which coincided with a visit by the owners. I arrived via commercial airliner into nearby Ketchikan. The oil men arrived in a private jet. Two had left their wives behind and brought their girlfriends. Their arrival in the jet, and subsequent shopping trips to buy everything from rain gear to television sets, put Ketchikan into an uproar.

At the lodge, I watched from a distance the all-night drinking and hot tub parties, and I overheard long, loud conversations about politics and resources. Two of the oilmen had long-term business ties in Alaska and held various gas and oil leases. For the first time, I began to understand the concept of Alaska as a colony, a place not in charge of its own destiny.

Maybe I began to think about my destiny. A friend once said people like he and I weren't meant to have normal lives. I didn't agree. I still don't. But I guess I just wasn't ready to settle down.

Perhaps leaving an otherwise good marriage wasn't the right idea, but once I left our home, I found there was no returning. Another friend described the experience as boarding a train for which there were no stops or disembarking or going back.

That quiet Sunday morning, with the newspaper series "Family Secrets" on the floor in front of me, I felt something powerful. There was no going back from this, either.

Anchorage Daily News

ANCHORAGE, ALASKA, SUNDAY, OCTOBER 18, 1987 — PRICE 50 CENTS

FAMILY SECRETS

Daughter tells her story of life with an Anchorage crime figure

The teen-age girl picked up the telephone, dialed the newspaper, and asked to speak to a reporter. She was angry. She wanted to know why, in a three-paragraph article about the

By KIM RICH / FIRST OF 3 SUNDAY PARTS

Nancy is fine

1st lady undergoes surgery for cancer

By SUSANNE M. SCHAFER
The Associated Press

A matter of policy

Gulf attack raises questions for U.S.

By DAVID B. OTTAWAY and MOLLY MOORE
The Washington Post

Walsh plans to give businesses break

By DAVID POSTMAN
Daily News reporter

index

weather

Newspaper series art for "Family Secrets."

CHAPTER 7

The Right Stuff

W hen I looked at the sheets of newsprint containing my life story, I felt a turbulent range of emotions. Part of me felt great sorrow as I thought of my mom and my dad and how much pain and loss had led up to that moment.

My other feeling was fear. I'd now put my entire past out there for the world to read. What would be the result? Was it the right thing to do? How would people react? Did I get it right? Was my research thorough enough?

Another fear was less rational. In the final days of writing the story, I had been overcome with a fear that I, too, might be in danger of being killed by my father's murderer.

My father had gotten into what was called the "massage parlor" business, a small but growing sex industry that cropped up in the early Seventies in Anchorage. The parlors were usually based in homes outside the city limits. For a short time, there were essentially no laws against them; they fell into a gray area. My father and others like him saw massage parlors as a way to make a fortune off the thousands of pipeline workers expected in Alaska. Instead of striking it rich, my father was killed on the orders of a group of people angered by his takeover of Cindy's Massage Parlor. They thought he had cheated them.

The killer was alive. He had been paroled and was living in Valdez, a small town south of Anchorage. He had killed the last two men who had crossed him. What would he do to a reporter, a daughter exposing him and his crimes all over again?

I met with Howard Weaver and tried to explain how I felt. I knew I was not writing about my father to avenge his death or retell the trial of his killers. My story was about my father's life and my life with him.

Then it dawned on me: "Do we have to use the killer's name?"

The killer was no longer a public person by journalistic standards, and to reprint his story could damage his current life and reputation. "Say what?" fellow reporters asked.

I knew it sounded crazy for a reporter to act this way. The crimes were public information and had been covered extensively by the local news media at the time. Criminal cases—files and trials—are open to the public. Reporters and newspapers have to be careful not to invade someone's privacy without a larger, compelling need to reveal something the public has a right to know. A convicted murderer could hardly make such a claim.

"Victim of a violent crime" is a phrase I would never use to describe myself. But I was. In general, I eschewed the notion of being a victim. I also understood that I did not want that fear or any other to define my life.

I thought of my favorite writer, Tom Wolfe, and his book *The Right Stuff*, about the origins of the US space program. The title came from how military test pilots quietly viewed their calling. You either had the right stuff, or you didn't. You were either tough enough to be a test pilot, or you weren't. Nothing more ever had to be said.

Newsrooms are filled with some of the same thinking. Working in a newsroom is also a calling. It's a brotherhood and sisterhood. Reporters must have the right stuff. They must be fearless.

But no other reporter I knew had ever been challenged to do what I was being asked to do: interview my father's killer.

The state trooper who had led the investigation and elicited a confession from my father's murderer after some two dozen jailhouse visits backed me up. "Don't go near him," he said.

I didn't want the killer in my consciousness. I didn't want anything from him, nor did I need anything. By the time I had finished researching my father's death and the trials of all those involved in the conspiracy to kill him, I didn't need to hear firsthand what happened. I knew it. I didn't need the killer to give me his version of events. I'd already read the transcripts.

And I didn't need an apology or, worse, any kind of relationship with him. He was like Darth Vader from *Star Wars* to me: he represented the dark side of life, and I did not want it in my world.

I didn't have to say much to Howard to convince him I didn't need to use the killer's name. And if a nationally respected Pulitzer Prize-winning editor like Howard Weaver agreed with me, then I was doing the right thing. He told me we could use the killer's initials in the story and explain why we—fearless reporters and editors—were doing so.

Not everyone in the newsroom agreed. But I figured that when they had to consider interviewing a loved one's murderer, we could talk.

ONE OF THE stabilizing influences in my life at this point stemmed from another aspect of my father's past. While researching the series, I learned of my father's Jewish roots. I decided it was time to know that part of my heritage.

I began attending the local synagogue, Temple Beth Shalom. I celebrated the holidays with Jewish friends. I even enrolled in a Hebrew class. I felt a deep resonance with the Jewish faith and found guidance in the synagogue's rabbi, Harry Rosenfeld.

Rosenfeld's accepting, easy manner and quick wit made it easy for me to negotiate difficult moments, such as Shabbat dinner with Jewish friends. One Friday night, my friends began the dinner asking everyone there to tell how they grew up celebrating Shabbat with their families. I was mortified. I had nothing to say, as my father didn't practice that faith or any other. Somehow, I managed to avoid my turn.

Later, I asked Rabbi Harry, as he liked to be called, what I should have done.

"Answer the question. If it had been me there, I would have said, 'playing football,' because that's what we did every Friday night," Rabbi Harry said.

WHILE I WAS researching my story, I would often hear from another Anchorage friend, Jeff Lowenfels. He was—and still is—the newspaper's longtime gardening columnist.

Lowenfels, tall and lanky with a ready smile and laugh, is one of the most upbeat and energetic people I've ever known. He's one of the funniest too, one of those guys who'll pull out a clown's nose and pop it on his face if he's around a group of kids.

Jeff grew up in a rich suburb of New York City, the sort of place that's home to people who own entire broadcast networks. Jeff's undergraduate degree was from Harvard, but he would never tell you that. He did have a letterman jacket left over from being on the school's cross-country ski team. But three of the letters are missing from the school name, leaving only "ar ar."

When he finished law school in Boston, Jeff came to Anchorage with his wife, Judith Hoersting, who is an artist and nurse. Their flight from the East Coast was initiated after their first date. They had been riding bicycles in the city when Jeff was shot during a mugging. Judith, a nursing student at the time, saved his life. In the hospital, Jeff told Judith of an old proverb that holds that if someone saves your life, you are responsible for them for the rest of their life. They married, had two children, and have been together ever since.

I had told Jeff and Jude a little about my dad's story as I was working on it. Jeff loved it. The Monday after the last of the three-part series ran, Jeff phoned me at my desk in the newsroom.

"Are you ready? I'm going to send this off to my friend Kenny Kaufman," Jeff said. Kaufman was a major Hollywood producer living in New York City. He and Jeff had attended summer camp together as boys.

On deadline and completely uninterested, I replied, "Sure, Jeff, you do that."

After I hung up, Jeff called his old buddy, who quickly tried to dissuade him from faxing what Jeff insisted was a story Kaufman would love.

"Jeff, please don't do this to me," he said. "I get calls like this all the time from my relatives, my grandmother, and so on..."

Jeff was not to be deterred, and he faxed off a thick stack of pages. After only a few minutes, Kaufman called him back and said, "I laughed, I cried, I want it."

I was out of the office working on a story that afternoon. I returned to my desk to find a line of phone messages across the top of my computer screen ordering me to "call Jeff Lowenfels ASAP." I knew at that moment something big had happened.

The next day, I sat in Jeff's office in a conference call with Kaufman, who offered me $10,000 for an option on the film rights to my story.

Dead silence.

"I know. You're overwhelmed," Kaufman said.

To say the least. I was stunned. Kaufman explained how it worked: in exchange for the money, I would sign an option agreement good for a year that gave his company the right to produce a film based on my life. He offered to send a packet of information and videos of films he'd made.

Just before we hung up, I said, "That's great, but I always wanted to write a book."

Famous first words.

I had no idea what I was saying, but Kaufman said he knew of a good literary agent for me.

I went back to the newsroom and immediately spoke with Howard. Figuring we needed some advice, Howard contacted his friend Joe McGinnis, the well-known nonfiction writer and novelist.

Howard had met McGinnis when the writer came to Alaska to research and write *Going to Extremes*, about Alaska during the pipeline days. McGinnis has since written twelve books and is most known for *The Selling of the President 1968* and a true crime series. Several of his works had been adapted into TV miniseries.

Something happens when your ship comes in. You buck up. Somehow, I knew that saying, "Gee, this is really neat," was not a good idea. These people were serious.

Ironically, just a few months earlier, I had been wondering if I was in the right field. At one point, I considered ditching journalism. I actually took the LSAT test and began researching law schools while I was working on the biggest story of my journalism career.

But now, it looked like I was on the right track. I began researching the business of publishing and Hollywood, buying the right sort of books to understand what I was dealing with. Soon, I got a call from a woman with a crisp English accent at what is considered one of the largest literary agencies in the world.

"We very much agree with Joe that your story would make an excellent book," the woman said.

Agreed with Joe? She refers to one of the biggest-selling writers in the world as "Joe"? He'd already called them on my behalf? I was floored. I've got one guy wanting to pay me a bundle of money for my life story, and a woman with an English accent talking about a book.

Holy jackpot, Batman!

There was only one thing to do: go to New York City.

A FEW DAYS later, the producer put me in touch with another literary agent who specialized in representing journalists writing books.

I planned a trip to New York City to meet with all of them—two literary agents and the producer. I'd never been to New York and was intimidated by the prospect. After visiting family in Washington, DC, I arrived at Grand Central Station by train. I had no idea about the city's geography and even less about getting out of the train station. It took me an embarrassingly long time—and help from a friendly Amtrak employee—just to find the exit.

My hotel was right across the street, and I discovered just how small a hotel room can be. My window overlooked a mishmash of other buildings and what I would later discover was the side of Macy's at Herald Square.

My biggest fear that night was not whether I would make a good impression but if I would figure out how to flag a cab. Now, it's not as if I wasn't prepared. I knew enough to give a cab driver an intersection, not an address. I had read up on not getting taken advantage of by city slickers. I knew I should keep my hands on my purse while it was slung over my shoulders. Ha! Muggers, I showed you!

Beyond my caution rode a wave of excitement. New York City was mythical to me. I had spent much of my late childhood, teen years, and on dreaming of going there. This was the city of *Fame*, where I could attend the High School for the Performing Arts. This was the city of my favorite childhood television show, *Family Affair*, in which a rich uncle and his butler strived to raise three orphaned children. To me, New York City was *That Girl*, the TV sitcom about a young, single woman making it on her own. This was the city of dreams. My dreams. New York was "where I'd rather stay," as the line went in the ridiculous TV sitcom *Green Acres*.

The only problem was I was afraid to venture out into the great city. When I finally did so later that afternoon, I looked up and down

The New York City skyline, southern tip of Manhattan Island, mid-1990s. I took this photo from the water when I went to visit the Statue of Liberty and Ellis Island.

Seventh Avenue and was struck by one thought: it's just a city. I had been to Seattle and Phoenix, Los Angeles and Denver. The only difference, I told myself, was that New York was a really big city. Some of my fears were allayed.

"Hey, Kodiak!" shouted the bellhop, who had been talking about Alaska with me. He opened the door to a cab he had hailed for me. I gave the cabbie my intersection and sailed off to meet with the producer Ken Kaufman.

THE MEETING WITH Kaufman was informal and friendly. I barely remember it, except that he asked if there were any Broadway plays I wanted to see. My choice was *Starlight Express*; I had read about Andrew Lloyd Webber's latest musical, which was performed on roller skates, and figured it was not likely to tour Anchorage anytime soon.

He then asked where I would like to go to dinner. Only one place came to mind—the place where I'd been told you could watch commercial jets come in for landings at a lower elevation than you, Windows on the World in the World Trade Center.

Kaufman had family plans, so he excused himself and left me with a friendly young assistant. Together we went down to the subway, where—just like in the movies—the trains were all covered in graffiti. Windows on the World indeed felt so high, it was almost dizzying.

The next day, I had time to kill before attending *Starlight Express*, so I walked down Seventh Avenue. I had a map I'd discreetly pull out of my pocket from time to time, but I really had no idea where I was going. After a few hours, I turned to go back to the hotel. I was tired and my feet were sore. But I had no idea how to flag down a cab.

I continued to walk until it grew dark and began to rain. I started to panic. I finally decided to find a store, go in, and see if they could call me a cab. I happened to turn off Seventh into SoHo, another place I'd read about. I walked around taking in the gallery signs and windows, until the rain forced me to duck into the only shop that was still open.

Like Alice down the rabbit hole, I found myself in a place where I seemed to have suddenly shrunk—or perhaps everything else had grown giant-sized. Six-foot No. 2 wooden pencils stood near giant five-foot Crayola crayons, enormous silver paper clips, and a pink rubber Eberhard Faber eraser as big as a medium-sized dog.

I had stumbled into Think Big!, a pop art store. I was in heaven. I had been reporting on art and artists in Anchorage and had come to know the various arts movements and great works of art. I had always loved visual art and had been drawing since I was young. I suppose I considered becoming an artist, but I think I grew up too poor to look at it as a serious career.

The Think Big! store was the perfect place for me. I couldn't have done better that day if I had meticulously planned every detail. I bought as many items as I could carry. The clerk was kind enough to walk me to Seventh Avenue and show me how to get a cab.

THAT NIGHT, I saw *Starlight Express*. When the show let out, I marched my newfound cab-flagging skills over to Seventh Avenue and began flagging like a pro. And I flagged, and I waved, and I held my hand in the air, but I didn't know that getting a cab at 11 p.m. in the theater district was not going to happen. I figured I'd walk back to the hotel. I was at about Forty-Second Street, and my hotel was near Thirty-Fourth street, a little over ten blocks. Easy for someone who jogged every day.

As I began to walk, I stumbled on another discovery—Times Square.

The old Times Square, long before it was renovated and upgraded for Disney and parents with children. Thanks to crowds that filled the area, I felt safe. I basked in the glow of the famous neon. I also kept moving and stayed wherever there were people. As I neared the hotel, I could see Macy's. It was the holiday season and the massive department store had a laser light show on its exterior with giant teddy bears and gift packages. It was almost magical.

From that moment on, I was hooked. New York was my kind of town.

THAT YEAR, RICH Mauer, a senior investigative reporter and dear friend and mentor in the newsroom, suggested the *Daily News* nominate "Family Secrets" for a Pulitzer Prize in feature writing. They did. I deeply appreciated Rich's vote of confidence. That year, Howard Weaver was on a Pulitzer panel. He later told me that when voting began on the finalists, "Family Secrets" was one of the last stories on the table.

That I came close was good enough for me. My parents would have been proud. Certainly, if they were around, they would be amazed that within a few days, I would have two publishing agents vying to represent a book based on their lives and deaths.

Soon after my trip to New York, I met with an agent in Washington, DC. Rafe Sagalyn of the Sagalyn Literary Agency was known for representing journalists, including many Pulitzer Prize winners.

"You are sitting in the catbird seat," Rafe told me during our lunch. "You can't go wrong no matter who you choose."

So I chose him. His confidence in my story and his experience working with journalists told me he understood how journalists think and work. The literary

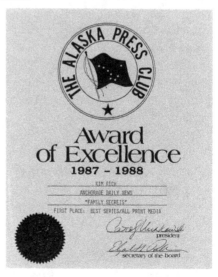

Award of Excellence
1987 – 1988

KIM RICH
ANCHORAGE DAILY NEWS
"FAMILY SECRETS"
FIRST PLACE: BEST SERIES/ALL PRINT MEDIA

president

secretary of the board

One of the state and regional awards granted to "Family Secrets."

agency I'd met with in New York had asked me to produce a sample chapter that would "sing," and then they would decide if they thought I could write a book. I knew that firm wasn't the right one for me. My gut said to go with Rafe, so I did.

Soon after, I went to Los Angeles to meet again with Ken Kaufman, the film producer, and visit family. The trip felt as if I were coming full circle in my life. Kaufman mentioned this feeling to my literary agent.

"Kim is coming home," he said, noting how my parents had started out in LA. I was born there, and now my life story was going to be the subject of a TV film produced there.

Everything seemed to be falling into place in a way I could never have imagined. What could go wrong?

Everything.

THE DAY OF my meeting with the producer, I borrowed a cousin's car—a beat-up clunker. "I appreciate the offer, but I can't drive this to Beverly Hills," I said at first. But it was too late for a rental, so I hopped into the dented, dirty red sedan and sped off from Burbank.

My lunch date was at a swanky, hot Hollywood spot in Century City, off the Avenue of the Stars. I was determined to be punctual, but I couldn't find a spot to park. I had no change for a parking meter anyway. I had no choice but to use the valet parking. As I pulled into the lot, all I could see was a sea of shiny luxury carts.

Later, a friend noted the scene was straight out of the film *Beverly Hills Cop*, where Eddie Murphy's Detroit detective character experiences a similar moment. As he hands over the keys to his junker, he remarks, "Be careful with it. This is what happened the last time I parked here." I didn't have a clever line in my pocket. But to my surprise, the friendly valet acted as if nothing was out of the ordinary. I rushed out of the car and into the restaurant to meet Kaufman.

We were seated on the second-floor balcony overlooking the main dining area. We chatted and scanned for the occasional movie star. But I'm mostly Italian, and I talk with my hands. At one point, my enthusiastic gestures knocked a heavy salt shaker off the table. As if in slow motion, it flew across the railing and down, down, down onto the classy dining area below.

Kaufman and I stared at each other, both resisting the urge to lean over and see where it landed. A few moments later, the waiter brought back the flying salt shaker. Fortunately, it had not landed on anyone's head. I wouldn't need to pay for some starlet's plastic surgery.

DESPITE HIS INITIAL interest, Kaufman didn't use his one-year option on the film rights to my story. In the meantime, I kept learning everything I could about the publishing and film business. I called writers I knew and read books on the subject. Eventually I learned that film options could run out. You needed a major agent to get a major book contract, and then the rest—including a film—would follow.

Rafe said I needed a book proposal, about a twenty-five-page, double-spaced summary of the book. I spent six months trying to write it late at night in the newsroom after my workday was done.

Rafe and his staff rejected draft after draft. He couldn't understand why I couldn't quite get the hang of it, and I was beginning to doubt myself as well. But finally, we created a document that managed to tell the first fifteen years of my life, culminating with the murder of my father. Rafe began shopping the proposal and within a few days, he had several offers.

It was late in the day when he called to tell me about the big offer, which required we either accept or turn it down right away.

"It's a home run," he said. "Maybe not with the bases loaded, but a home run, nonetheless."

We accepted the offer. It was a wise move. Rafe had given my proposal to one of the top editors in the business, Paul Bresnick at Doubleday. Paul had worked with some of the biggest celebrities and stars in the world, including a number of professional athletes. He had a book that was one of the all-time best sellers in nonfiction. He was laid-back, cool, and despite his New York roots, he got excited over little things like celebrity sightings—just like me!

I would sign my contract with Doubleday a few months later, in January 1989, in order to finish out the year at the newspaper.

WHEN PEOPLE HEARD I was writing a book, they'd say things like, "Alaska's hot!" or "Books about Alaska are big," or "Everyone wants to do a movie in Alaska."

A dear friend and writer, Tom Bodett, the folksy-sounding voice of Motel 6, started his writing career in Homer, Alaska. He began by doing humorous spiels about small-town life on National Public Radio. He eventually went on to write books based in Homer (and incidentally, Rafe Sagalyn was his agent).

As a feature writer, I was once assigned to do a profile of Tom. I drove to Homer, about 225 miles south of Anchorage, to meet with him. At one point in my hippie teen years, I had dreamed of a life in Homer: living in a cabin, growing my own food, making my own pottery dishes. In fact, many people do just that. So when I met Tom, with his short hair, blue jeans, and flannel shirt, drinking a beer and looking like a regular guy, I was surprised.

We spent most of our time together talking about writing. He described what he did as somewhere on the lowest rung of the literary ladder. I'm not sure I agree with that, given the long-heralded tradition of folksy humor writing. If Tom was on the lowest rung, I wasn't even on the ladder! But not once did he say, "Alaska is hot! I'm going to write about it."

The idea of Alaska as a hot topic probably stems from the lineup of major American writers who have ventured north to write about Alaska, including Joe McGinnis, John McPhee, and James Michener. Alaska was hot because those authors were hot, with huge, established careers.

When people talked to me about the novelty of writing about Alaska, I would point out that writing about family was nothing new, no matter where you were from.

"Woody Allen started his career writing about his average New York City middle-class Jewish family," I said. My other hero, Nora Ephron, took the breakup of her marriage and turned it into *Heartburn*, one of the wittiest and most scathing novels of the times. I didn't pretend that I had the material or talent of either of those writers, but as a journalist, I knew good stories were all around.

Then there were the people who might comment on the dysfunction and tragedies in my family and say soothingly, "Writing a book will be cathartic." I hated that word. It implied, "You are different," or "You have issues you need to work through, but the rest of us are A-okay."

At least, that's generally how Defensive Me interpreted such comments. It took me a long time to realize why I didn't like that assumption: it diminished my parents and what I thought I was doing. I was not only writing their story but my own.

Once, I was asked to speak at a memoir-writing class. I began my talk by saying, "I'm just lucky enough to have a father who was murdered and a mother who went insane." The handful of mostly middle-aged women in the class stared at me in silence, their mouths hanging open and eyes wide. "She's speaking ironically," the instructor said, leaping in to reassure her shocked students.

It's the story I was stuck with. The story I lived. If I could have crafted my own childhood, it would have looked a lot different.

ALL THIS—THE IDEA that Alaska was a hot topic, or the notion that I might exploit my own childhood, or that I was writing the book as a form of therapy—went out the window the day I asked my editor, a highly successful publishing house editor in New York City, why he wanted to do my book.

"I lost my father at a young age," Paul said. "I want to do what you are doing."

WHEN IT CAME time to leave the newspaper to go off and write the book, the newsroom gave me a party. Colleagues took me to lunch, and some said they were jealous of my chance to get paid to write my story, my Great American True Story.

How did I feel? The first day, I sat in my home office and cried.

I'd never felt so alone. I hated it. Then Jeff Lowenfels got his law firm to rent me a small office in some unused space. This went better, as I became friends with the firm's staff. But I still missed the noise, chaos, and camaraderie of the newsroom.

I was given a time frame of about two years to finish the book. Part private eye, part cop, and mostly a reporter working on my own story, I spent every day trying to uncover my father's life story. I had never met any relatives from his side of the family, except a grandfather who came to Alaska when I was about five or six. The memory was so faint I wasn't sure it had actually happened.

With such a tight turnaround, I had to write while I was researching, creating a memoir that became part mystery novel. My contract had me paid when I handed in the first half, and would again when I turned in the second half. I had an advance that was more than enough to support me for a couple of years and pay for long-distance calls, express mail queries, and travel. I mapped out a work schedule that involved about six months of continued research, and then I had to begin writing. I created a production schedule that called for X number of pages to be written per day, week, and month.

Keep in mind that there was no Internet, no cell phones, and no cheap airline flights from Alaska in the late 1980s.

My first travel was to meet with my mother's family to tell them in person about the book. Naturally, they had concerns, including revealing my mother's maiden name—Chiaravalle—and hence identifying my male cousins who bore that name.

One cousin asked if I was going to use real names. He was worried about his privacy, and I respected that. Mostly, I struggled to explain my aim in writing the book. It was for my parents, whose lives were cut short. I stressed that I had enough training as a journalist to be fair. I had no intention of blaming or embarrassing my mother's family. I was not writing the book as an exposé or to settle any scores.

I asked them to trust me. I can't say I would be any less concerned if someone was writing a book that would include my personal life or family members. To their credit, not one of them asked me to stop writing the book. It's as if they knew that day would come. I think they had as many lingering questions about my mother's illness as I did; it was the most controversial issue in the book for them and for me.

My digging eventually led to the discovery of relatives on my father's side of the family. They were all welcoming and warm and talked to me. Only one frightened me—one of my father's paternal uncles, who was alleged to have Mob ties. My phone rang one day, and when I answered, a deep, gruff voice said only, "Is this Kim Rich?"

"Yes," I said.

Click.

He hung up.

It was unnerving. Then I realized who the caller probably was and how he got my number. Another relative had apparently told him I had shown up at their house, so my uncle called to make sure I was who I said I was. I had run into the same kind of reaction when researching the newspaper story.

For one interview, I traveled to Oklahoma City to visit a man who had once been married to my dad's mother and adopted my dad. We sat at a kitchen table with the tape recorder between us. I'd start the recording, ask a question, and get a short answer, followed by, "Well, that's about all there is to say." Then he'd reach over and hit the stop button on the recorder.

I'd gently reach back over, flip it on, and ask another question.

"She was nice. ... Well, that's about all there is to say."

Off went the recording. And so on. This might have gone on all day if his wife hadn't come in and chided him into talking to me.

"She needs answers," she said. "Talk to her."

He did. And so did most people I contacted.

THEN THERE WERE people who contacted me. One was the brother I had never known.

When my father married Bridget in 1973, she was pregnant. The baby boy was born after my father was kidnapped. I had seen him as an infant, but when Bridget left my life, I never knew what happened to him.

For most of his life, John Rich III was raised by his grandparents in nearby Eagle River. Bridget's addictions left her unable to raise him, and she died when he was young. One day, he spotted my byline in the *Daily News* and sent me an invitation to his high school graduation.

We happily agreed to meet each other. As soon as he opened the door, we both had a lot of questions answered. He saw that what he had suspected was true—my father was not his biological father. Bridget and my father were white. My brother is black. That didn't matter to either of us. From that moment, I was his sister and he was my brother, and we remain very close.

I ALSO NEEDED to uncover my mother's mental health records to explore her conditions and diagnoses and how her life played out after she left my father and slipped irrevocably into schizophrenia.

The last person I thought of in any of this was me. I never thought of it as my story. It was theirs. I felt uneasy when writing about myself as a child, never mind the painful childhood memories.

In order to get through the research and writing, I took the "me" out of it so I could get it done. I treated the book as another journalist might.

One friend said reading the book was like reading a mystery as I searched to uncover the secret of my parents' lives. Later, some critics—mostly women—faulted me for not being emotional enough in the writing. Maybe. I had been a journalist, not a creative writer. But even now, I'm not sure I would have changed a thing. I'm not sure I was capable of adding my emotions. I don't think I would have had the stamina or the ability to get through it. I got the impact of the tragic elements of the story, and I didn't think my comments were necessary.

I never imagined the costs of taking a journey through the past. Eventually it all hit me—the collapse of my marriage, the stress of the book, and perhaps even reliving my childhood led to a clinical depression. It lasted about a year or more.

I probably got by as long as I did because I ran every day. In the winter, I would cross-country ski on trails near my office. I'd work in the morning, take a lunch break, ski or run for about forty-five minutes, then go back to the office to work the rest of the day and sometimes the night.

At some point, my first counselor diagnosed me with post-traumatic stress disorder, like a soldier. She described my childhood as a "war zone." I had survived, but as with combat veterans, I would one day have to deal with the emotional consequences.

There might be some truth to that. I got through the tumultuous time immediately surrounding my father's death by staying tough and by refusing to give in to feelings of fear and abandonment. In some ways, I was glad to be away from my father's temper and his lifestyle.

I don't know if PTSD was the correct diagnosis or if it was just popular at the time. It didn't matter. I kept working and researching and writing every day. I knew this was a dream of mine—to write about my parents—and I wasn't about to screw it up.

I was also dating for the first time in nearly a decade, and it was a disaster. One guy dumped me and went Antarctica to work. Another, a West Point graduate, went to the Gulf War. The emotional ups and downs of my single life probably contributed to the depression.

When my first counselor moved to Seattle, I found another. She had me keep note of how I was feeling. After a couple of weeks, I read aloud my one-line notations in my date book. I discovered I had been crying nearly every day. I met with a psychiatrist who prescribed an anti-depressant. Within a couple of weeks, I was my old self. Within six months, I was off the medication and fine.

I could not believe the difference. I credit both the psychiatrist and my therapist with getting me through the research and writing of *Johnny's Girl*. I felt like I owed them my life.

MEANWHILE, I WAS learning a lot about book publishing. The editor who buys your book for the publishing house doesn't actually do the kind of editing I was used to in the newsroom. Instead, authors often hire their own editors to help develop a story, find plot holes, cut irrelevant details, and fine-tune the work.

My agent suggested a writer and editor he knew, Mike Dolan. Mike was perfect. He was from Washington, DC, and had long roots in the district. He was funny, wickedly smart, and an excellent editor. He made the task doable and less lonely. He got the story. He got me. Years later, I remain close to Mike and his family.

With Mike's help, I was done with the book by 1992. I turned it in to my publisher and decided what I was going to do next: go to graduate writing school. I researched the best schools and decided I'd start there, get rejected, and figure out where to go next.

Eventually, I learned about the Masters of Fine Arts (MFA) program at Columbia University in New York City, which has a nonfiction component that is one of the best in the country. I sent away for the information packet. It included a handsome black-and-white booklet with photos of Dodge Hall, which housed the film, music, theater, visual arts, and writing programs. My teenage dream of attending a performing arts school in New York City could actually come true. I wasn't exactly in high school, though; I was in my early thirties, an age when most people are settled into marriage and families.

My editor Paul Bresnick said I had already done an MFA in writing my book. He was right; most who enter the program do so with the hope of getting their manuscript worked on and published, since the school is in the heart of the literary world and publishing industry.

I figured I had a lot to learn. I had always wanted to live in New York, and here was a chance. Plus, I thought I should be close to my publisher when the book came out, which was scheduled for the spring of 1993. Rafe had long told me I would need help to market the book and that I needed to befriend the publisher's publicist to make sure they paid attention to it.

The only problem in all this was that I first had to be accepted into the program. Part of the application process involved sending in writing samples. I sent in a part of my book.

I was overjoyed when I got the news: I had been accepted.

I was going to the Ivy League. I was moving to New York City. A friend of my father once said that my dad would not have been too thrilled with a daughter who was a reporter. But a writer?

"Johnny would have liked that," he said.

The only downside was that I had recently met someone. And it seemed serious.

I FIRST MET Bill during the summer of 1991. I was roommates with David, a longtime friend and former colleague from the radio network who had decided to go to law school. David had a split-level, four-bedroom house in an upscale part of West Anchorage. When I began working on my book, he offered to let me live in the basement rent free.

One night that summer, I went out with a group from David's law firm. One of them was a paralegal named Bill Large.

Bill was originally from the Chicago area. He told me he had graduated from the Massachusetts Institute of Technology and then drove to Alaska on a lark. He basically did it to avoid taking a job in finance on the East Coast, the kind of job many of his fellow MIT grads had been recruited for.

Of course, there's also a story about a buddy of his calling him a sissy for selling out to the temptations of the corporate world or not being courageous enough to drive to Alaska on a dare. To prove his friend wrong, Bill jumped in his truck and drove north.

I didn't think Bill was my type. Plus, he was ten years younger than me. I had dated two younger guys, and both relationships ended disastrously. I swore I'd never do that again.

Besides, the two of us could not have been any more different. I'm five foot two; he's more than a foot taller, at nearly six foot six. I'm dark-haired, emotional, and loud, and I love to dance. Bill hates dancing, has strawberry-blonde hair, and is shy. Once, when he went to introduce himself to a college volleyball player after a game, he got so nervous that he unconsciously began taking off his shirt as he walked across the gym.

I grew up in Anchorage and have roots in California. Bill was from the northwest suburbs of Chicago. My sensibilities are West Coast/Pacific Northwest alternative. His? During his senior year in high school, Bill had a mohawk. He and a buddy would hitchhike into Downtown Chicago to go to concerts by hardcore underground rock bands like Black Flag or Husker Du. He still had the mohawk haircut in the photograph that accompanied his application to MIT. His major was political science—far from my own interests in music and literature.

By the time I met Bill, he had been accepted into Harvard Law School. He had something of a buzz-cut hairstyle and drove a monster truck of sorts that was so far off the ground, he had a rope ladder to help passengers climb aboard. When off work, he wore colorful bandanas wrapped around his head, blue jeans, big-lug leather boots, and a flannel shirt tied around his waist—just like all good grunge members of his generation.

You couldn't accuse Bill of being a snob, and he certainly didn't look like a stereotypical Ivy League grad. When I heard he was going to Harvard, my response was, "Who, him? That guy?!"

Once, I ran into Bill and a friend at a University of Alaska Anchorage hockey game. I told Bill I had studied at UAA and competed in cross-country running. He mentioned he had rowed crew for MIT. I knew he was Harvard-bound. "What are you? A Kennedy?" I asked.

And the rest was still not history.

Bill developed a serious crush on me, but it took months of hanging out as friends before I agreed to date him. A logical person, he argued his case with comments like, "I don't see why you won't date me. I'm nice, I'm smart, I dress okay. I like you."

I'd never met a guy who tried harder. We became friends because one of my first impressions of him was how at ease I felt in his presence. I thought he would be fun to hang out with—as a friend. And he liked my dog, Treadwell the lab. Bill let Treadwell hang out at the condo he shared with another paralegal-soon-off-to-law-school roommate.

By the first of the year in 1992, I had sent in my manuscript. I had moved in with one of the families that had taken care of me when I was a teenager and when I was in college, the Johnsons. Floyd Johnson had passed away a number of years earlier, and Hazel was living alone in their four-bedroom home in East Anchorage.

Once again, I had a room in a basement. It was fine. My dog could stay there, but Treadwell seemed happier with Bill and his roommate, where I spent more and more time.

Finally, Bill and I became romantically involved, as they say.

MONTHS LATER, IN August of that year, we were southbound. I flew to Chicago. Bill drove his red Eagle Talon coupe down the Alaska Highway, known as the Al-Can, since it goes through Canada to connect Alaska to the rest of the United States.

We met up at Bill's mother's house outside Chicago. After visiting for a few days, we embarked on our road trip for the East Coast via Florida.

In researching and writing *Johnny's Girl*, I was reunited with my paternal grandfather, John Rich, Sr. I found him living in Miami Beach, where he had been since World War II. We instantly became close; I was his only grandchild, and he was the last living direct link to my father. We spoke weekly on the phone, and I went to visit as often as I could.

Bill and I decided we could drive down to see Grandpa, enjoy Florida for a few days, and then drive back up the coast to New York and Boston. I would go to grad school at Columbia University, and Bill would go to Harvard Law. It was a great plan.

The only problem was that it was hurricane season, and we were about to head straight into one of the biggest and most deadly hurricanes of all time—Hurricane Andrew.

My then-boyfriend Bill Large and me, visiting the Statue of Liberty and Ellis Island. While living in NYC, I explored and visited every part of the city and its many famed landmarks.

CHAPTER 8

New York, New York

*I*t was a journey that was so fraught with peril, even Lewis and Clark might have turned back.

First, there was there was a slight problem in Orlando, where we stayed overnight before heading into Miami to visit my grandfather. We booked ourselves into a then-popular national franchise motel. Once we got settled into our second-floor room, Bill went downstairs to get a soda from the vending machine on the first floor. I called his mother to check in, using the room telephone. In the middle of our conversation there was suddenly a deafening *BANG*. The line went dead, and the lights went out.

Silence.

A moment, then the phone and the lights came back on.

"What the heck was that?" I asked Bill's mom, describing what had just occurred.

We were still on the phone a minute later when Bill wandered in the door. He looked dazed.

"What's up? You okay?"

"I think I got struck by lightning," he said.

"What?!"

Bill had been putting a quarter into the vending machine when suddenly he, too, heard the loud bang. Next thing he knew, he was on his butt several feet away from the vending machine.

We surmised that lightning hit the roof and traveled through the vending machine; the force of the bolt threw him away from the machine.

"Are you sure you are okay?" I asked.

Bill examined his arms and lifted his T-shirt, where he had a small bruise on his lower abdomen. He insisted he felt fine.

His mom, who was a registered nurse, was still on the phone with me. She insisted we go to an emergency room, because lightning can damage the heart and disrupt its rhythms.

I hung up the phone, and off to the nearest ER we went. Upon arriving, we were given a form to fill out. Under "Reason for Visit?" Bill wrote, "Struck by lightning."

The doctor said Bill was lucky to be alive. Months later, we would settle a small lawsuit against the hotel chain for not having a lightning rod and not having the building properly grounded. In the meantime, assured that Bill's heart was ticking along just fine, we continued our journey.

The next stop was Miami Beach. We arrived in late afternoon, took a walk along the boardwalk, and then went out to dinner. My grandfather's one-bedroom apartment was small, so I booked us a hotel up the coast a bit. It was a lower-priced motel in Dania, twenty-five miles north of Miami Beach.

This was our next mistake.

The drive along the coast highway seemed to take forever. We finally arrived close to midnight. We pulled into a darkened parking lot, where beer bottles and trash were strewn about. Two men were fist-fighting outside the motel office. The only way to check in was from outside. You spoke to the night clerk through bulletproof glass and slid payment through an opening, as if you were buying a movie ticket.

After getting our room key, we drove around the back to our first-floor room. We talked about leaving, but we hadn't seen any hotels with vacancies nearby. It was late. We were tired. We decided to stay.

I turned to go unload the car, the back of which was filled with our clothes, computers, a portable TV, cameras, and all our necessities.

Me on Miami Beach, August 1992. This was just before Hurricane Andrew was within hours of making landfall.

"No, leave it all out there," Bill said. He didn't want anybody to spot us bringing valuables into our room. He figured if anyone wanted to steal anything, let them get it from the car. This is how MIT guys think.

The room seemed so dirty that we left all our clothes on, including our coats, as we reclined on the twin beds and turned on the TV. The few local stations the motel carried all broadcasted the same thing: live news updates on the approaching Hurricane Andrew, which was certain to make landfall within the next twenty-four hours.

It was August 15, 1992. Andrew, a Category 5 hurricane with sustained wind speeds of up to 165 miles, had already caused major damage in the Bahamas and Louisiana and was headed straight for the Miami area.

We both slept fitfully, watching the news updates and wondering if and when we should get back in the car and grab my grandfather. At some point, it became clear a massive evacuation order was in effect for South Florida, especially areas along the water such as Miami Beach, where my grandfather lived.

In the morning, we drove to Grandpa's apartment. We insisted he either come with us or go to a nearby shelter. He refused to do both. Authorities were preparing to close all bridges to Miami Beach that afternoon. Bill and I either had to leave or get stuck in Miami Beach for an indefinite period of time. Forecasts for Andrew's destructive force called for widescale massive destruction never before experienced.

We argued with my grandfather to come with us. Once up the coast, we could figure out what to do next. But at the moment, we had to get out and get out quick. All lanes of I-95—which stretches from Miami all the way north to the Canadian border—were already jammed with bumper-to-bumper traffic to Orlando.

But Grandpa was adamant. He was not going to leave the second-story apartment where he had lived for decades. His building was one of the neighborhood's older ones, in mid-Miami Beach. The small building was surrounded by towering condominium buildings that had long ago blocked the view my grandfather's unit once had of the actual beach. Called "The Lakeside," it was a somewhat rundown but clean refuge for a group of elderly men and women, some younger disabled residents, a Vietnam vet, and others with meager fixed incomes and long histories in Miami. Over the years, I had come to know the landlord and most of my grandfather's neighbors, who helped keep an eye on him and called me whenever anything was wrong.

My grandfather, then in his late seventies, had begun to show signs of early dementia over the past year. I had him assessed by his doctor and even a social worker to see if he should be moved to an assisted living home. Stubborn and independent, he refused to consider moving. His doctor said he was still fine to live on his own, but for not much longer.

That's where things stood that frenzied and panic-filled day.

My grandfather's neighbor, the middle-aged and friendly Vietnam vet, assured me he would take care of my grandfather, as he and most of the other residents were going to stay put.

I called the Miami Beach Police Department to see what they thought I should do. I spoke with an officer familiar with my grandfather and the building. He assured me he would keep an eye on them.

Bill and I then raced between neighboring small grocery stores and bought up what was left of bottled water, batteries, fresh food, and anything we thought my grandfather might need.

Fearing we were doing the wrong thing, at one point I suggested Bill just pick up Grandpa and physically carry him to the car so that we could take him with us.

"I can't do that," Bill said. "It would humiliate him."

108 *A Normal Life*

I knew Bill was right. Plus, I was afraid my grandfather would pitch a fit and try to jump out of the car. He was clearly beginning to lose his mental faculties and would sometimes go into a rage about little things, anything from someone stealing a bottle of Tylenol he could not find to insisting his next-door neighbor was spying on him. These episodes came and went as they do with early dementia, but my grandfather's demeanor that afternoon made it clear he would not leave his apartment. Period.

Finally, with minutes to spare, we said our goodbyes. I was crying as Bill and I got into our car and sped off to join the exodus out of South Florida—tens of thousands of motorists all headed to Orlando.

The driving distance between from Miami to Orlando is 235 miles, usually about a three-and-a half-hour trip. It took us ten hours in traffic that was literally bumper-to-bumper nearly the entire way. We arrived in Orlando around midnight. Listening to local radio stations the entire way, we kept track of when Andrew was expected to make landfall and where, and got updates on hotel space in Orlando.

By the time we got there, all eighty thousand hotel rooms in the city were filled. Not a single room was available.

After making a pit stop, we decided to keep driving north into Georgia, where we hoped to find a hotel room. Sometime in the middle of the night, we made it to Brunswick, another three hours north, and stopped at the first hotel that had any vacancies. We booked a room, paying full price though it was nearly dawn, with checkout at eleven. We didn't care. We got in the room and collapsed.

THE NEXT MORNING, I called my grandfather. Amazingly, the phones were working. Miami Beach and the City of Miami were spared the worst of Andrew's impact. The hurricane landed in Homestead, a suburb south of Miami.

"I should have gone with you!" Grandpa shouted over the phone.

Indeed. The hurricane blew out a large window in his living room, and fierce wind and rains pummeled his building throughout the night. But he and his friends were safe, which was all that mattered.

Relieved, Bill and I continued our journey up the coast without any incidents. Two days later, we drove into New York City via the George Washington Bridge, or as locals call it, "the GWB." Like most New

Yorkers, I instantly fell in love with the architecture of the handsome, grand bridge that spanned the Hudson River. But as we circled off on the exit ramp, we saw it—an abandoned car fully engulfed in flames.

We hoped it wasn't an omen.

I HAD ALREADY made several visits to New York City and had a couple of friends there. I counted on them to make my transition easier. But no sooner had I arrived than they each announced they were moving away, one to Connecticut and the other to Wisconsin. Bill, meanwhile, was headed for Harvard.

I was on my own.

I doubt many of the tens of millions of tourists who annually visit New York City make the trek to visit Columbia's campus. I certainly had not. It's a long haul up the Upper West Side via any mode of transportation—subway, bus, or car—and well off the beaten path of the city's more popular tourist attractions.

The moment I set foot on the campus, I fell in love with it.

The large urban campus sits on thirty-two acres. North to south, it encompasses an area between 110th Street and 120th Street. East to west, the campus is between Broadway and Amsterdam Avenue. It is a giant fortress of sorts, rising above the surrounding neighborhood. The main gates open off 116th Street; inside is a wide promenade, including the broad steps leading up to Low Memorial Library, which has appeared in many feature films and television shows.

I had always regretted that I hadn't gone to a large university outside Alaska. Attending Columbia University in the City of New York—its official name—became that for me. I passionately embraced it, despite some initial disorientation and homesickness, stifling heat and humidity, and the discovery that the suite housing I'd signed up for was basically a coed dorm.

Columbia undergraduate students live in campus dorms, but graduate students have a wide range of rentals available through the university. All along the Upper West Side near Columbia are blocks upon blocks of ubiquitous eleven-story, post-World War II apartment buildings. Many of those within a few blocks of the main campus are owned by the university. Over the summer, Columbia invites prospective graduate students to visit the campus and tour housing options. The university also offers students coming from abroad—or in my case, from Alaska—the option of selecting housing by mail.

I decided I didn't want to have to set up a new apartment needing kitchen supplies, furniture, and the like, so something called "suites" seemed appealing. These were located in a building not far from campus, evidently reserved for students from the College of Arts & Sciences.

I selected a suite that offered a room and shared kitchen and bathrooms with other students. Bill had nothing but good things to say about suites. He had seen the Harvard suites. They were located in elegant, restored older buildings with fully furnished shared living spaces that offered fireplaces and fine art.

"At Harvard, the suites have these chairs with HARVARD on them," he said, describing a scene of New England charm. Naturally, my mind conjured up something you might find in a nice bed and breakfast in the Vermont countryside.

Once signed up, I was excited to see my new home as quickly as possible. Remember, this was before the advent of the Internet. Most of what I knew about Columbia and my potential housing was gleaned from the school catalogue and phone conversations with Columbia employees. I must have failed to ask for details about my housing.

Bill and I arrived on the weekend. Along with some friends, we decided to head uptown to where I'd be living and take a peek at the building; I couldn't move in until Monday.

When we got there, the front door was locked, so we peered in through the glass door. The lobby was shockingly dirty and littered with trash. (We didn't know that workers inside were sprucing up the place for the students and creating a mess in the process.)

As we stood there, an elderly man with long gray hair and a beard and a dark overcoat—in August—walked up on the sidewalk. We stepped aside so he could go in. But he froze, staring down at the ground and grumbling under his breath. He became increasingly agitated by our presence. We tried talking to him, but it only seemed to upset him more. We knocked on the door, hoping to summon someone. Quickly, a polite younger man appeared. He came out and gently helped the elderly man inside. Then he returned, explaining to us that the older man was schizophrenic and would not enter the building if people were by the door.

Oh.

He also explained that when Columbia bought the building, it was being used as an "SRO"—Single Room Occupancy—building for the disabled and mentally ill. Many of the building's original residents still lived there as part of the sale agreement. None were dangerous, he assured us.

After he left, one of my friends turned to me.

"There's *no* way you are living in this dump," she said.

But I had to, at least for a month, according to the housing officials I called the next morning. With thousands of students arriving at the campus and moving in, the rules stated that you could not transfer housing until at least October. They allowed everyone to get settled before letting students to move.

I made do with the situation, which fortunately improved when it came time to move in. By that time, the workers had finished, the walls had fresh paint, and the wood floors were refinished.

My suite consisted of a bedroom with a twin bed, a small wooden desk, a small closet, and one window. I was a few floors up and near a corner, so I could see out well enough. The one thing the room didn't come with was air conditioning.

No air conditioning. In August. In New York City. And I was from Alaska.

I had no idea how to dress for hot, humid weather. As soon as I stepped outside, I'd be a sweating mess. I came to appreciate why New Yorkers left the city in summer, especially in August. I came to call it "pea soup" weather, because that's what the air felt like to me—a big, soppy soup you could hardly slog through.

I bought a small fan for my room's lone window. It helped at night. I managed to go running if I left early enough in the morning. But I also was able to get off the concrete sidewalks by heading west to Riverside Park, along the Hudson River, only a few blocks from where I lived.

Riverside Park, with its dirt trails and pathways, became one of my favorite places in New York. I could run down to the waterfront and a small boat harbor where a smattering of houseboats reminded me of Juneau.

I ONCE READ that New Yorkers spend little time in their notoriously tiny apartments. I was no exception. I tried to make mine as livable as possible, but it was a challenge. My room was one in a long hall of other rooms. There was a small kitchen at the end, which was occasionally the source of rancid smells and unattended cooking. I used the bathroom with great trepidation. Before I showered, I'd scrub down the stall thoroughly. Most of the other student residents spoke Chinese, so casual conversation was nearly impossible.

I counted down the days until I could get out of there.

Maybe it was the heat. Maybe I looked at what the whole thing was costing me. Or perhaps I was tired of the stress of learning how to do everything anew, whether it was trying to do laundry or finding the best place to shop for toilet paper.

Whatever it was, I got on the phone one night with one of my best friends and said I was fed up and wanted to go home.

The next day, I marched into the office of Stephen Koch, the chair of the writing division, and laid out my woes and insecurities. Within a day or so of my meeting with the department chair, the housing department agreed to speed up my move. As if that wasn't enough, the department granted me fellowship money if I stayed.

Of course, I did.

In the days before classes began, I gradually met fellow students. During one of my first visits to the department, I ran into Jerome Gentes, a handsome young man who came from Northern California. He, too, was enrolled in the Columbia's nonfiction program. He was working on a memoir of being one of eleven children adopted by his parents. We became instant friends. He also seemed older, though not as ancient as me.

Despite meeting Jerome and a few others, I still often felt like quitting. When I complained to Bill, his response was to offer to pay all of my student loan debt whether we stayed together or not.

What?! Never in my life had I heard such a thing. It was the most generous thing a boyfriend had ever said to me. He was a keeper.

WHEN AN EDITOR friend at the *Anchorage Daily News* heard that I was moving to New York City, he gave me a freelance assignment to write a fish-out-of-water magazine-style story for the paper's Sunday section.

He advised me to write it soon after arriving, before everything that I was experiencing as new became routine. While I began my classes, I

The cover of the Anchorage Daily News' *Sunday magazine, December 1992. Photographer and friend Fran Durner, who grew up in the city, took me to the Plaza Hotel for Afternoon Tea to capture my experience of one of New York's treasured activities.*

also started work on the story. A photographer from the *Daily News*, Fran Durner, got the assignment to shoot the photos.

Fran was originally from New York. Her parents still lived there, and she visited them often. I was friends with Fran, and once she got there, I learned a lot about New York. She even booked us afternoon tea at the Plaza Hotel. This was a New York tradition, and I knew I should dress up. On this occasion, Fran took the photo that would run on the cover of the Sunday magazine: me sipping tea with the elegant and regal décor of the Plaza in the background.

I was far from home, and by that point, I loved it. I loved every statue in the city, I loved walking down the streets, I loved the shopping and the hustle and bustle. I was awed to see women wearing clothes that came out of the pages of a fashion magazine. I was surprised the first time I realized that department stores had whole sections devoted to this clothing designer or that—people I had only read about. I couldn't believe the selection of shoes at Macy's or Bloomingdale's or any of the larger department stores. The shoe departments were bigger than some of the stores in my hometown!

What I didn't already know about New York, Fran taught me. She told me about the Central Park Zoo, which had a polar bear exhibit.

"There's a polar bear in Central Park?" I asked her.

Not long after I arrived, a longtime friend from Alaska called to say he had an extra ticket to some tribute concert at Madison Square Garden. Would I like to go?

I had adopted the notion that I was to say yes to every opportunity to explore the city.

"Who's playing?" I asked.

Tim, who was a lawyer working in media law, wasn't quite sure. It was some kind of tribute to Bob Dylan. It sounded like other musicians doing Dylan's songs or some such thing. I didn't feel all that excited. I might have been worried about the long commute downtown to the Garden. I always worried about getting home late at night. While I preferred the subway for its speed and economy, I nonetheless felt intimidated about riding it late at night. But this would be my first visit to the famed arena. So, I met Tim at his Midtown office, and we took a cab to Madison Square Garden.

The event looked to be sold out. As we looked over the program, we were stunned to see just how big an event it was. Billed as "Columbia Records Celebrates the Music of Bob Dylan," there were nearly thirty major rock, soul, country, and folk singers and musicians scheduled to perform. They included everyone from Eric Clapton and Neil Young to The O'Jays, to Willie Nelson and Rosanne Cash, her father, Johnny Cash, and his wife, June Carter Cash. There were rock stars and bands such as Ronnie Wood, George Thorogood and Tom Petty & the Heartbreakers, grunge rocker Eddie Vedder, and Chrissie Hynde. And, of course, Bob Dylan himself.

Together on stage or alone, each performer did their version of a Dylan song. It may have been the biggest lineup of acts either Tim or I had ever seen. I spent the evening in a state of perpetual awe, thinking, *Only in New York City.*

Throughout the evening, I would get up occasionally to walk around or stand. At one point, a man stood next to me. He was wearing a nice-looking button-down shirt, and on the pocket was embroidered, "Brooks Lodge, Alaska."

Never had the world seemed so big and yet so small.

I SAVED THE program from that night. I collected brochures, pamphlets, and guides to everything I did in New York, whether it was a general museum visit or a special exhibit, such as "The Art of the Motorcycle" at the Guggenheim Museum. I kept ticket stubs from concerts or shows, especially from popular events such as the *Christmas Spectacular starring the Radio City Rockettes.*

I took note of dining at popular restaurants of the time, whether it was Elaine's on the Upper East Side or The Russian Tea Room in Midtown. Bill and I even got tickets to see Frank Sinatra at Radio City Music Hall. Knowing that Sinatra was in his late seventies, we figured it might be the last time we could see him. The concert was on a weekend. Bill drove down from Boston, as he often did.

We dressed up and went to Radio City, where we marveled at the crowds of men in sharkskin suits and women in fur coats. We felt as if we had stepped into the early Sixties. I kept thinking about my parents and how they would have loved this. Bill had grandparents who were of my parent's generation, and he shared the same thought.

We headed up to our seats in the balcony. The opening act was stand-up comedian Don Rickles. This was a once-in-a-lifetime event.

The concert hall slowly filled up as it got closer to the start time. Once everyone was seated, an awkward silence fell over the hall as everyone anxiously awaited the start of the show.

Suddenly a male announcer's voice was heard.

"Ladies and gentlemen, Frank Sinatra will not be performing tonight due to an illness."

Like everyone in that hall, Bill and I were momentarily shocked.

Did we just hear what we think we heard?

No one walked onto the stage. There was just a voice explaining how to get a refund and that another concert would be booked at an unknown later date.

We looked at the people around us; they couldn't believe what they just heard, either. The lights came on, and in disbelief, people began getting up and walking slowly out.

We just sat there, letting the ramifications of what we just heard sink in. We were likely to never get another chance like this. We couldn't have been more disappointed. We were less concerned about getting our money back than losing a chance to see Sinatra.

Months later, I heard a radio ad for another Sinatra concert. I immediately called Bill. We were thrilled until we checked the calendar. The new show was booked on a school night for Bill. He had classes he could not miss the next morning. But on the morning of the show, Bill got out of classes and declared: "I'm driving down!"

He decided he could not miss Sinatra, so he would drive down from Boston, go to the concert, then drive back in the middle of the night. On a good day, with fair weather and light traffic, the drive from Boston to New York took about four hours.

Fortunately, Bill liked long-haul drives. He was a fan of listening to sports games, talk radio of any kind, and old radio dramas or comedies. I swore the guy was out of his era and had tastes more like his grandparents'.

It was a good thing Bill liked to drive. I swore off driving to Boston after my first visit. I took the train up, which was fine. I loved the city. I saw all the tourist sites. We even attended a Red Sox game; eventually we would see the Celtics and the Bruins hockey team. I appreciated Boston's famous sites, including walking the downtown Freedom Trail, taking in all of the famed Revolutionary War landmarks, from the Old North Church to the route Paul Revere rode to warn the colonial militia of the approach of British forces. I even went running along the Charles River, one of my more memorable jogs. I kept noting how people I passed would stare at me. I wondered what it could be. When I finished, I mentioned it to Bill.

"You wore that hat?" he asked.

"That hat" was my Yankees baseball cap.

Growing up in Alaska, a place without professional or few college sports teams, I was unaware of how serious sports rivalries were. I was lucky no one knocked it off my head. I had gone running in a New York

Yankees hat deep in the territory of their baseball archrivals, the Red Sox. I never made that mistake again.

While I loved Boston, I think I only went up twice to see Bill. That's because he was living in his old fraternity house. It was a handsome, historic building that had been restored and even featured in films because of its grand staircase and huge stained glass dome.

Well, the main living areas had been restored to their original turn-of-the-century splendor. The living quarters and bathrooms were derelict at best. Most large bedrooms and other areas had long been filled with makeshift wooden dividers and homemade lofts to accommodate members of the fraternity. It reminded me of living in Juneau in half-built homes and my old float house. I can't even talk about the bathrooms.

For Bill, it was a great deal. He could live there rent free as the resident advisor. He took to the role with gusto. But the place was just too manly and dirty for me. I got a hotel room my second time up and stopped going after that.

So Bill often drove down to New York. But even so, I was surprised that he would drive down for just the evening to see a concert. But then again, it was Frank Sinatra.

We went that night, and the show did go on. It was everything we'd imagined. The men in sharkskin suits and the women in fur coats were back. The disappointment of months before was replaced by memories of the sight and sound of a great showman.

Not long after, I heard that Sinatra had stopped touring. Things went like that in New York.

CHAPTER 9

The Writing Division

Although I wilted in the heat, battled being homesick, and endured crummy housing, I still loved being at Columbia. I felt inspired every time I walked through the tall, wrought iron gates on either end of its promenade. I loved the buildings, the trees, and the sculptures around campus.

My favorite building was St. Paul's Chapel, an Episcopal church that was a popular tourist attraction as well as a wedding and concert venue. With its northern Italian Renaissance revival architecture, Byzantine interior, domed ceiling, and many stained glass windows, it often drew me in to recoup from a busy day or just to cool off. Every time I entered, I would stand under the inscription written along the lower part of the dome that in part quotes Corinthians 13, turning my head as I read: "Faith. Hope. Charity. But the greatest of these is charity." These words, coupled with the large black-and-white photographs of some of America's greatest writers that hung on the walls of the Writing Division classrooms, defined my life at Columbia.

Under the fixed gaze of classic writers such as Mark Twain, Virginia Woolf, William Faulkner, and Ernest Hemingway, we students sat in workshops to discuss each other's work or listened to professors discuss the five major themes in literature: light versus dark, order versus chaos, man versus nature, civilized man versus uncivilized man, realism versus surrealism.

There were about a hundred students in the MFA program. Most were fiction or poetry students, with only a handful of others who were studying nonfiction with me.

During one lecture, the then-chair of the writing program declared to the class, "No one should write a memoir when they are this young!" or words to this effect.

He looked over at me and added, "Unless you're Kim Rich."

Everyone laughed, including me.

THE SCHOOL OF the Arts program was housed in Dodge Hall, near Columbia's main gate at 116th and Broadway. Directly across the street was the campus of Barnard College, the all-women's school that opened in 1889 to counter Columbia's refusal to allow women to enroll in the all-male school. (Columbia began admitting women in 1983.)

Across the promenade from Dodge Hall is Pulitzer Hall. It is home to Columbia's Graduate School of Journalism, which also houses the Pulitzer Prizes and publishes the *Columbia Journalism Review.* I had looked into attending the journalism program until I learned it was for students seeking to become journalists, not people who were already professionals.

The School of the Arts building then included a visual arts program, the theatre arts, film, and writing programs. Each department occupied a different floor of the building. Nothing was overstated about the Writing Division and its small, plain offices; the only thing that distinguished it as the Writing Division was a bulletin board with book covers of past and current students' published works.

The program is built on a series of workshops, seminars, lectures, and master classes taught by veteran agents, editors, and writers. The school advertises itself as offering courses created "for writers by writers who discuss student work and examine literature from a practitioner's perspective, not that of a scholar or theorist."

We students basked in the glow of visiting writers, listening intently to their anecdotal stories about the writing life. Nothing seemed off limits. Susan Cheever talked about her father's homosexuality; Philip Roth kindly answered a student's earnest question about how he worked by actually outlining his working day; Columbia alumnus Richard Price talked about the pitfalls of once being a writer with too much time on his hands.

One course was broken into several sections where we studied writing about food with a renowned *New York Times* food writer. We even studied under one of the best-selling children's book authors of all time, Jon Scieszka, author of *The Stinky Cheese Man* and a graduate of the program.

Other classes were taught by a mix of writers who worked for the *New Yorker* magazine, the *New York Times*, or other esteemed entities. It wasn't long before we students talked of working for the *New Yorker* or other literary magazines.

I was reading more than a hundred pages a night at times, trying to get through the reading lists from my classes, all of which entailed the greatest works of the twentieth century. It was strenuous, draining, superb.

My living arrangement improved when I was finally able to transfer to new housing. I found a two-bedroom apartment occupied by a social work graduate student from Colorado. She spoke fluent Spanish and French as well as English. I had never met anyone who seemed so unassuming yet was so well educated. Her name was Ellen, and we got along well.

The apartment was huge by New York standards, with a separate kitchen, bath, living room, two bedrooms, and a long hall. We were on the fourth-floor front of a building with a doorman. Like my first New York apartment, it housed mostly students, plus a few residents who were allowed to remain after Columbia bought the building.

On the other end of our street was Morningside Drive, where the university president's residence was located, and across from which sat Morningside Park, a known hangout for drug addicts. We were advised not to go there, especially at night. I was amazed at how a single block could transition from safety to danger, especially after dark.

The Cathedral of St. John the Divine was a few blocks away, and across from Riverside Park, where I ran to and from every day, was St. Peter's Cathedral. The heart of Harlem was only a few blocks north along 125th Street. The area we were in was both wonderful and a little scary. Harlem wasn't so much a concern, but the dozens of halfway houses in the area were.

Residents of some of these routinely panhandled along the corner of my building and across the street in front of a small food market. Those of us who lived in the area came to know them by name. We'd give them spare change and occasionally buy them cups of coffee and soup from the market.

New York City, Fall 1992. Here I'm about to open the main entrance to the apartment building where I would end up living for most of the three years I attended Columbia. I transferred to this building after a month of putting up with my "suite" dorm room a few blocks away.

The first time a regular asked me to get her some soup as I was walking into the market, I bought a can of soup.

"What am I supposed to do with this?" she asked when I handed her the brown bag with the can of soup in it. I thought she wanted to take it home to cook and felt a bit stupid for not realizing she meant take-out soup from the deli counter. Anchorage didn't have much take-out.

But that's how living in New York City went. I had to learn a whole new way of being. The first time I went to pay for something at a magazine stand, I stood by patiently waiting my turn—which never came. My companion, a New Yorker, grabbed my money and assertively waved it at the clerk. Lesson learned.

During one of my early visits to the city, I accidentally bumped into an elderly man in a crowded space in front of a small electronics store. He began pushing against me, shouting in a language I didn't recognize. I managed to break free and get out as he yelled and then spat at me. Onlookers stared as I stood there dazed. Later I realized he thought I was trying to pick his pockets. It took me awhile to get over feeling rattled by that run-in.

Yet despite the occasional harshness of big city life, New Yorkers always surprised me with their helpfulness and friendliness. Once when taking a subway to Midtown, I walked out of the subway tunnel and came up in the middle of an east-west street surrounded by buildings. The closest intersections, which would tell me where I was, were too far to see from where I stood. Go left or right?

As I stood trying to decide, a woman walked up from out of the subway stairs and asked if I was lost. My first instinct was to say no, since I had learned to be always on guard in the city, but I quickly realized she was sincere. "It's hard to know what direction to go in from some of these stops," she said and then directed me to my destination.

That was New York. Hot and cold. Good and bad. But I loved it. A colleague from the newspaper once asked me, "What's it feel like to live in New York City, the place to be?" She knew that life in Alaska always required explaining to strangers or family members in the Lower 48. Now I was living in a place that was universally recognized.

One night, I went to hear a friend's band play at a neighborhood bar. A man got on the stage and shouted out to the crowd.

"Welcome to the greatest bar in New York City!" he yelled. "In the greatest city in the United States!" The crowd roared their approval. He went on. "The greatest bar in the greatest city in the greatest country in the world!" The crowd went wild. And there was still more. "This is the greatest bar in the greatest city in the greatest country in the greatest world in the galaxy!" The noise was deafening.

And that was how I felt living in New York City.

CHAPTER 10

Circling the Center

*I*n the fall of 1992, the galleys for my book were delivered to my apartment. I remember holding the copy in my hands and feeling the weight of its power. I knew once I let go of it—signed off on it— my life would be forever changed. Did I really want to reveal all of my family's dark and terrible secrets? Was my writing any good? Could I endure critics? What would they comment on? What could I expect?

I felt frozen. I couldn't seem to begin reading it. Each time I tried, my mind raced all over the place.

I would hang on every page, rethinking what was written. I would never get through it in the few days I'd been given for review.

Then I remembered a classmate who was a voracious reader. Ed was the program's youngest student. He entered the school at age twenty. He was an only child, dark haired and fiercely intelligent. I liked Ed and especially his parents, who saw me as the one to look after their Edward. Because I was one of the oldest in the program, Ed's parents thought of me as his protector in the big city.

I picked up the phone and called him.

"Ed, I just got the galleys to my book. Can you read it for me? Can you tell me if I can let it go?"

Ed came right over and picked up the book. He read it overnight. The next morning, he came over.

"I loved it!" he exclaimed. He went on and on to tell me how good he thought it was. But it was his final remark that stayed with me: "I love how you used your father to write about your mother."

SINCE WRITING THE NEWSPAPER ARTICLES that led to the book, I always thought I was writing about my father. But I had hoped that my mother's story might also reach people, conveying the tragedy of her life. She had the courage to be a good mother during the most important years of a child's growth and development, from birth to three years old. Her unwavering love and devotion saved me. Yet, no one was able to save her from a life that either contributed to, missed, or mistreated her clinical depression. At age eighteen, she received her first shock treatments.

She was unlucky. It's never been easy to suffer from a serious mental illness, not historically, not in the middle of the twentieth century, not now.

One of the things I love about journalism is its ability to help bring about change. I was passionate about reporting, especially if I felt what I was doing could make a difference, right a wrong, highlight an important social issue or problem. I believed firmly then and now in the news media's role as a government watchdog and champion of the underdog. At one point in college, I thought I might want to be a social worker. I loved sociology. I loved learning the why of things. In journalism, I could investigate all these areas and more.

I thought writing about my mother might help others like her—or like me.

Maybe I just wanted to know how I was or was not like her. She was creative and artistic. During her institutionalization, she sent handmade Christmas cards to her family. They saved them and gave them to me years later. She drew and colored the cards and envelopes. On each, she created a smiling Santa Claus face surrounded by candy canes and branches of holly. She used bright red, green, and white markers or paint. She left large parts of the envelopes and cards white, exhibiting the elements of balance, design, and arrangement in art. She clearly had artistic talent, something I, too, exhibited early in life.

When I was in elementary school and bored in class, I would draw page after page of elaborate ball gowns or beautiful dresses. Around the same time, like a lot of little girls in the late Sixties and early Seventies, my favorite toy was my Barbie doll. Barbie and the television set kept me from feeling lonely as an only child with a father who was rarely home. With Barbie, I could create whole new worlds—Barbie's workplace, her home, her boyfriend Ken, and the wonderful clothes they wore.

My mother loved chic, fashionable clothing and bright, sparkly costume jewelry. Like many of her generation, she had a set of real pearls. She had a silver mink stole. She had a one-shoulder, long-sleeved black dress that I was given by my aunts who saved my mother's things. Somehow it got lost over the years. Boy, would I love to have that dress. She invested in expensive clothes even while living in Alaska. Despite rough edges, adults in Alaska still managed to dress like adults in any big city. The town always had a lively night club scene.

That was my parent's world. I have photos of me as a newborn with my mom in full makeup, including red lipstick, sitting bleary eyed on the corner of the bed, dressed in beautiful lingerie. When I was a toddler and preschooler, she took photograph after photograph of the two of us. In

My mom with me as an infant in Los Angeles, 1958. Here she is, getting by with no sleep, but still managing to do her hair and makeup and be a dedicated and loving mother.

every single one she is beautifully dressed. To her, "casual" meant a pair of form-fitting plaid capris with a coordinated short-sleeved cashmere sweater. That was her generation, the early 1960s, the cocktail culture, a time when men nearly always wore suit jackets, if not a full suit.

My mother was petite and slim—five foot one-and-a-half inches tall. I found her weight in her psychiatric records—105 pounds. I am her exact height and, at times, her exact weight.

When I was researching and writing my book, I took regular

walks with a friend named Averil. She was a lawyer and married to another lawyer who later became a judge.

During one of our walks, as I talked on about some latest thing I'd learned about my dad, she asked, "But what about your mother?"

I fell silent.

"I don't remember much about her."

"How old were you when you lost her?" Averil asked.

I explained how when I was six, my mother and I fled Alaska to return to her hometown of Ironwood, Michigan. Almost immediately, she was gone, hospitalized. At times, she was placed in a nursing home for care. For the next three years, our visits were rare. I was nine the last time I saw her. She died five years later, institutionalized in a large mental hospital in the middle of the Lower Peninsula of Michigan, hundreds of miles away from her family. Thousands of miles away from me and any friends she had in Alaska.

"Six? She raised you until you were six," Averil said. "That's a lot of years. Important years in a child's life."

Averil, who had two children, went on to explain to me just how critical those years are. Later, I spent the first of many sessions going over the two scrapbooks my mother created from my birth until I turned about five—or until she began to become seriously ill, right after I turned six.

Being a mom, Averil could spot the work of an attentive, loving mother. As we went over the pages of my mother's scrapbooks, she pointed out different pictures and would ask questions like, "Who do you think picked out that dress for you? Dressed you? Who bought all those toys? Who placed them on those shelves? Who did your hair like that? Who threw that birthday party? Invited all those children? Got you that red plaid dress with a white apron and the number four on the front?"

Averil's observations and insights were a revelation to me and began to open more memories—some good, some bad—of my early years with my adoring, loving mother.

"Look how in every photo with you, she's kneeling down at your level," Averil noted in pictures of me in my Halloween costume, or Easter dress, or Christmas jammies.

Averil looked and saw a woman who was an excellent mother. She saw a child who loved her unconditionally. That was probably how my mother managed to hold it together as long as she did, despite an illness and condition destined to destroy her life by her mid-twenties.

As schizophrenia does.

Her middle twenties.

I was in my late twenties as I began work on my book and for the first time fully understood why I had not had children yet. For the first time, I understood how huge a loss, how catastrophic, it was effectively to lose her forever at age six.

I was more like her than I could have imagined, genetically hardwired with a creative bent. Fortunately, I had ducked inheriting

My mom and me. Note how well she always dressed.

schizophrenia because I was symptom-free at a time when the illness typically surfaces in young women. At one point, I was told my risk of having it was 25 percent. Some might say I was lucky. But I think my mother's absolute, all-consuming, solid parenting, nurturing, and boundless love was what made the difference. All the difference.

My grief over her loss is and will always be endless, tucked deep inside in a place I rarely visit but which surfaces in visceral and profound ways.

Thus, I was only slightly surprised when my graduate school friend Ed declared what he saw as my book's true purpose.

I can still see his face when he said, "I love how you used your father to write about your mother."

I sat back thinking, *He is right.*

He went on to say the book was fine and I could send it back to my publisher feeling assured it was okay to let it go.

THIS BECAME ONE of my first lessons about writing: sometimes we circle the outside of what it is we truly need to say. The professors in my writing workshop classes commented on this again and again when discussing a student's writing.

After hearing from Ed, I made a list of anyone I thought to check with regarding their part in the book. This involved everyone from members of my mother's family to the lawyer who represented the man convicted of killing my father. The lawyer got him off on another previous case, a murder with a sensational trial that occurred less than a year before my father's own death.

I sent portions of the book to some and read parts to others, all with the disclaimer that I was checking facts as well as letting them know what to expect. I probably contacted a handful of people involved in what I considered hot spots in the book. I told them that if they had any issues with what was written, we could discuss their concerns, but if what was written was correct and necessary to the story, it stayed.

Most people I contacted had no problem with what I had written. I sent the parts about my mother's family to my oldest cousin and his wife. I thought I had been fair to them regarding how they dealt with my mother and her mental illness. They were no worse than most at that time.

My cousin and his wife called. Their only concern was a line in the book regarding my mother's two sisters. My mother was the youngest in the family. The oldest was Sandra, then brother Tony, followed by Lena, and then my mother. They were all born in Ironwood. Tony left right after high school and went out to Los Angeles, where three of his uncles had settled at the turn of the twentieth century. He stayed, and met and married a local Burbank girl. Eventually, my mother went out to live with Tony and his wife, Luce, and finished high school at Burbank High. It was in California where she eventually met my father, and they married in 1956, when she was twenty-one and he was twenty-two. They had me two years later, and within my first year, they moved to Alaska.

My mother's sisters stayed in Ironwood, a small former copper-mining town on Michigan's Upper Peninsula. My Aunt Sandra lived most of her life in the same house where she had grown up, a long, rectangular building that had once been a store. It was dim, half empty, and spooky to a child. Aunt Lena married and lived only a few houses away, down a small hill, in a charming wood-framed house set in a large sloping yard.

I had noted in the book that during arguments, when Aunt Lena would leave my Aunt Sandra's house, Aunt Sandra would often shout something after Lena to the effect of "You go back to your house down the hill."

Out of everything that was written about my mother's illicit activities, her mental illness, and more, only one thing stood out that the family feared might upset my elderly aunts: the line about "the house down the hill."

Like most families, it's often the little things that cause rifts and resentments. Aunt Sandra would have probably liked a home of her own, away from her Old World Italian mother, in a small but attractive house like Aunt Lena's. Instead, she lived in a giant old building that dated back before the Depression and seemed to be to be filled with ghosts. In a way, it was.

I didn't want to upset my aunts. I was close to both of them, and the line was unimportant, so I took it out.

Not long after that call with my cousin, I sent the galleys back to the publisher for months of legal review. The front cover was created, the fonts were chosen, and other details tied up. It would be nearly six months before the book would be released.

I settled into my New York routine, writing and reading every day, attending classes, having dinner or drinks with fellow students, seeing Bill on the weekends, and running every morning along the Hudson River.

CHAPTER II

Being Published

*I*n the spring of 1993, *Johnny's Girl* was released. Working around my class schedule and spring break at Columbia, I embarked on a small publicity tour, mostly to the Pacific Northwest and Alaska.

I got to visit my beloved Juneau and see old friends. In Anchorage, the Dodge family allowed me to use their home for a book premiere party. People from my present and past lives were there. A notice for the party was advertised in the newspaper, and hundreds showed up. It remains the biggest and best party of my life. One friend said, "This is the best party Anchorage has ever had!"

When I was a teen, I wanted heaven to be a place where all your friends and family members gathered forevermore. That party was pretty much it.

During my stop in Seattle, I stayed with some friends, both of whom were journalists. One, Marla Williams, had worked at the same TV station in Anchorage where I did my college internship.

My publisher's publicist had given me printouts of each media event

I was to attend. I was scheduled for an interview and appearance on a local Seattle program. "Radio," my instruction sheet said.

So I threw on some casual clothes, and Marla drove me to the station. She wondered why I hadn't dressed up.

"It's radio," I said. "No one will see what I'm wearing."

She asked me again what station it was. I told her.

"That's television," she said firmly.

My itinerary was wrong. I was about to appear on a local morning TV show hosted by a pair of local broadcast celebrities in front of a live studio audience.

Marla's house was too far away to drive back and get new clothes. Hastily, we worked on my hair and dusted me off. At least I was wearing a sport coat that day. Marla and I may have even switched some clothing.

With no time to spare, I was ushered out of the green room and onto the live set. Marla took a seat in the front row of the audience section.

Being underdressed was the least of my problems. Marla and I repeatedly had to stifle the urge to crack up. I struggled to figure out which camera to look at, and I tried to be polite as it became clear that the hosts had not even glanced at the book. It's not that I was offended and expected them to have read it; I just had trouble answering questions unrelated to the book I had written.

I do not have a poker face. Back then especially, I found it hard to hide my emotions or reactions. The camera repeatedly caught me unprepared, rolling my eyes, or making a grimace. Marla was reeling in laughter.

I WAITED AS each review came in. My biggest thrill was when the *New York Times Book Review* featured *Johnny's Girl* in a half-page review—half a page!—written by one of my heroes, nonfiction writer Cyra McFadden.

(Later, I met with the editor of the book review section. When I asked why she had chosen to have my book reviewed, she had a surprisingly personal reason: "I had a college roommate from Alaska.")

The *New York Times* review was a huge achievement. My agent Rafe and editor Paul were delighted. I couldn't believe it. I've joked that my tombstone will read, "She was reviewed by the *New York Times*."

The review was mostly positive. I had been told by an editor who worked there that, at least back then, they generally didn't print bad reviews of first-time authors; they just didn't run the review. However, it wasn't entirely glowing. McFadden took me to task not on the writing but on my own reactions to my life. I was surprised that she would take exception to some of my own thoughts, feelings, and conclusions, and I admit that I felt miffed. A postcard from my editor Mike Dolan said it all: "What did she expect you to do–weep and moan and bitch for 300 pages? Fuck reviewers."

The postcard still hangs over my desk.

The legendary postcard, which still hangs in my office and always makes me laugh.

OVER TIME, THOUGH, I realized that one might expect to be critiqued when reviewed by the *New York Times*. I'm grateful my writing has held up, despite the reviewer's perception of my emotional life.

I might be an anomaly. I never felt victimized emotionally or psychologically by my past, in part because of the love and attention I received in my early childhood. Perhaps, too, it was because my teen and young adult years were spent in Anchorage at a time of great optimism and economic growth.

Perhaps I didn't say everything there was to say about my sometimes conflicted feelings about my father, who stood large in my mind. I do know that when it came time to write of how he hit me—beat me—on a handful of occasions, I felt at a loss. I had left the house and reported him to the authorities, and the hitting stopped. But years later, I still did not know how to feel or what to say about his actions. Does such an act erase a daughter's love of her father? Should it? I figured out that while I understood the source of his uncontrolled rage—his having been passed from one foster home to the next as a boy—I had pulled away from him when I became a teen. I focused all of my anger on him and everything I thought he was and what he did for a living.

Understanding someone's actions doesn't make them okay. He beat my mother, too. That makes him a domestic bully of the worst sort.

But it was his unwavering love and bond that also gave me the strength to be who I am and to walk a relatively straight path right out of the underclass into which he was born. Johnny Rich was the illegitimate son of an unwed mother. His grandparents were Russian-Polish immigrants probably fleeing prosecution for their Jewish heritage. They despised their teen daughter's lover, an Italian man so emotionally flawed that he never married. My father's story ended tragically, but he wanted a better life for me.

THERE WERE OTHER criticisms of the book, some hard and some easy to take. Oddly, none criticized the writing, but some continued McFadden's focus on my own feelings. Women reviewers tended to think I wasn't mad enough, bitter enough. Male reviewers were uniformly supportive. Many were probably fathers themselves and perhaps relieved that a father could screw up as much as my dad did and still have a daughter come back to write a loving memoir.

Phew! they must have thought. *At least I'm not as bad as that guy!*

Nonetheless, my editor and I were thrilled when the *Los Angeles Times*, *Glamour*, *Mirabella*, CNN, National Public Radio, and other major media outlets chose to review the book.

For a shining moment, I was a star in Columbia's writing program. One of my workshop teachers, veteran writer Patricia Bosworth, hosted a book party for me at her high-rise Midtown apartment.

This may have been the highlight of my time in New York. Not only did she invite fellow professors and heads of the program but also my friends and fellow students. It was in the middle of this party that I felt I had finally become a New Yorker. I was *That Girl*!

THAT SUMMER, AS I had done each year, I went home to Anchorage and worked at the *Daily News*. I loved being able to go home and do what I loved—work in the newsroom with my friends and colleagues.

In the fall, less than six months after my book's release, I got a call from my agent that Hallmark wanted to option *Johnny's Girl* for film. Without hesitating, I said yes. I felt I could trust the quality of their work.

Before I knew it, the project went into preproduction. They were adapting the book for a company called Signboard Hill Productions, a part of Hallmark. The head of Hallmark's Hall of Fame films was head of this company. Filmmaker and writer John Kent Harrison was hired to adapt and direct the movie.

John broke a cardinal rule: he called me.

Film directors and writers are often reticent to contact the original authors for fear they will become obstructionists in the project. Book authors are frequently unhappy with how their books are adapted for film. I understood the process and didn't have a problem with it. I had even begun taking a screenwriting class at Columbia. I had read enough to know that the only part of the process I could control was choosing the right production company.

Perhaps my career as a journalist made it easy for me to work with John. I was accustomed to working with editors and have always enjoyed positive relationships with them. Journalism, like film, is a collaborative process. A reporter works in conjunction with an editor in being assigned or proposing a story, the angle to pursue, the writing, its length, editing, and dealing with all legal and ethical considerations.

I did not expect the same exchange in watching my book be adapted to film. One writer described the process akin to sitting in the stands at a football game and being powerless to do anything about what's happening on the field.

John called me that fall of 1993, while I was home at my apartment in New York. One of the first things he told me was how Hallmark pitched the project to him. "John, we got a father-daughter story for you," he recalled, himself a father to two girls.

We hit it off right away and had a far-ranging talk about my book and life. A native of Canada, John had a feel for Anchorage's last-frontier-town atmosphere in the 1970s.

"If you really want to get a feel for the place, you need to visit

Anchorage," I told him.

Soon, the producers flew both of us to Anchorage. For a week, I took him to see all the places in the book I wrote about and to meet my father's friends, former lawyers, and others. We went everywhere I could think of, including a strip club.

I wanted out of the dingy, smoke-filled place the moment we walked in. It brought back too many bad memories. *Research. We're doing research,* I kept telling myself.

John loved the old night clubs and restaurants and cafes of my father's era. I learned a lot watching him talk to people. He was intuitive, and like a good reporter, he could talk to anyone.

During one of our last nights, we met some friends of mine for dinner at one of Anchorage's newer restaurants, an uptown, hip kind of place. It was not at all the sort of night club or restaurant that existed in my father's era.

In the middle of the evening, John turned to me. He wanted to leave the trendy restaurant and go back to my father's old haunts, to "old" Anchorage. For once, I felt joy at visiting these places.

Later, when the script was completed, John sent it to me. I had no idea how to read a script or what to look for. It was important to John that I like it.

I did.

Our talks had unearthed things that weren't even in the book. He talked to me about writing, asking who I read and which writers were my early influences. I described first falling in love with writing in middle school through the work of Walt Whitman. As it turned out, one of John's first films was the award-winning movie *Beautiful Dreamers*, a film about Whitman's visit to a nineteenth-century Canadian institution.

The adaptation of my book to film also led to a new turning point in my own career. I began to study screenwriting at Columbia. I remember running into some fellow students in the Writing Division's student lounge. I showed them some of what I had learned, and one remarked, "I just learned more about writing than I have in an entire year."

Whether that was true or not, my introduction to John Kent Harrison marked another turning point in my life and work.

MOST STUDENTS IN the Writing Division arrived with a thesis or book they were already working on or had written and were using in workshops. Technically, the program does not allow for the use of previously published material. All material must be written while in the program. This rule kept me from using parts of *Johnny's Girl* in workshop. This was fine with me. I wanted to develop my next book.

For those of us in the nonfiction program, pieces read in workshops became the basis of or part of a student's thesis—150 pages of publishable prose.

There was one student who took a work of fiction and labeled it nonfiction because she felt she had a

Me standing at a Writing Division bulletin board in Dodge Hall at Columbia. Soon after I arrived, the department assistant tacked up a cover of Johnny's Girl *along with other book covers written by graduates of the program. Seeking to be a normal student, I was grateful, proud and slightly overwhelmed by the recognition.*

better chance at getting a nonfiction book published. Some students had "fish out of water" tales of studying abroad. There were several "fictional" stories of young female college students engaging in destructive affairs with much older professors.

For others, writing projects stemmed from extraordinary experiences in their lives. One of my best friends in the program, Laura, grew up in Japan, where her Ohio-born parents were missionaries. She went to college in Japan and spoke fluent Japanese. She was working on a book about her experiences working for Honda Motor Company, both in America and in Japan (*The Accidental Office Lady*). She led a movement to do away with the restrictive and sexist clothing and attitudes toward women working at the company. Another student had worked in Africa; one had canoed the entire length of the Hudson River, and so on.

I struggled to find a thesis until one presented itself uninvited—an adventure involving my paternal grandfather, John Rich, Sr. Growing up, I had only vague memories of meeting him once as a child. While researching *Johnny's Girl*, it took me over a year to track him down. When we finally made contact, my grandfather was in his late seventies, slowly going senile and in failing health. He lived alone in Miami Beach, in the same apartment he'd lived in for decades.

Then, on Thanksgiving Day in 1993, the unimaginable occurred. My grandfather was kidnapped by Gypsies.

CHAPTER 12

Grandpa and The Gypsies

My grandfather's apartment building was in an area of Miami Beach that I called "Mid Beach," a few blocks of modest apartment and condominium buildings between the rich high-rises of North Beach and the area that was then being renovated into trendy South Beach. His neighbors were a mix of drug dealers, immigrants, and elderly living on meager Social Security checks; most had fading memories and rapidly expanding vulnerabilities.

I knew nothing of Grandpa's assets except that, shortly after I found him, he had me take him to the bank. There, he put me on a $10,000 certificate of deposit. I tried to resist, insisting I had not come down for his money.

"I know that," he said. "That's why I'm doing it." I realized that by having my name with the bank, if something were to happen to him, they would know to call me. So I let the arrangement stand.

I knew my grandfather was slipping, of course. What I didn't know or anticipate was that he was a prime target for exploitation.

"Gypsies" was the word one of my grandfather's neighbors used. They were a pair of women—a late-middle-aged mother and her daughter, probably in her mid- to late thirties. Through some sleuthing and use of my reporter skills, I later learned they were originally from the Ukraine. They had come into the United States from East Germany after the fall of the Berlin Wall.

During one of our regular phone calls, Grandpa announced, "I met a German millionaire!" He couldn't have been more excited.

"That's nice, Grandpa," I said, figuring he'd met someone during one of his daily walks along the Miami Beach boardwalk.

He told me his new friend owned hotels "all up and down Miami Beach." He wanted me to meet her and "do business" with her. He'd told her I had a book that had just been published and that I lived in New York City. He said she was there in his apartment, and he put her on the phone.

Tanya, as I'll call her, spoke no English, and I spoke no whatever-it-was she was speaking. Was it Russian? German?

Hel-lo, Houston to Kim? An alarm should have gone off in my head. The arrows on the internal warning meter should have been spinning wildly. I should have smelled smoke. But no. I was happy he had a new friend. I always worried about him being alone and lonely.

Plus, my grandfather made friends easily. He knew all the local small business owners. He was a man of distinct habits. Every morning, he ate breakfast at a Cuban-owned diner on his block. He didn't speak a word of Spanish, and the times I was with him, no one in the place seemed to speak much English. But the regulars, all Cuban-Americans—some retirees from the neighborhood, but mostly construction workers—waved and said hi to my grandfather. He ate dinner every night at a Denny's restaurant a block away from his apartment. He was a good tipper, and while he ate alone, he always chatted up the waitresses and waiters.

The staff at his bank all knew him by name and waved and smiled when he came in. He was a big flirt, always complimenting men and women on what they were wearing or their nice smiles. Every holiday season, he would give presents to all the tellers at his bank. His favorite gift was faux perfume that he ordered over the phone in bulk, and he'd go around giving a bottle to every woman he came in regular contact with.

He loved to be around people, and everyone loved him. Many times, he would take me with him here and there to meet all of his friends. Obviously, most of the relationships were superficial, and indeed, he was lonely.

Knowing that Grandpa was in failing health, I had already taken measures to get him into an assisted living facility. His name was on a waiting list for a place down the street from his apartment. A friend from Naples, Florida, offered to keep an eye on him if he lived closer to her, but he refused even to consider moving.

I had visited Grandpa's doctor to talk about his failing mental health and was told he was still okay to live on his own, but that was going to change. The doctor believed my grandfather was suffering from a series of minor strokes that were slowly eroding his mind.

I even had a social worker do an assessment, a service in fairly high demand in the area for distant family members trying to take care of their elderly loved ones. She, too, found him competent to live on his own for the time being. I was advised to keep a close eye on him. So I did. His neighbors all knew me and had my phone number. Hence, it was a neighbor who called the night before Thanksgiving.

"Kim, you better get down here. There're two women hanging around your grandfather."

Something inside clicked.

A few days earlier, my grandfather had complained about missing money. I figured he was withdrawing money and forgetting. I had gently tried to assure him his accounts were fine and that no one was stealing from him.

On another recent occasion, he had become uncharacteristically enraged on the phone, attacking me and calling me vile names, accusing me of taking all his money. I was stunned. He had never talked to me like that before. I was angry and hurt, but I instinctively knew his failing mental health was behind the tirade. I had recently been to a Miami conference on Alzheimer's disease and learned about a condition called Sundowner's Syndrome, where those suffering from senility grow paranoid, agitated, and aggressive at night. Perhaps that was the problem, I thought.

But then came the call from his neighbor. "Gypsies," she called the two strangers.

I immediately phoned my grandfather to see what was going on. The moment I mentioned the women, he flew into a full rage. I tried to explain my concern.

"I married one of them!" he yelled at me and hung up.

I sat back, trying not to panic. My mind was racing. It all began to add up. On one visit, I had noticed that he left his mail and his bank statements on top of the television set in his living room.

Anyone could see it.

The women could see it.

But married one of them? He'd only met them a few weeks earlier.

I tried calling back, but no one answered. Earlier, he had given me a phone number for the women. I called it. I was amazed when the daughter, Olga, answered.

"Who are you, and why are you hanging around my grandfather?" I demanded. "I know one of you married him. I am calling the police."

Olga accused me of taking my grandfather's money. My name, she said, was on his bank accounts. I had no idea my name was on his checking or savings accounts. I had never touched the accounts, and I assured her that bank records would prove I had never withdrawn his money. I tried to explain that it was common for the elderly suffering from dementia and memory loss to withdraw money from their accounts and then forget they had done so. But I was getting nowhere with her. I got mad.

"I'm coming down right away," I announced.

She hung up on me.

I called my grandfather's neighbor back. She said she would keep an eye on his apartment.

A short while later, the neighbor called again. She said the women had come to my grandfather's apartment and then left with him.

"Left with him?" I asked in disbelief, simultaneously kicking myself for calling Olga.

The neighbor had tried to talk to my grandfather in the hall, but the women hurried him away. Grandpa seemed confused and talked about going on a trip. Except along with his suitcases, they also had his ancient black-and-white TV set. Why would they take the TV on a trip, I wondered.

I hung up and called the Miami Beach Police Department. An officer got on the line. I tried to explain I was calling from New York City and what had happened. I told him everything I knew, including that my grandfather had married one of the women who took him away from his apartment.

The "married" detail made things a lot harder. Try explaining the disappearance of an old man and his new wife to a disinterested cop, who must get calls all the time from distant relatives worried about their elderly loved ones.

"So?" said the officer who took my call that night.

Some of the details from those first hours after his disappearance are a blur to me.

What I remember best is he lectured me about all the families that just forget about their elderly family members until something bad happens. He insinuated that all some families care about is their inheritance.

"So what if he married? Maybe he's happy," I was told.

Great, I thought. *Now I'm suspect.*

I tried to explain that my grandfather was a lifelong bachelor and everything that occurred was out of character for him. Plus, I was sure he had no money except a CD for $10,000 with my name as the beneficiary. No sooner had I said that did I realize I was not helping my case.

I assured this officer I was a person of integrity, a former newspaper reporter, and I believed my grandfather might be in danger. I told him about my book and challenged him to look up who I was. The officer became slightly more empathetic and advised me to get down there right away.

Right away meant the next day.

The next day was Thanksgiving.

I was hosting Thanksgiving dinner for our group at Columbia. More than a dozen friends were scheduled to come. Bill was driving down from Boston that night to help cook. And now my grandfather was missing. Or kidnapped.

Could his life be in danger? Or was this one big misunderstanding? My reporter's training taught me to look at every detail. I replayed all the events and conversations in my mind from the last few weeks. I even wrote down everything I knew.

It occurred to me that perhaps the language barrier had created a situation in which Tanya and Olga didn't understand that my grandfather was half senile. What if in trying to impress them he talked about being a "big shot," as he would call it?

I learned that my grandfather told the neighbor a few days earlier that he had married Tanya in order for her to stay in the country. Her visa had expired.

The same neighbor said she overheard my grandfather and the women saying I wanted to put him in "jail."

Jail? Was this some twisted conclusion his demented mind had conjured up in a panic that night? Did he get this idea because of my earlier efforts to move him into an assisted living facility? Did the women think that was the case, or did they want him to believe it so he would leave with them?

Nothing added up, except one thing: the women were up to something. Or as my cousin, a retired detective from the Los Angeles Police Department, would say, none of the arrows were pointing in the right direction.

THAT NIGHT I was a nervous wreck while waiting for Bill to arrive. I was also angry. I felt as if I had become embroiled in some farce you might see in a movie. I felt as if I were back in my father's world.

Later, when word got around school, both my screenwriting professor and chair of the film department told me to keep them posted. This story was movie material.

But it felt personal and awful. I fought the fear that I might never see my grandfather again. In more rebellious moments, I asked myself why I should bother. My grandfather had chosen the life he had. Why should I do anything more than what I had already done for him?

My grandfather, like my father, lived on life's edges and in the underworld. Aside from serving in the military in World War II, he had worked as a bookie for much of his life. He had told me of his travels to Cuba and his hasty departure when rebel troops were closing in on Havana.

Now he was in a mess that reminded me of life with my father, where bizarre and terrible things happened on a regular basis.

Despite all I had done and as far as I had come, here I was, on the eve of Thanksgiving of 1993, dealing with a missing grandparent. Maybe he had chosen to disappear. Yet I couldn't stand to think that he might need help, and I was the closest family he had.

BILL ARRIVED THAT night, but there wasn't anything more to do until I could talk to the police in the morning. I prayed they would have some answers by then.

The next morning, the plot thickened.

My grandfather's neighbor called to tell me that the women and my grandfather had returned to his apartment. Here's something these women clearly did not know or anticipate: if you take a person with dementia away from their familiar surroundings, they will decline, become even more agitated, and—in my grandfather's case—likely throw a huge fit. Once the evening wore down and he was tired, he would just want to go home to his bed. As with many elderly in his condition, routine was the only thing keeping him from completely losing it.

And he must have lost it. Because whatever was going on, the women arrived back at his apartment. The neighbor had heard them in the hall and came out in time to witness my grandfather opening the door to his apartment.

"I've been robbed!" he yelled when he saw that his TV was missing. Clearly, he didn't remember packing or leaving with the TV. With that, the three of them left again. The only good news was that these two women had an elderly, irate ex-bookie with a foul mouth on their hands.

Most of the morning, I was in a panic. Once I got the latest report from Miami, I knew I had to go south, but I couldn't focus. I did the only thing to do: I made the bed. With my thoughts racing and struggling to keep from falling apart, I began making the bed.

Bill walked into the room. "What are you doing?"

"Making the bed."

"You don't have time for that. You've got to get to Miami."

Oh, yeah. That's right. But I did not want to go. This whole thing did not seem as if it could end well.

I called the police again, hoping for news. They had arranged a welfare check at my grandfather's apartment only to discover no one was home. I spent the morning trying to find an affordable last-minute flight to Miami.

While everyone was arriving for Thanksgiving dinner, Bill took me to the airport.

I ARRIVED IN Miami early evening. A friend picked me up at the airport, and we promptly drove to my grandfather's apartment.

Grandpa didn't have much, but he always kept his small apartment neat and tidy. A handful of framed photos of him and family members sat on an end table in the living room. His small kitchen was always wiped clean, and on a narrow glass shelf above the bathroom sink, his hair comb was always lined up next to his razor and a small round mirror, all in a row.

Not today. When we walked in, my grandfather's apartment looked ransacked. Clothing and personal items were missing, as if hastily packed. Sure enough, the TV was gone. Then I found a clue to my grandfather's worsening behavior: a pile of his bank statements.

The most troubling discovery was that my name was indeed on the account. Then I made an even more shocking discovery—there was about $40,000 in the account. Or there had been. In recent weeks, large sums of money had been withdrawn.

There were about six months of statements folded together. He must have gone to the bank to get copies. Did he do so at the behest of the women? Most of the paperwork showed a regular pattern of cash withdrawals of small amounts here and there. His most recent statement, however, showed a couple of larger withdrawals. Was he spending the money on Tanya and Olga? Taking them out? Giving it to them?

I went to the Denny's restaurant where he regularly dined. There, and in other places he frequented, workers recounted seeing the women with him in recent weeks.

THE NEXT MORNING, the first thing I did was go to the Miami Beach courthouse. I prayed that there was no marriage license, that he hadn't really gotten married.

No such luck. There I confirmed my worst fear: my grandfather had indeed gotten married only a couple of weeks earlier to Tanya, the older woman. Yet in the intervening time, neither had moved in with the other. This affirmed what the neighbor told me: it was a marriage of convenience for the sake of US citizenship.

At some point during my first twenty-four hours in Miami, I called the social worker who had done the assessment of my grandfather. As I tried to summarize the facts, I ended by saying, "I'm not sure what's going on."

"I know what's going on," she said matter-of-factly.

Her name was Ronnie. I had liked her from the moment I met her when I hired her to do the assessment of my grandfather. She was an attractive, slim woman in her late forties or fifties, with highlighted short blonde hair and a no-nonsense attitude. She'd worked decades in the social services in Southern Florida and knew all too well the kind of scams and abuse that can victimize the elderly. Ronnie was the first person to grasp what was going on. She'd seen it all, from gold diggers to so-called "black widows," women who would marry elderly men and then kill them off for their fortunes.

"If that's what is going on in my grandfather's case, these poor women are in for a big letdown," I told Ronnie. It occurred to me that my grandfather, who naturally resisted the idea he was going senile, may think he was conning the women. Who was conning who?

Either way, short of hiring ex-Navy SEALs to go rescue my grandfather, Ronnie told me my only recourse was to file in court to have him declared incompetent. She gave me the name of a lawyer. I called him immediately and got an appointment to see him later that day. Then I contacted Grandpa's bank and asked them to freeze his accounts. They did so.

I met with the lawyer after five at his office. He listened intently while I told him everything I knew. He said he would draw up the papers immediately. His payment would come from my grandfather's assets, as was customary in such cases.

I left his offices knowing I had done everything I could.

MY GRANDFATHER NEVER showed up at his apartment again.

Within a day or two, I got the name of a lawyer who represented Tanya and Olga. We arranged a telephone conference. I had a bad feeling about this lawyer, so I asked a friend from Alaska to sit in on the call. He was a seasoned businessman and entrepreneur who knew how to deal with lawyers.

The conversation went sour fast. The lawyer accused me of harassing his clients by calling them repeatedly. I tried to explain I had only spoken to them once or twice. I wanted to speak to my grandfather, who was with his clients.

"Mr. Rich never wants to see you again!" the lawyer said sternly. He accused me of stealing my grandfather's money.

I don't know if it was his tone or what he said that hit me the hardest. I completely fell apart. I started crying so hard I could barely talk. My friend, who never lost his composure, calmly explained who he was and how long he had known me. He assured the lawyer I had never taken my grandfather's money.

The lawyer then asked for my address. My friend refused. The call ended sharply.

"Why didn't you just give him my address?" I asked, afraid we had offended the lawyer.

My friend explained that probably the only reason the lawyer wanted my address was to send me some kind of letter regarding harassment charges.

"I am not going to make his job any easier," he said. Every minute the lawyer spent trying to get my address would cost his clients money.

That was my first lesson in just how hard things were going to get.

AT SOME POINT, I found out the full names of Tanya and Olga. I went down to the clerk's office at the state courthouse building in downtown Miami and ran their names through a search of all civil lawsuits filed in Miami in the previous five to ten years. I didn't have to go back very far. A handful of lawsuits filed by banks were listed either against the women directly or against companies they owned. I copied down the list of cases and went to the clerk's desk to ask to see the files.

The clerk on duty saw Olga's name scrawled on the edges of my list. She recognized it. *Of course*, I thought. If you are in the business of bidding on foreclosed properties, you become a regular at the clerk's office where the case files are kept.

I immediately played dumb, figuring Olga and Tanya were likely dropping in there all the time. The clerk asked if the name on my sheet of paper was the same as the person she knew.

"Ah, I don't know. I was told to come get copies of these files by my boss," I said. I also had never actually seen the women, so I had no idea what they looked like. I decided to ask. "What's your person look like?" I added.

The clerk described a woman of average height, dark hair, maybe in her thirties. "Mustache," she added, motioning with her index finger across her upper lip.

I fought the urge to laugh. "No, I don't think so," I said shaking my head.

OLGA AND TANYA had moved to Florida around the time of Hurricane Andrew. Olga ran a business that bought up foreclosed, condemned, and/or abandoned properties—homes, condominiums, and the like—at auctions held regularly on the courthouse steps.

Most of the properties were from the city of Homestead, south of Miami. Hurricane Andrew destroyed 25,000 homes and severely damaged 100,000 more in South Florida.

Like all large natural disasters, a reconstruction boom followed. The women were simply trying to do what many others were doing—cash in on the aftermath of disaster. Even my friend from Alaska had moved to Florida with a construction company seeking work after Andrew.

However, from the court records, it looked as if no payments were ever made on any of the properties Tanya and Olga bought. It seemed the plan was to sell them before the banks had to go through the lengthy process of repossessing the homes.

WHAT FOLLOWED THAT day in the clerk's office was a series of events seeking to declare someone incompetent, a ruling that judges often hesitate to make.

I tried to get the Florida Department of Health and Human Services involved. I thought they should at least investigate the women and the surroundings in which they were keeping my grandfather. A worker I spoke with couldn't be less alarmed. When I tried to explain my grandfather's declining mental health, he shouted, "I've seen old people living in filth like pigs, and I still couldn't do anything to help them!"

When the authorities failed to do anything, I turned to the one entity I knew well: the news media. I spoke at length with a reporter from the *Miami Herald*. Unfortunately, what was happening with my grandfather seemed to be a common occurrence in South Florida.

I WAS JUST unlucky enough to have this happen to my grandfather a few years before a wave of such incidents hit the national news and "black widow" stories became headlines. But in 1993, my case sounded like just another gold-digger-versus-distant-family story.

I also called longtime *Miami Herald* columnist and author Carl Hiaasen. I was a huge fan of his work. I couldn't have talked to a nicer guy. I'm sure the fact that I was a fellow journalist assured him I wasn't a nut. I'm equally sure that the more I explained my grandfather's situation, the more I must have sounded like one of those people who routinely call newsrooms wanting to report UFO sightings or government conspiracies.

When my newspaper series came out, a woman had called the newsroom with some story about having something that belonged to my father. I spoke with her and invited her to meet. My editor came with me; we worried this would be something difficult to see or deal with.

The receptionist showed her to the conference room. My editor and I entered the room and introduced ourselves. When we asked what she had, she pointed to a large sand and wood candle she had put on the table.

"He's in there," she said. It quickly became clear she was not well and was convinced that my father's spirit inhabited the candle. We politely led her away and thanked her for her concern.

That's how I must have sounded to anyone whose help I tried to enlist or who I thought should be involved in the safekeeping of Miami's most vulnerable residents. I worried that's how I sounded to Hiaasen. But he was exceedingly polite and apologized for my situation, one which he said was all too common in Florida.

I was left with no choice but to wait out the process of trying to have my grandfather declared incompetent. It was not going to be easy. First, my lawyer and others warned that my grandfather would likely hate me for it. Families left with no other choice are torn apart by the proceedings, which can become adversarial and antagonistic. Usually, though, the sick family member is indeed in need of oversight and help.

The court appoints a lawyer for the allegedly incompetent person. This is done to forestall the rare occasions when family members might be seeking Grandma's Social Security checks or pension or whatever. In my case, Olga and Tanya's lawyer filed to be my grandfather's attorney. The judge agreed to that, even when we pointed out the conflict.

I was told the court might strip my grandfather's rights slowly, such as the right to drive or manage his own finances. But the right to marry, live where one chooses, and even vote are liberties the courts are loath to take away.

As THE COURT date approached in November, I became increasingly nervous about seeing my grandfather again. I had not seen him since he had disappeared with Tanya and Olga. By their accounts, he hated me and never wanted to see me again. Even knowing he was not in his right mind didn't assuage my sense of hurt and loss.

I waited in the lobby outside our assigned courtroom. I knew my grandfather would be with the women. I was scared to see him. What would he do when he saw me? Yell at me? Call me names? I knew how vile and belligerent he could become when pressed. No doubt the women had told him I had filed to have him declared incompetent. He could not be happy about this.

But what else could I do? Nothing seemed right, and if he was in some kind of danger, I was the only person to do anything about it. I had to at least assure myself that he was okay.

I had gone over everything in my mind many times. If the women truly wanted to be with my grandfather, great. All the better for him to have them in his life. If they wanted his money, that couldn't happen. It would have to be put in the hands of a court-appointed guardian.

It was clear to me from that first talk with their lawyer and their court filings that these women either did not experience my grandfather's senility the way I had or they wanted desperately for him to be deemed competent. If he was not competent, the marriage might be void because he was not in his right mind at the time of the ceremony. Tanya could be deported.

That MORNING, I was sitting in a lobby to the side of the elevator landing. I heard the elevator door open and braced for the fit of rage I expected.

My grandfather shuffled into the lobby, walking slowly and with great difficulty. He looked terrible, as if he had aged years since I had last seen him. He suddenly spotted me. And then he smiled.

"There you are! Where you been?! I've been looking all over for you!"

I rushed to his side and we hugged. His eyes teared up.

"I'm right here, Grandpa," I said.

I directed him to a chair and sat next to him. Olga and Tanya hovered nearby. They must have been as shocked as I was by his positive response to me.

It didn't take long to figure out what was going on. When I was out of sight, I was out of mind. Whenever the subject of his granddaughter came up, he did not make the connection between the actual me and the person he was being told was doing him all this harm.

It hit me hard to realize how much his Alzheimer's had progressed. I knew that leaving his routines and longtime home would cause a decline. I just didn't expect him to be as sick as he was. He looked rail-thin and haggard. His clothes seemed more worn than usual. He was unshaven, and he badly needed a haircut. He had no idea why we were all there.

I think it was at that first meeting that Olga, the daughter, gave me a gift. It was a book, one that held out the promise of the American Dream: *Wealth Without Risk*, by Charles J. Givens.

Givens was a self-styled financial planner, motivational speaker, and infomercial real estate guru who rose to national prominence in the early 1990s. His lavish life was even featured on the television program *Lifestyles of the Rich and Famous*. Although he was later disgraced and sued for consumer fraud, at the time of this court hearing Givens's book was clearly a roadmap for Tanya and Olga.

It was obvious that they came from impoverished circumstances. Their clothes looked as if they came from a thrift store, worn and in need of laundering. Their shoes were little better. I felt a great deal of empathy for them.

But still, we were adversaries, and my grandfather was caught in the middle. Whenever we were all together, my grandfather's relationship to me was clearly intact. Away from me, given whatever he was told, he supposedly ranted and raved about me.

Welcome to senility.

Not a lot happened during that first court hearing, except for one moment that told me all there was to know about my grandfather's state of mind. The judge was reading a history of the case and got to the part where my grandfather married Tanya. The minute he heard this, my grandfather shouted out, loud and clear, "Yes, my wife! I married her!" He pointed across the table to his "wife."

My grandfather John Rich and me outside his apartment building in Miami Beach, early 1990s.

I was stunned. I couldn't believe my luck. His lawyer looked alarmed, as well he should have. He gently asked my grandfather not to speak up in court. The lawyer then asked the women to keep him silent.

I've already won my case, I thought.

When my grandfather impulsively pointed out his "wife," he didn't point to Tanya—who indeed, records showed, he had married at the Miami Beach courthouse. Instead, he had pointed to her much younger and more attractive daughter, Olga. My grandfather's mind was so far gone, he had no idea which one he married.

A follow-up hearing was scheduled for several weeks later.

CHAPTER 13

It's All Material

$\mathcal{S}$oon after the court hearing, Bill and I got together with the women and my grandfather for a meal at a restaurant. It was probably a Denny's, my grandfather's favorite. I think our lawyers suggested the meeting.

I struggled with trying to decide whether Tanya and Olga were as confused as I was by my grandfather's shifting mental state or whether they were indeed my enemies. I wanted to believe the former and hoped it wasn't the latter.

Conversation was hard, as they spoke broken English. I tried to explain that my grandfather was quite sick and that what they had done by taking him from his familiar surroundings made him even more senile. I wanted to believe they could and would take care of him should he continue to live with them. I wanted my grandfather to have a wife and loving family around him. I was willing to chalk up the events of the past few months to one big misunderstanding created by an ex-bookie who may have well thought he was conning these two "millionaires."

Maybe he was in love.

But the meeting went sour, and at one point the conversation got heated. It was difficult to understand Olga's broken English, but Bill and I both felt threatened by her anger and her use of the word "destroy." The women were determined to keep my grandfather's marriage to Tanya from being nullified.

They left with my grandfather. I stood in the parking lot and watched them go, shaken by the message I got.

I returned to New York to resume my classes.

A few weeks later, Tanya and Olga took my grandfather to the emergency room for some reason, and he was hospitalized. I rushed down and saw that he had been transferred to a nursing home.

It was a small victory. It wasn't the best place nor the worst—a multifloor unit near one of Miami's waterways. It had a view of the water, though the immediate surrounding area was a mix of closed businesses and low-rent residences. The facility had some private apartments; a caring, bright young social worker on staff; and typical nursing home activities—movies, card games, arts and crafts, and meals in a dining room made to look like a restaurant.

On my grandfather's floor—the Alzheimer's/dementia unit—I would pass residents in the hall while they were sitting outside their rooms. The women were often dressed up as if they had an engagement to attend. They might sit for hours, their purses held on their laps. At first I thought it odd, but I soon realized these were the routines of a lifetime. My grandfather, though he hadn't driven a car in years, would still stop to look for his car keys before we'd leave his room to go to the dining room.

I made a habit of talking to the residents and made friends with some. I developed a relationship with the staff, especially the activities director and the head of the home. All understood my grandfather's precarious situation and kept a watchful eye out for Tanya and Olga should they return.

But since my grandfather had yet to be declared incompetent, there wasn't much to do if he decided to leave. He still had that right.

Yet we all knew that every time his living circumstances changed, his mental health would decline. I decorated his room as best I could with things I had salvaged from his apartment. I even bought him a new TV.

I prayed I could keep him at the facility before the next scheduled court hearing.

The reporter in me questioned every event, every conclusion, until I could find multiple sources to back what I was learning about the women. I was still shaken by Olga's threat. I felt an old familiar fear creep back into my life.

I felt afraid for my life, as I had when writing about my father for the newspaper, as I had the day I thought one of my father's old enemies was following my car after I had interviewed him. This fear is hard to describe and can only come from the kind of vulnerability felt by people who've been the victims of violent crime.

Was I willing to risk my life on this thing? Should I just walk away and let my grandfather's fate play out? He had created a life far removed from his many family members who lived in his home state of Connecticut.

He once had an older brother who lived with him in Miami. His name was Bobby. I got the feeling Bobby was the leader of the two, the more handsome and charismatic. But he had died many years before.

When I was doing research on my book, my grandfather put me in touch with his sister. She and I became close, and I visited her often at her assisted living apartment an hour or so north of New York. I had called her when my grandfather first went missing. She thanked me for looking after her distant brother.

There were other siblings and nieces and nephews—most of whom my grandfather had never met. He also had another brother who lived in Northern Florida, but they had nothing to do with each other.

I was mad as heck that after leaving my father's world behind, here I was on the fringe of society again, dealing with events and people I wanted nothing to do with. Many times, I thought about walking away. Where was he when I was growing up? What did I owe him?

"You can't," Bill would say. "He's got no one but you."

In *Johnny's Girl*, I had chronicled finding him and how much joy it brought us both. He hadn't known that my father was dead. Or my mother. It was shocking to him. Bill thought that news alone was a huge setback to my grandfather's mental health.

When I returned to New York after getting Grandpa settled in the nursing home, I met again with the chair of the Writing Division program, Stephen Koch.

"I feel like I'm in one of those made-for-TV movies," I said, describing how terrifying it was to be up against everything with no one believing you.

He said something I'll always remember: that it was frightening and hard to be a hero.

I didn't think of myself as a hero.

He and Bill were right, though. I couldn't walk away. I would wonder the rest of my life what happened to my grandfather. And if something bad happened to him, I would never forgive myself.

As I feared, after I left Miami, Tanya and Olga went to the nursing home and convinced my grandfather to leave with them. And off into the night they went.

AN UNEXPECTED CONSEQUENCE of the whole mess emerged from the people looking at this story from the outside. The chair of the film school at the School of the Arts loved my grandfather's story. He saw a movie in it. So did my professor in my screenwriting class.

Ditto for John Harrison, who was directing the film production of *Johnny's Girl*. I spoke to John several times a week as the film was in preproduction and scheduled to begin filming the spring of 1994. During one conversation, I described the latest development in my grandfather's case.

"Take notes!" John said. "It's all material."

Material for a horror story, maybe. The entire episode was a nightmare.

I had one break over the Christmas holiday when visiting with a friend in Chicago. My friend Ginny was someone I had initially met over the phone when I was researching *Johnny's Girl*. Trying to locate a relative, I had called a theater in New York where she worked. I didn't find my relative, but instead I met Ginny. We became fast friends.

Ginny was petite, with a bright smile and a pixie haircut. She might not look imposing, but she was one of the smartest people I know. And one of the most generous.

By Christmas of 1993, she had left the theater and was in law school. We reunited near Chicago, where Bill and I were spending the holidays with his mother and her husband. One evening when we were talking in

Bill's mother's kitchen, Ginny listened intently as I ran down the latest on the Grandfather Saga.

At that point, everything seemed to be going badly. How much longer could I keep going to Miami and missing classes and generally wear myself out? It had been more than a year since my grandfather had disappeared. I had been told that by the time a family member has to drag an aged relative into court to be declared incompetent, they usually are. For the most part, these things moved along swiftly. Nobody I talked to had ever heard about a situation such as mine, where the allegedly incompetent had an attorney fight to *not* have their client—who was so clearly quite senile—incompetent.

"What about politically?" Ginny asked. "Do you know anybody with political power?" See what I mean about her being smart?

It had never dawned on me. As a journalist who had to strive to remain impartial and unbiased in many parts of life, especially involving politics, I would have never envisioned myself doing what people do all the time: contacting an elected official for help on a matter involving a state or federal agency. Such thinking had long been trained out of me. I was and still am a dyed-in-the-wool, old-school journalist. I was brought up in a newsroom filled with hard-nosed, tough, cynical editors who were ethical almost to a fault.

A source offers to buy coffee? You pay. Those nice business people you wrote about send flowers to thank you? The flowers go straight to a local nursing home. As reporters, we could accept no gifts or gratuities. And under no circumstance could we use our position as journalists to exact some favor, privilege, or even a cut in line from the world at large.

So turning to someone of political power for help? Nope. Never would have thought of that. But Ginny, who had long worked in fundraising for nonprofit theaters, understood well how to get things done.

I had explained to Ginny that the women were in the United States illegally. I had been advised to report them to the Immigration and Naturalization Service.

Guess what happened?

Nothing.

I probably called the INS a few times. More than a few times. Probably a lot. I was, after all, an ex-newspaper reporter. A *Daily News* colleague once said that if I were an animal, I'd be a wolverine. All soft and cuddly looking on the outside, but on the inside? Wolverines are one of the most vicious of mammals and will attack creatures many times larger than themselves.

This was still a time when the US Coast Guard had its hands full rescuing Cuban refugees from rickety rowboats or plucking lucky survivors from the seas. Miami is a gateway city for immigrants and refugees fleeing economic hardship and political instability in Central and South America. The Miami INS office is a bit busy. About the last thing its employees probably wanted to deal with was a senile grandfather who'd run off with a couple of European immigrants living in the country on expired visas.

Ginny listened to my latest diatribe about how slow and preposterous the court proceedings had become, how the police refused to investigate the women by saying it was an immigration service matter, and how the INS was doing nothing to help with an obvious violation of immigration law. Ginny grew up in an Irish-American Catholic household in Wisconsin, where civic duty and involvement in one's community was as important as attending mass every Sunday. Well, almost. She knew how the system worked. She knew that when a government agency doesn't respond to a registered voter, elected officials often will.

So get out your score cards.

I just happened to come from a state with a relatively small population, around 600,000 at the time. I also happened to be from a state with one of the most senior and powerful men in the US Senate: Senator Ted Stevens.

I also happened to have written my book in rented office space at the law firm where my dear friend Jeff Lowenfels worked. One of the founding partners of the law firm was Bill Bittner, who was also a friend. Bittner's family had long roots in Alaska. Early in his legal career, he worked as a prosecutor and was the assistant DA on one of the cases involving one of the men involved in my father's murder. Bill Bittner's sister was married to Senator Stevens.

I couldn't have been more connected if I was a Kennedy.

I was out of options, and my grandfather was declining fast. He wasn't able to care for himself, and no one else was doing it for him.

It didn't take me long to place the next call.

AFTER THE HOLIDAYS, I returned to New York. Within days, I got a call from a kind staffer in Stevens's office. They would be looking into the matter.

Soon after I got a call at eight in the morning. It was a man with a deep voice and official tone, the kind that police officers use when pulling you over for speeding.

"I need to speak to Kim Rich," the man said.

"This is she," I answered, half fearing what the call was about.

He introduced himself as head of the INS office in Miami. He said he had a Congressional Directive on his desk. "Just who *are* you?" he asked.

The conversation went something like this:

"So, there're these women—"

"I know who they are."

"Well, I'm not sure what their immigration status is—"

"I know what it is."

"Oh, okay, well…"

Without saying much, he confirmed what I thought had been going on. The women were using my grandfather simply to stay in the country. Somewhere in the conversation, he told me that he had never before received a Congressional Directive to investigate a matter.

Later, when I called to thank the staffer in Senator Stevens's office, she assured me that what they did was what they would do for any constituent.

Perhaps.

All I know is soon after that call from the head of the Miami INS office, I flew to Florida. I was to be part of a sting operation of sorts. The INS would pick up Tanya and Olga, but they wanted to make sure I was there to take my grandfather. My attorney was floored that the INS was taking such swift action. So was pretty much everybody north of Key West, I think.

I called the nursing home and was able to get his old room back (hoping he might just ease back into living there).

I arranged to meet Tanya and Olga and my grandfather for breakfast at a restaurant. But instead of appearing there myself, I was to wait across the street at another restaurant while officers took the women into custody. Everything proceeded smoothly. Tanya was given a "voluntary deportation," meaning she had to leave the country on her own.

We still had to conclude the incompetency hearing. The women and their attorney hoped to preserve the marriage.

As I had expected, the judge declared my grandfather partially incompetent and took away some, but not all, of my grandfather's rights—most importantly, his right to handle his own money. He could still decide where he wanted to live. His money, what little was left, was placed in a trust with a state agency charged with overseeing his care. Of the roughly $40,000 he had in savings, most of it went to legal fees for both sides of the case, court costs, and for the times he was housed in the nursing home. A state agency established to help the elderly

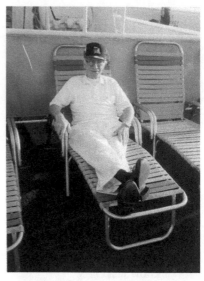

My grandfather reclining on the deck of a cruise ship in the mid-1990s. After the whole affair with the other women was over, I bought us an overnight cruise to the Bahamas. It wasn't a luxury one, but it was good enough. I'm not sure where I got the idea to take a senile man on a cruise. Thankfully, I met and made a lifelong friend onboard and with her help, I managed to survive.

with no loved ones to handle their affairs was granted guardianship of my grandfather's Social Security and any other money he had.

Tanya and Olga said they loved my grandfather and wanted to him to live with them. He chose them.

Did they really want to live with my aging, senile grandfather? This was a question I discussed with the head of the guardianship program many times. The program director assured me of one thing: Tanya and Olga knew they were being watched. My grandfather was at least safe from harm. The women had to ask formally for any funds needed for food, housing, bills, and so on. At one point, they requested about $7,000 for a trip to Hawaii. The request was denied.

A couple of months later, the Homestead police got a call from a security guard about an elderly man who was wandering the streets. The old man said he lived in Miami Beach. That was miles away. The police picked up my grandfather, who just happened to have a business card from his case worker at the state guardianship program. Tanya and Olga were evidently living in the neighborhood, but my grandfather couldn't say where.

That was it. Whether the women intended to lose him or he wandered out the door, it was just what the guardianship and I had expected. They could not properly care for nor supervise my grandfather. The guardianship filed with the court to take full custody of my grandfather. He was sent back to the nursing home.

My grandfather's grand adventure with the so-called "Gypsies" was over.

CHAPTER 14

✒ *Crossroads*

I had my grandfather housed safely in the nursing home in Miami. I visited him frequently and he did well. It was time to get back to living my life.

My book was not a runaway best seller, despite the kind declaration by Jerome, the first friend I made at Columbia.

"A book in every book sack on the subway!" he predicted gleefully.

Johnny's Girl was, however, widely reviewed, and I could live with that. The small book tour the publishing house arranged was enough of a taste of fame for me. I was sent to Anchorage, Juneau, and Seattle. I got to see all my old friends in Juneau and was recognized from the visitors' gallery in the Legislature. I was deeply honored.

In Anchorage, at one book signing, I sat behind the table as a string of elderly women lined up to get their books signed.

Oh boy, now I'm going to get it, I thought, fearing these old-time Alaskans might not take too kindly to my descriptions and story about Anchorage. In trying to describe the kind of people who moved to

Book party release of Johnny's Girl at the home of the Dodge family in Anchorage, 1993. The Dodges opened their home to hundreds of people—their friends, mine, ours, my adopted family members, colleagues, sources, childhood buddies, and even associates or friends of my dad. From left to right: local attorney Bruce Roberts, me, and colleague Bruce Melzer.

Anchorage around the time my parents did, I knew many were misfits, or black sheep, or in dire need of a fresh start. I recognized, too, there were also many drawn to the adventure of it all and the lure of the outdoors, even in the late 1950s, long before the back-to-nature movement of the 1970s took hold in popular culture.

But each and every one of the ladies praised the book and briefly told me their own Alaska story.

As each of the elderly women thanked me for writing my book, I realized that people read into a book their own experiences, finding themselves in a word, or a sentence, or on every page.

When I would later speak to high school classes, there were teenage girls who told me they read my book multiple times.

I remember that at twelve, I read *Love Story* over and over, the first and only romance novel I've ever read. I saw the film version—about the tragic love story between a rich Harvard law school student and a working-class women's college music major—six times.

Six. Times.

I saw it so many times at the same theater that when the film ended its run, I asked the theater manager if I could have the poster hanging in the lobby. I put it up in my bedroom where I could stare dreamily at the star, Ryan O'Neal. *Love Story* was what every tween dreamed of—except, of course, the part where the girl dies. It was worth rereading and rewatching. But my book about my family?

Nothing could have been more flattering than the words of the young students who approached me that day. I still receive emails from other young women, or people such as the airline executive from Chicago, or a military public relations specialist from the Midwest, or those I went to school with who thought I got it right (or even wrong).

My agent Rafe said publishing a national book would open doors and change everything, and he was right. Even if not every New York City subway rider had a copy of it in their hands. If that had happened, I'd be penning this book from my Malibu beach house. But I'm not.

While the publication of *Johnny's Girl* opened many doors and created many opportunities, it also brought profound pain for some and offered me a glimpse of a darker side of life I've never wanted any part of. This is why I never read the newspaper accounts of my father's death nor attended my father's killer's trials. It's also why I moved as quickly as I could away from the dark side, as I saw it, and into the light.

That light was being in New York City and being done with the whole damn grandfather episode and about to go to the set where *Johnny's Girl* was being filmed.

As part of my film contract, I was flown to Vancouver, British Columbia, to spend up to a week on the film set. I was put up at Le Meridian in a large room so beautiful that no sooner had I checked in than I was calling friends and inviting whoever could get away to come stay with me. This was a once-in-a-lifetime event, and I wanted to share it. I must have asked everyone I knew.

I rode to the set each day with John Harrison and the second unit director. We arrived before 7 a.m. and often left near midnight. The schedule was exhausting, and I was amazed that no one seemed to mind the long hours.

John had sent me a copy of the script months earlier, after he finished the adaptation. Since I had begun studying screenwriting, I understood the demands of dramatic writing versus the long form. As such, the storyline in the script was condensed to about the last half of the book and centered on the years I returned to live with my father. In real life, that was between ages nine and fifteen. But for the purposes of the film, that time was compressed to a few weeks.

The script also changed the actual circumstances of how I came to live with my bachelor father. In real life, my mother had been institutionalized. In the film, my mother dies, and I am shipped from Los Angeles to Alaska to live with my father, my only relative.

I didn't mind any of the changes. As my publishing house editor said of the film, "It feels like the book."

While on the set—and upon every viewing since—I felt the film captured the spirit and tone of the book. John once remarked that he wished it had been optioned for a theatrically released film rather than a TV movie. This would have allowed the story and filming to be grittier, better capturing the seamier sides of the story.

Perhaps. I was glad it was as it was.

Thanks to my many conversations with John, the film has elements in it that are part of the true story but never made it into the book. For example, he remembered the conversation we once had about my love for the works of Walt Whitman. In the film, he included a scene of my character reading Whitman's *Leaves of Grass*.

I even got to appear in a cameo in the film. I played a school teacher. In one quick scene, I can be spotted walking across a hall in the background while scolding a student. My hair, makeup, and costume were hardly flattering. I was given a bouffant hairdo, horn-rimmed eyeglasses, and a drab tweed skirt.

In a more inspired moment, I almost played my own mother—at least, her voice. In the book, I wrote about a recording I have that my mom made soon after she graduated high school. The 78-rpm record was made in what was known as a Voice-O-Graph booth while my mother and a friend were looking for work in Chicago.

On the film set, we decided to try using my voice for what's on the record. It seemed fitting and even profound. But since I'm not an actor, I wasn't able to emulate the right tone to capture my mother's voice and the inflections of a young teen. A professional handled it instead.

WHILE I WAS on the set, the movie was being filmed in two or three on-location sites as well as in a vast sound stage built to recreate one of the homes where my father and I lived. (We moved at least once or twice a year in the six years we lived together.) One set was a large room made to look like one of my father's gambling houses.

When I arrived, the film crew was on the first of two location shoots, in the middle of a six-week shoot. I was greeted warmly by the crew and cast members. They even had a director's chair made with my name on it that was placed next to chairs belonging to the stars and director. I still have the canvas top with my name, plus a deck of playing cards with the words *Johnny's Girl* and a pair of aces, the film's logo.

During my first days of shooting, the set was in a rundown part of Vancouver filled with businesses like low-rent strip clubs. The area was so known for crime that, late one night while driving back to our hotel from the set, we were pulled over by the police.

Speeding? Busted tail light? No, the officer saw that there were two men and a single woman in the van. John introduced himself and showed his identification and passes from the film set, and the police officer apologized. Evidently, he thought I was a hooker with customers who'd just picked me up. The irony was not lost on us.

The neighborhood chosen for the shoot included a former crack house. Location scouts had spotted the vacant, two-story, wood-framed home. They had it cleaned out and decorated to look like a house where my father and I might have lived. It was painted a drab beige with dark brown trim and was next door to an auto body shop set up by the film's set designers and building crew. Both buildings sat on a narrow alley across the street from a windowless, concrete block wall belonging to an actual strip club. The film used the bar's back door to stand in as a door to my father's night club.

The night club set was inspired by Le Pussycat, which my father ran for about a year sometime in the late 1960s. It featured acts such as the Jades and J'Adorables, a seven-member review with four guys in suits in the band and three women dancers who fronted them on stage. The trio of pretty dancers wore costumes and performed routines to covers of popular music, eventually stripping down until they were topless by the end of their set. I still recall the band's cover of Paul Revere and the Raider's "Indian Reservation (The Lament of the Cherokee Reservation Indian)" while the dancers pranced in Indian headdresses—and not much else.

That was real life. But the film was being created by a subsidiary of

Hallmark and filmed for television. Thus, in the movie, my dad's club was depicted as a go-go bar with girls who danced in go-go boots and skimpy, bikini-like costumes with lots of fringe and sequins.

The on-location site was every bit as seedy and crummy as some of the areas I'd actually grown up in. It felt like the Anchorage I knew, too. I was there in March, and it was cold. Many days dropped down to freezing temperatures. I borrowed a heavy winter coat from the costume department.

On set, John introduced me to his assistant, a woman named Ruth Atkinson. She was a slim Canadian with shoulder-length curly blonde hair, bright blue eyes, and an easy way about her. When she wasn't busy, she showed me around and introduced me to the various members of the crew and the actors on set. Ruth also introduced me to the script supervisor, Tracy Young, another Canadian. Tracy told me she had grown up a lot like me, with a father who was murdered when she was growing up. The three of us became friends that day, and we still are.

When I wasn't talking to Ruth or Tracy, I walked around the set chatting up the crew, all of whom were friendly, and asked everyone about what they did and their role in the project. Through my talks with the costume designer, my character ended up wearing clothes that were identical to ones I would have worn as a teen. More than a few people on the set noted that writers don't usually talk to the crew, sticking mostly to themselves. They are what is known as "above the line" talent.

I became fast friends with many on the set that first day, and those friendships have lasted all the rest of my days.

Like everyone else, I got a daily printout of the call sheet listing which scenes, actors, costumes, extras, and so on were needed and when. I quickly absorbed the rhythm and order of the set. I felt a sense of awe as I watched the one hundred or so members of the crew move about their jobs.

All these people are working on a story I wrote about my parents, I thought, amazed by it all. *If only my parents could see this.* If only.

Shortly after my arrival on set the first day, John waved me over to a group of people. He thrust me forward, and I suddenly found myself standing right in front of Treat Williams.

I had been nervous about meeting the actor who was cast to play my father. I had long been a fan of Treat's work, beginning when I saw him portray a character named Berger in the film version of the musical

Treat Williams and me on the set of Johnny's Girl *the movie in Vancouver, Canada, March 1994. Treat and I talked a lot, and I was honored by Treat's dedication in getting his portrayal of my father right. (Photo courtesy of and copyright 1994 by Capitol Cities/ABC, Inc.)*

Hair. Treat gave me a hug and asked me to follow him. We went to his trailer, one of several lining the alley. He pulled out his copy of my book, showing me how he'd marked it all up as he read it in an effort to get to know the man my father was. He asked me questions about my dad and ran some of his thoughts about my father's inner life by me. He got it.

What's more, Treat grew up in Connecticut, albeit a wealthier part of the state than where my father was raised. Right away I was struck with how much Treat resembled my father, with his handsome facial features and dark, wavy hair combed back. And as it would turn out, at the time *Johnny's Girl* was filming, Treat was forty-one years old. My father was forty the year he was killed.

Treat and I must have spent an hour or so in his trailer talking about my book and our families, but mostly about my relationship with my dad. I had never expected to have such a conversation and to become friends with the actor who portrayed my father.

The actress hired to play me was Mia Kirschner, an eighteen-year-old from Toronto. At the time of filming, she was only a few years

Me and actress Mia Kirshner, who portrayed me as a teenager in the film. I fell in love with Mia and found she captured my look and attitude from that time of my life. She even spoke of studying journalism and English literature at McGill University, where she later entered that fall.

older than I had been when my father was killed. Mia was on her way to being a star, and I was told she was often compared to Elizabeth Taylor in her looks. Probably because of her youth, Mia's mother was with her at all times while on the set. Both women were friendly and warm. I was struck with how pretty Mia was. She had long, naturally curly hair, as I did at her age. Like me, she was of Polish-Jewish descent on her father's side. We talked often. She was smart and headed to McGill University in Montreal. She also expressed an interest in journalism, as her father was a journalist.

I had less contact with other actors and actresses, some of whom were near the beginning of their careers and would go on to find success in major films.

READERS ARE GENERALLY not happy with film adaptations of beloved books, and I've heard from many who didn't care as much for the film as I did. But then, I was there to see the attention to detail that went into recreating my world. On the sound stage sets, I marveled at how much the rooms looked like rooms my father would have decorated and ones we lived in. It wasn't so much things that I might have described in the book but what the era felt and looked like. The set reflected the feel of my memories. Everything looked authentic.

That first day, I walked among the shooting areas, including inside the house meant to look like my own in the 1960s. The back door led to a fully decorated kitchen, then a living room. When I entered, I slowly

This set was used to represent one of my childhood homes. Here, I'm holding an old Alaska Magazine *the set decorators and props crew had found and used. Note I'm in my heavy coat again as there was no heat in the house for filming.*

took in the level of detail involved in making the house look authentic. On the refrigerator was a magnet from KYAK, a radio station I listened to while growing up. On a side table in the living room were copies of *Alaska Magazine* from the period. John told me he had gone through at least one set designer before finding the one who got the look he was aiming for. That look was my life.

A set of narrow stairs led up to a couple of rooms, including one that was supposed to be my dad's bedroom. The room was off limits, with a strip of tape across the doorway and a sign reading HOT SET. This meant it was set up and ready for filming the next day. No one was to touch it.

A crew member saw me peeking in and said I could look around, but I should be careful not to move anything.

A double bed facing the door was in the middle of the room and nearly filled it. Across from it was a wooden dresser with a mirror, on top of which were photos of Treat Williams with a little girl. The photo was a copy of one found in a fake family photo album the props department crafted. In preproduction, at one point I was asked if I had any photos of my family I could share. I sent the large green scrapbook my mother had kept from my birth until I was about six. Fearful the original would get damaged during filming, the crew made the replica. The only difference between the two was the addition of a series of photos of Treat Williams with a young girl meant to be me as a school-age child. The album is used in scenes in the film where Treat and Mia look through the album together reminiscing about my mom.

Nothing like that ever happened in real life, though I wish it had.

The room was a time capsule of sorts. I sat on the bed, and for a few minutes it felt like it really was my dad's room. It reminded me of a dream I once had where I found him sitting on the edge of a bed. As I approached, his eyes shone back a bright blue. In reality, they were brown. That dream and others that occurred from time to time played off a similar theme though—that my father was alive. At first, I might've felt happy to see him, but soon I felt what I once learned in my college psychology class, cognitive dissonance. In the dream, he's alive, but I'm thinking, *But wait, do I have to go live with him again? Am I still in high school? This can't be. He's dead.*

As I sat in my father's reimagined room, I didn't feel dread or apprehension. I felt something akin to old grief, the kind that isn't hard to recall. I felt love. I sat there by myself for a few minutes, and for the first time in a long time, I cried.

Inside the room created to be my father's bedroom, I encountered old ghosts and some sorrow. Again, as throughout the filming and various on-location and sound stage sets, I felt as if I had traveled back in time. The attention to detail astounded me.

I ENDED UP staying an extra week. It was just too hard to leave. My friend Laura came and hung out on the set with me for a while and stayed with me in my luxury hotel room.

On my final day, the crew was shooting on the sound stage. John gathered everyone around as I said goodbye before leaving for the airport. The electrical crew, or gaffers, "pinned" me by giving me a wooden clothespin, an honor, I was told, awarded to few. I still have the pin.

I was asked what I might like to keep from the set when they were done shooting; I asked for the photo album. (I tried asking for the Cadillac used in the shooting, but that was probably too much.)

The night before, I had jotted an entry in the journal I'd kept since starting graduate school. With the crew gathered around, I thanked everyone for a great time and for accepting me as one of their own. Reading from my journal, I reminded them of the 1989 film *Field of Dreams*, in which an Iowa farmer creates a baseball diamond in the middle of his cornfield and brings the 1919 Chicago White Sox team back to life. To me, that's what it felt like to be on a film set, watching my long-dead parents brought back to life. It was my own field of dreams.

EVERY TIME I have seen the film since, it gives me pause. One day, I ran across the video on a shelf at a Blockbuster video rental store in Anchorage. Then there was the day I was doing housework with the TV on. I looked up from my vacuuming and saw that the movie was on a cable network.

The first time I saw it, though, was the most memorable. In New York, the movie aired on ABC TV over Memorial Day weekend in 1995. That night, a group of friends from the Columbia writing program gathered to watch it. We all cheered when the titles read, "Based on the book by Kim Rich."

That spring, I stayed in my Columbia apartment as I continued to work on my thesis during my third year in New York City. When in town, Bill and I would walk around and point to apartment buildings and imagine ourselves living there after school.

I depended on my summer trips home and stints working in the *Anchorage Daily News* newsroom to reconnect with my roots, something I have never wanted to lose.

Five of my fellow classmates in the nonfiction writing program and me at New York City's legendary Algonquin Hotel. Here, we attempted to recreate the so-called Algonquin Round Table. From left to right: Jay Elhard, Andrew King, me, Catherine Melissa Park, Laura Kriska Gunn, and Jerome Joseph Gentes. We all keep in touch, except for Andrew, who we sadly lost to suicide.

In New York, though, and particularly through the writing program, I became part of a group of students who regularly hung out together. We went to dinner, coffee, and even on trips out of town. Our ventures included expeditions to Shelter Island by ferry or drives to a favored professor's upstate New York farmhouse.

Some of us were in the nonfiction program; others were in fiction and poetry. We formed our own version of the Algonquin Round Table, meeting at the famed Midtown hotel where a celebrated group of New York City writers and others had met more than fifty years before. While some came and went from our group, we stood mostly at about a dozen at any one time. I was one of the oldest in the group, in my early thirties. Most of my fellow students were straight out of undergraduate school. They came from all over the country and the world, most from the best colleges, all with stories they were writing based on their lives to date. Each had some extraordinary tale to tell or the desire to live the life of a writer.

There at Columbia, we found inspiration in each other. In workshop, we read each other's works and talked about them. Other times, we shared earnest tales of bumping into the larger literary world off campus. Once, a friend and fellow student got to meet a famed *New Yorker* writer. We all listened breathlessly as he recounted his casual run-in with the then quite elderly Joseph Mitchell.

By my third year with them, I felt I had become a New Yorker.

I HAD A rule about living in New York: say yes to every opportunity. That meant that I got to see and do lots of things I never would have imagined doing. Bill had a college friend whose girlfriend worked for Hilton Hotels in California. She was working in New York the weekend of the New York City Marathon, and her company's lodging was booked solid. Thus, they put her up in the penthouse apartment.

She called and invited me to take a look. This was the kind of place you see in movies. A private elevator opened onto a wide, multistoried foyer with winding stairs that went up to the living room area. That room was wide and spacious, with modern furnishings and floor-to-ceiling picture windows that ringed the entire space. Upstairs were large bedrooms, one decorated in a jungle theme and another in French provincial, I believe. Each had its own master bath and huge walk-in closets.

Back on the main level, there was a kitchen, with a small bedroom off to the side for staff. Staff! Apparently stars and Arab sheiks with large entourages would stay there for periods of time. We tried to guess the nightly rate. It was light years beyond anything a penny-pinching graduate student could afford.

On another occasion, Treat Williams was in New York, and he invited me to a screening of a cable film project. As usual, my friend Laura was game to go.

Once we were ushered in, Treat waved from his seat from the middle of the theater.

"Hi! Come sit with us," he said.

So we did, in a long row of actors and actresses, Treat's agent, and others. Treat introduced us to everyone there.

Once we were seated, the lights began to dim. Laura turned to talk to a man on the other side of her just as the film was about to begin. She then turned to me and whispered, "He asked if you starred in the film with Treat."

I smiled. He thought I was an actress? Laura certainly had the looks, but me? *Cool*, we both thought.

ASIDE FROM THE occasional brush with fame and fortune, most of my time in New York was spent in my apartment writing and reading.

Nonfiction students were required to produce 150 pages of publishable material as our thesis. Mine was the story of my grandfather's Alzheimer's and his adventure with the Gypsies. I would hand in sections to my advisor for editing, get them back, and then rewrite. I was hoping to be done by the spring of 1995, when Bill was scheduled to graduate law school.

My advisor and professors at Columbia became new mentors to me. I had also become friends with Ken Reich, a veteran reporter with the *Los Angeles Times*. He was yet another person I had met while seeking out my father's relatives. Ken introduced me to a senior editor at the *New York Times*. These two remarkable individuals, much like my editors in Alaska, became mentors.

That winter, I reached a crossroads. I had turned thirty-seven and was about to graduate. My newspaper mentors envisioned me working at the larger papers. That was my dream, too. I had long wanted to work at the *New York Times* or the *Los Angeles Times* or any major metro daily

I talked to my advisors at Columbia, who frowned upon the idea of returning to daily journalism. Eventually, I would take their advice to live the writer's life. I wasn't exactly sure what this meant, except that one of the last things I did before leaving the film set of *Johnny's Girl* was make an agreement to cowrite a script with John Harrison about my grandfather's adventure. The day we shook hands on the deal felt like one of the luckiest days of my life. In essence, I would apprentice under John to learn screenwriting. One of my advisors at Columbia said it was like earning a second MFA in screenwriting. This decision felt like a natural extension of expanding my storytelling.

Whether or not it was the best decision, I'll never know. But something happened with screenwriting that I had not been able to do with the long form—I learned to write fiction.

The former head of Perseverance Theatre in Juneau, where I had done a theater practicum in college, would tell me that sometimes a person has to switch genres to break out of a mold.

I FELT I was coming full circle. I was born in Hollywood, California, and there I would return.

Not only was I born in Hollywood, I have more family there than in any other part of the country. My maternal grandmother had three brothers who settled in Southern California at the turn of the twentieth century. My mother's only brother, Tony, moved out to California at the end of World War II and stayed, marrying Luce, whose parents were also Italian immigrants. They had two sons, Paul and Ronald.

My Italian roots are so deep in LA that when my aunt and uncle celebrated their fiftieth wedding anniversary, not only did the original wedding party come, but their cake was baked by the same baker who made their wedding cake. His small Burbank shop is still open.

At one point, my cousin Paul, then a veteran Los Angeles Police Department detective, got up to give the toast. He looked down a long table filled with guests and thanked everyone for coming. He called out everyone's last names—the Chiaravalles, the Paolones, the Delisios, and so on. One tight-knit Italian family after another, all interconnected, all amazingly part of my roots.

Some of my earliest memories are of being with my mother in Los Angeles when she left my father the first time. I watched the funeral of assassinated President John F. Kennedy on my aunt and uncle's black-and-white television. I have faint memories of being with my mother and a man at dinner on the beach, someplace where I could hear sea lions bark against the rush of the night tide washing onto the shore.

My mom and dad met in California and probably should have stayed there. How different their lives might have been.

As a teen, I began traveling throughout California, from the coast to the vast central farmlands. By the time I was twenty-five, I had explored nearly every part of California. I have long loved the state and its scenic beauty and, of course, the weather.

So, with great enthusiasm, I began work on a script under John's tutelage during my last winter in New York. I made frequent trips to Los Angeles. The process would take a year, at the end of which his agent began shopping the script.

At the same time, I completed my graduate thesis. My grandfather's story became one of dealing with dementia and my family's difficult history. Like father, like grandfather. I wrote in *Johnny's Girl* about my father beating me as a teen. Years later, I encountered my father's rage in my grandfather. At times, my grandfather would become enraged and threaten to hit me. But I stood up to him and in a big voice told him, "Don't you dare. "

Meanwhile, with my book published, I was encouraged to seek freelance magazine writing work. I was able to get meetings with editors of leading women's magazines through my contacts at Columbia. One editor had read the review of my book and wanted to meet me.

As summer 1997 approached, I faced another crossroads. Once I graduated, I could no longer live in my Columbia-owned apartment. I would have to move on.

BUT FIRST, I had a graduation ceremony to go through. It was a beautiful, warm spring day as we sat outside on the common area of the campus listening to the graduation speakers. Then, those of us from the School of the Arts left to receive our diplomas on the stage of the school's theater.

The high point, though, came later. Our group got together to celebrate what we knew was probably the last time we would all be together in New York. We'd done many things in the city, but we had not yet been on the Staten Island Ferry. We planned to meet on campus and then go out for dinner and the ferry trip.

We ended up taking a detour. Someone in the group knew how to get to the rooftop of Butler Library. We knew being on top of Butler was not okay with school authorities, and I'm not sure why we felt we had to do it, but we did.

Butler, the school's main library, sits across the quad from the domed Low Library. There, the statue "Alma Mater" sits with the goddess Athena raising her arms in

Bill and me at Columbia University after my graduation ceremony.

welcome. New York City sprawls in every direction.

We ran from end to end of the roof snapping photos of one another with Columbia's environs in the background. Maybe we needed to see it all one last time as students.

The photos taken that day are some of my favorites. We are all smiling and laughing and together. For me, the day was bittersweet. I didn't know when we would all be together again, though we swore we'd have regular reunions in and outside of New York City.

Years later, some of my fellow students at Columbia would indeed find fame and perhaps some fortune as writers—and one of us became an A-list Hollywood director. With families to support, some would abandon writing altogether and stick with steady careers in law, public relations, and business. Some, in the long run, wouldn't make it. In the next twenty years, at least two I knew would commit suicide.

But that night, we ran high above Columbia, high above the names of great writers and leaders etched on the library façade—Homer, Plato, St. Thomas Aquinas, Dante, Shakespeare, George Washington, Abraham Lincoln, Ralph Waldo Emerson, Mark Twain, and, yes, my old friend Walt Whitman.

CHAPTER 15

A Normal Life, Round Two

*L*eaving New York was one of the hardest things I've ever done. It would be a long time before it would feel like the best decision I'd ever made.

During the summer of 1995, I made what can only be described as a crash landing back in my hometown. Bill went to Fairbanks for his clerkship, and I stayed in Anchorage. I worked part time at the *Daily News* and began teaching in the Communications Department at the University of Alaska Anchorage.

John Harrison and I worked on my grandfather's story for a movie script for a year. His agents attempted to sell it without success. We were disappointed, but I deeply enjoyed the experience and had learned a great deal. John encouraged me to teach screenwriting as a way to learn more, so I did.

Meanwhile, I put together a book proposal about my grandfather's story and eventually changed literary agents. I'm fairly loyal, and this was not easy. But Rafe wasn't enthusiastic about the grandfather story.

Alaska Pacific University, where I taught for more than a decade. I began teaching college right after graduating from Columbia. I love teaching. Here, I'm helping student Heather Thamm. (Photo courtesy of Alaska Pacific University)

Somebody—and I don't recall who—referred me to an agent with a large talent agency who liked the book. It didn't sell. Just as well. I wasn't sure I wanted to revisit that story having so recently lived through it. And I was busy. Busy avoiding going to Fairbanks.

During one trip, I actually found Fairbanks engaging and charming, if not cold. That trip, the temperatures only got down to minus twenty degrees.

Law clerks aren't paid much, so economical Bill rented a studio apartment in Fairbanks' historic Northward Building. The eight-story, steel-sided building was constructed in 1950 and, according to some sources, was the town's first apartment house. The H-shaped building originally featured shops and businesses on the first floor and apartments of varying sizes on the upper floors. A small bar on the first floor seemed to be the only functioning business in the place; I never saw anything else open.

In her 1958 book *Ice Palace*, American author Edna Ferber used the Northward Building as the pattern for the central building in her tale. Initially, this made the place sound appealing to me. It's part of a work of literature.

Bill's studio apartment could be termed literary in the sense that it actually had words in it—or, at least, the name of a popular brand of American whiskey—printed on a wall covered in gold-flecked mirror tiles. Historic all right, circa the 1970s, I believe. The dark-brown shag carpeting was from the same era, as was the dark-brown laminate fake wood paneling and dark wood cabinets in the tiny kitchen. The small bathroom had the type of industrial toilet you might find in an army barracks. It rather reminded me of the 736 Club. It made my suite at Columbia look like the Ritz-Carlton. I don't know what it was about Bill, but he seemed to have an attraction to the low-rent district.

I visited Bill's apartment once. That weekend I came down with a sudden, terrible flu. I awoke in the middle of the night vomiting violently. I arose from bed and fainted, and I kept fainting every time I tried to stand.

"Call the paramedics," I yelled at the sleeping Bill.

Once awake, he offered to go get his car. He drove a used 1980s Subaru wagon with a wire coat hanger for a radio antenna. As I said, clerkships don't pay a lot. Who was I to talk? I drove the base model Saturn, but at least it was new. Not only did I abhor riding in the Subaru, I knew it would take at least a half hour to warm it up in the frigid weather. Then Bill would have to get me—puking my guts out the whole way—down the creaky elevator, out the door, and into the car.

He relented and called the paramedics. From the floor, barely able to lift my head, I told Bill to grab me a warm jacket and some socks while waiting for help to arrive. Then a horrifying thought occurred to me: the paramedics might think I was puking because I was drunk. Or that I was a hooker. (I can't say I actually saw any there, but I figured the Northward was a place they might go.)

Yes, in the darkest of moments, I worried about how I might be perceived by the paramedics. Like it mattered. Like even those drunk or on drugs don't deserve dignity and respect and good care. I think I was delirious. Bill found it amusing that, once the paramedics arrived and placed me on the stretcher, I was telling them our whole life story all the way to the ambulance, desperately trying to put a sheen of respectability on the whole business. I know they didn't care, and I'm sure they'd experienced worse babbling from a semiconscious person in the middle of the night.

Did I mention it was twenty degrees below zero outside?

I admit, I had been curious about how that kind of cold would feel. So earlier that day I had gone running. Yes, running. I recall the temperature displayed on a time-and-temperature digital clock said it was minus seventeen degrees. Fairbanks boasts (if that's the right word) of much lower temperatures every winter, but that was a record for me. I was dressed in layers of running clothes: wool, down coat, face mask, insulated snow mittens. I looked like the Michelin man. Somehow, I managed to get in a thirty-minute run.

During my run, I kept hearing what sounded like a loud clap behind me as I went down a residential street. The houses were small, one-story ranches with garages that faced the street. I kept looking behind me to see where the sound was coming from. I eventually realized it was the echo coming off the garage doors from my running shoes hitting the hard, frozen street—*clap, clap, clap.*

Intriguing as that weekend was, I never went back.

THAT YEAR ENDED, and fortunately Bill moved down to Anchorage, where he accepted his first job with a boutique law firm based out of San Francisco. He had worked for one of the partners when he was a paralegal before law school.

We got a one-bedroom apartment in the Bootlegger's Cove area of Anchorage, and less than a year later, we bought our first house. It was a ranch-style three-bedroom home in the downtown area of Anchorage known as South Addition. We paid a whopping $137,000 for the charming log home built in the late 1950s. It had a compact, handsome yard ringed in tall birch trees and a wooden fence. In the backyard stood a majestic weeping birch tree, along with a group of lilacs and other shrubs. The house sat on a small rise that offered just enough elevation to see a part of the Chugach Mountains bordering Anchorage to the east.

I called our first house the "lawyer's starter home." Throughout the years, various lawyers in town had bought this particular house and had upgraded different parts of it with whitewashed interior walls, a fireplace with bright red ceramic tile, and blonde wood flooring. Most of the windows had been upgraded except for a few original paned windows that added extra charm.

That house—perhaps like all first couple homes—became the center of frequent dinner parties and holiday celebrations for the six years we owned it. I learned it had always been a popular gathering place. Kay Fanning, former publisher of the *Anchorage Daily News*, once told me how she had interviewed Walter Cronkite in the backyard when he came up for the annual state press association conference. Other guests talked of attending Kentucky Derby Day parties in the home under a previous owner who would later become Attorney General of the State of Alaska. The house had good vibes, as they say.

We threw small but fun Halloween parties, inviting all our friends and their children. We'd strew dry ice by the front door to create fog, put speakers outside, and play a recording of scary Halloween sounds and music. Inside, we'd watch classic horror films such as the original 1931 *Dracula*, starring Bela Lugosi. We'd then throw on Mel Brooks's *Young Frankenstein* followed by the most recent hit horror film.

Those same close friends would come to our annual Easter party, where we all dyed Easter eggs, and to our Christmas party, where Bill, who loves to cook, made a traditional holiday meal featuring homemade Yorkshire pudding.

IN AUGUST OF 1997, we got married.

The proposal came quite unexpectedly, in the middle of a nonstop flight from Miami to San Francisco. We were not alone. We were escorting my grandfather to Alaska.

After settling into our first home and jobs, we had decided to bring Grandpa up to Anchorage. He needed full-time nursing care for his heart and dementia, and I wanted him closer to me. I researched places in Anchorage and found a room in a small assisted living home.

Getting him out of his room in Miami and onto an airplane required the kind of logistical planning that would make even a five-star general balk. First, I had to gain full custody of my grandfather. The state guardian was happy to assist, and the whole thing occurred in a brief court hearing.

I worried whether I was doing the right thing by taking Grandpa away from all he had known for most of his life. The head of the guardianship agency had no such doubts.

"He's going with his loving granddaughter," he said.

"But what if he dies in the middle of the flight?"

"He'll die happy," he replied.

Besides, I added to myself, *he could die at any time for any number of reasons*. That convinced me it was worth it.

Next, I had to take Grandpa to a doctor for a checkup and to make sure he was healthy enough to make the trip. The doctor said sure. He even gave me some mild sedatives should my grandfather become agitated during the long day of flying.

I then consulted the Alzheimer's Association, as I had done on many issues relating to my grandfather's care, on how best to prepare him for the move. I knew that disturbing his routine would upset him and likely cause him to react badly. The social worker I spoke with had brilliant advice: do not pack up his room, she instructed. Quietly pack up any immediate necessities when he was out of the room, but leave the room exactly as it was. Once I had him out of the building, have a friend quickly pack anything that needed to go on the plane with us. Later, I could make arrangements for the staff to mail anything else we wanted to keep and give away the rest.

Since Grandpa had virtually no short-term memory at that point, it almost didn't matter if I told him anything prior to the day of departure.

Because we were flying three of us from Florida to Alaska, we used frequent flyer miles to make the trip affordable. The downside of this was that we had to book a route that had us stop and change planes, and we'd get into Anchorage past midnight. It was going to be a long day.

The morning of the flight, a close friend and I arrived at my grandfather's room.

"Grandpa, we're going on a trip!" I said as cheerily as I could.

My friend and I had planned our arrival for the morning, when Grandpa was most likely to be up and in a good mood. We feared that he would object and refuse to leave. We got lucky. He was game.

By saying "trip," I was implying a vacation. I'm not sure where I said we were going, but I made it sound like it was short and that we'd be back soon. The main thing is we got him to the airport, and the excitement of the whole endeavor got us all the way onto the plane without a hitch. In fact, once seated and buckled in, Bill and I looked at each other and couldn't believe it had worked.

Well, it mostly worked. During the first leg of the journey, my grandfather could sit by a window. But after changing planes in Denver, we were flying on a wide-body jet and seated smack dab in the middle.

Somewhere in the middle of the second leg, Grandpa grew tired and wanted to go to his room, which was now about two thousand miles away and thirty-five thousand feet down. He tried to get up. We got him to sit back down. We pointed out whatever was on the video screen in front of him. We took turns engaging him in conversation. Bill had a particularly tough time of it as my grandfather—as he began melting down—decided that Bill was some old gangster and began talking to him in "tough guy" language, accusing Bill of trying to con him. I got Grandpa's attention and changed the subject just as things started to get a little ugly.

Now and then, we'd take out the sedative bottle, read the instructions, count the hours, and say, "Good, he can have another!"

We tried to encourage Grandpa to nap in his seat. At some point, after many attempts on his part to get up and go to his room, I thought, *Fine! Go to your room. Go ahead, the door's up there!*

Finally, after God knows how long, he fell asleep. Bill and I were exhausted. I'm not sure how much time passed, but Bill turned to me, leaned over my sleeping grandfather, and said, "You're going to need some help with him."

Duh. Isn't that what you're doing? I thought groggily.

"I mean, like, help. Like, together."

I finally got it. "Are you asking me to marry you?"

"Yes."

I DON'T RECALL when my grandfather woke, but somehow, we made it all the way to Anchorage. Once on the ground, he was again sound asleep. We got a wheelchair, drove him home, and put him on the couch.

The next day, we got him to the home I had selected. It was a large, privately-owned facility with about a half-dozen residents.

Grandpa hated it.

He was a big-city boy. His assisted living facility in Miami had worked because it was in a high-rise with lots of people. It reminded him of the apartment building where he'd lived for so many years, with the city all around.

In the quiet Anchorage facility, he moped. He fought with the caretakers. Before I could plan to move him, he became ill and had to be hospitalized.

It was the best thing that could have happened to him and us. First, the doctor at the hospital asked me what medications my grandfather was on. I showed him the daily medications I had brought from Miami, which I'd been told were to help with his agitation. It turned out that the medication was for people with psychotic symptoms. The doctor suggested taking Grandpa off it to see what happened. At least he was in a hospital where they could handle any adverse outcome.

Nothing happened. If anything, Grandpa's mood improved. He felt safe and secure in the hospital. He had no fits of rage and no outbursts with the staff.

When it came time to discharge him, he was to go to a nursing home for continued care. Normally such news is not good news. Most nursing homes are not the kind of place anyone wants to end up. Unless you happen to have been in Anchorage at that time and were going to the Mary Conrad Center.

The day before he was to be transferred there, I went out to see the center, meet staff, and sign paperwork.

The Mary Conrad Center was a new facility operated by the Sisters of Providence Health Care System. From the moment I drove up, I knew Grandpa would love Mary Conrad. It was built to resemble a ski lodge or country club. The outside had handsome wood siding, with angles and points and lots of windows. Inside, low wool carpeting covered the flooring. Guests entered a reception area that fronted a large room with vaulted ceilings and, again, windows everywhere.

When I had looked at homes for my grandfather in the past, my test was to ask myself, "Would I stay here even for just a night?" At the Mary Conrad Center, with its warm wood surroundings and decidedly non-nursing-home look, my answer was a resounding *yes*.

Mary Conrad was both an assisted living and nursing facility comprised of a group of "pods," areas jutting off from the main entry and lounge area. The living areas were apartments set around a center area in each pod. Unlike so many facilities I'd seen, there wasn't a single strip of linoleum or the smell of cleanser—or worse, urine—anywhere in the building.

From the moment my grandfather arrived and for the five years he lived there, he never once complained or caused a problem. The only issue was that he wanted to wander out the doors.

In traditional nursing homes, a loud buzzer or alarm might go off when a patient leaves unescorted. These, of course, frighten the hell out of the residents. At Mary Conrad, a song is played whenever someone tries to go out an exit door: "The Happy Wanderer." The one that goes: "I love to go a-wandering, along the mountain track."

MY GRANDFATHER'S DESIRE to go a-wandering probably stemmed from a desire to do what he had done for years—go out for morning coffee at the Cuban diner near his old apartment building, or stroll along the Miami Beach boardwalk, or have dinner at the nearby Denny's.

I had learned it was best not to shock him with reality that might upset him. For example, when Grandpa would bring up my father, I wouldn't say that he was dead; I learned to change the subject. For someone with dementia, hearing bad news—even news from the past—is like hearing it for the first time. They start grieving all over again. Of course, by the next day they have forgotten it and have to be told—and grieve—yet again.

Sometimes Grandpa couldn't find something and would lapse into accusing someone—anyone—of, say, stealing his shoes, I learned to say empathetic phrases like, "It's hard to lose things, isn't it?" Often those with dementia are referring intuitively to their personal losses of memory and other issues; like anybody, they just want someone to listen and sympathize.

At one point, I thought how caring for my grandfather had expanded my own capacity for patience, a quality I hadn't much of for most of my life. I theorized that caring for him was good practice for caring for children.

Soon after moving Grandpa to Alaska, I realized that if I had children, I might not have the time or energy to devote to him. So I began visiting him as much as I could. I went at least once during the week, if not twice, spending evenings at the Mary Conrad Center watching television or walking around. We both loved the movies. Every Sunday, I would take him to a matinee at a nearby theater. Just getting out, riding in a car, going to the theater—all of it—stimulated his senses and made him happy. I knew that he might not completely understand what was happening in the movies we saw. But in studying screenwriting, I'd learned that films have emotional beats throughout in each scene. These beats take viewers on a journey. Even lacking short-term memory, my grandfather could grasp each beat of the story, whether it was an up moment, or down, or a love scene.

The hours we spent together were so much more than what we'd had when he lived so far away. It felt like the right amount of time. But when talking to a friend, she told me she visited her grandfather in his nursing home about once a week. At first I thought that was too little, until I realized she had children to care for.

I had thought that in some ways, my care of my grandfather was akin to caring for a child. This had occurred to me even while I was at Columbia. But after my grandfather was finally settled in a place where he could thrive, Bill and I decided it was time to start a family.

I SHOULD HAVE been a wedding planner; I like to plan weddings. This was my second marriage, so I briefly wondered if it was appropriate to plan a big church wedding. But it was Bill's first, so why not go all out?

Ours was scheduled for August 9, 1997.

It was something of a group project. My close friend Carolyn helped me get started and hosted my bridal shower. I pored over the latest issues of *Martha Stewart Weddings* and *Brides* magazines for inspiration. That was the new me—the wolverine as a blushing bride!

Bill and I drew up a guest list that topped 250 attendees. We chose what we felt was the perfect venue—the Quarter Deck atop of one of the towers of the downtown Hotel Captain Cook. As with the rest of this landmark Anchorage hotel, the Quarter Deck was built to look like its namesake aboard one of the ships sailed by eighteenth-century British explorer Captain James Cook. We liked the warmth of the wooden interior and the sweeping views of Anchorage from floor-to-ceiling windows. It was such a unique setting that when the hotel called to say they were planning to remodel the space and wanted us to move to a regular banquet room, we balked. We insisted we had to have the room as it was. The hotel agreed to postpone the project until after our wedding.

We hired a jazz band and had the hotel caterer create a polar bear ice sculpture. A photographer who worked at the *Daily News* shot the wedding; I wanted the pictures to have a candid and news-like quality. I had a cake made and decorated to match one I had found in a *Martha Stewart Weddings* magazine: white with white frosting and real purple pansies.

This time I had three bridesmaids: a best friend from my reporter

Central Lutheran Church in Anchorage, August 1997. Bill and I crack up as we head down the aisle after our wedding ceremony.

days at the Daily News, my best friend from New York, and my best friend from Columbia. Why torture them with having to wear a stereotypical bridesmaid dress? I helped select a simple black Ann Taylor tea-length dress that could be worn again and again. One friend even remarked that the wedding had one flaw: "The bridesmaids' dresses were too tasteful!"

As in my first wedding, my dress was off the rack. It was a simple pearl-colored, floor-length satin slip dress with long, silk gloves. It was reminiscent of what Carolyn Bessette wore a year earlier in her wedding to John F. Kennedy, Jr. Hers was a $40,000 designer gown; mine cost considerably less. I even copied Bessette's leafy bouquet studded with lily of the valley. The gorgeous Carolyn's marriage to John Jr. appealed to me in the same way Jackie O's sense of style was admired by the women of my mother's generation. It was my way of doing something my mother—highly fashionable in her day—would approve of.

Close friends came from Columbia and from Illinois, Wisconsin, California. Everyone I knew at the *Daily News* was invited. My Uncle Tony and Aunt Luce, along with my cousin Paul, made the event especially memorable. Luce and Tony rarely traveled in those days. I've always been close to them, and years later, after Tony died, Luce told me how they had wanted to adopt me when my mother became ill.

We packed our downtown Lutheran church with friends and family. The guest of honor was my grandfather. With one friend to help launch him from the back and another to help seat him at the front of the church, he walked me down the aisle.

A friend and former neighbor loaned us his vintage black Corvette as the getaway car to take us to the reception. There, it was a joy to dance with my grandfather. He had lots of dance partners that night. I'd never seen him up so late, having so much fun.

Bill and I paid for the event ourselves and somehow managed to keep costs down. In his typical quotable fashion, Bill said afterwards, "If we could have this same party every year for $10,000, I'd do it."

ONCE WE FINISHED our honeymoon in Victoria, British Columbia, our thoughts turned to a family of our own.

I've always loved children. I have always been able to talk to them and enjoy their company. I never thought I didn't want kids. I just wasn't ready, I would tell myself. I probably also feared I would end up being a bad parent or putting my kids through what I went through. I joked, "Why pass these genes on to anyone?"

Plus, despite once owning *Our Bodies, Ourselves*, I was clueless about my biological clock. At age thirty-nine, mine was definitely running down. Coming of age in the Seventies, in the rise of the modern women's movement, I had always assumed that not only could I do it all, but I could have it all at any time of my choosing. And then I could finally shop at Baby Gap! I was only doing what all the Hollywood stars of my generation were also doing in the late Nineties—having babies. It almost seemed that a baby on one's hip was the latest fashion accessory. Easy. I can just decide to have a baby and bingo, I win!

Then my inner voice said to me one day, "Those celebrities you're reading about, in love with their babies and enjoying life to the fullest? They are at least a decade younger than you."

Oh.

I actually had this conversation with one friend.

"Bill and I have decided to start a family," I said.

"That's great. I hope everything goes well," she said.

Western Washington State, August 1997. Part of our honeymoon included visiting Olympic National Park, the site of our first camping trip years earlier when we were still dating. We are sitting on a ledge near Hurricane Ridge Visitor's Center.

"What do you mean 'hope'?" I asked.

"Just being older and all," she said.

"So?! I'm in good health, I'm fit. I exercise. I don't smoke or drink. Plus, Bill's younger," I said.

"Ah, it's not the guy's age that matters," she said.

Pause. Silence. More silence. More.

"Say what?"

Yeah, yeah, I had heard of the biological clock. I guess I knew it starts dinging at about age, um, forty? Wrong. Try thirty-five. Try being at the top of the Matterhorn ride at Disneyland at age 34 years and 11 months and 29 days and 23 hours and 59 seconds. Hit thirty-five, and you are abruptly slammed to the bottom.

That's what the curve on medical charts looks like for a woman's fertility between the ages thirty-four and thirty-five. That's exactly what it looked like on the drawing my doctor did on a piece of paper in his office: a line that starts near the top of the page and plummets straight to the bottom of the graph.

Did they mention this in my eighth grade sex ed class? I don't think so. Or maybe the problem was not having a mom around to remind me of this simple fact of life or not having a dad loudly longing for a grandchild.

The fact is, not once did I question the idea that I could have children whenever I decided I was ready.

During one visit with my gynecologist, my kind doctor tried to remind Bill and me of all we had—each other, wonderful careers, a new home, at least one decent car, and the rest.

"Not having a child won't change all that," he said. "You don't want to be one of these couples who goes to the ends of the earth, trying everything to get pregnant."

"Oh, no," we both muttered, shaking our heads. We are not that kind of people. *Not us. No way. We're practical. Pragmatic. Just checking this thing out. We're good either way. Yep, that's us. Cool. Collected. We're with you, Doc,* we thought as he continued.

"I've seen couples desperate to have a child."

Nope. Not us. We're not those people, all sad and all. Either it's meant to be or it's not, right? Right? we said, thought, felt, knew.

This fertility pep talk came after six months on a fertility drug with no luck. Six months of charting that time of the month, when it was the best time to try and conceive; six months of running around trying to get back to our bedroom on short notice to try and conceive; six months of taking my temperature every single morning in trying to conceive; six months that had begun to feel like a lifetime. At thirty-nine, I knew if we had any hope of doing it on our own without serious medical intervention, six months was tops.

My biological clock had run out. Then, to add to the dire message of the day, some recent blood work didn't look so promising. Without getting all medical about all this, let's just say that my fertility company was closed for business.

"Uh-huh," I said, nodding and trying to absorb what the doctor was saying. Trying to look and seem smart about it all. Oh, no, we weren't going to let this ruin our lives. No way. We get it.

Bill and I walked out of that appointment dazed. Or at least I was. And to be honest, I was a little disappointed. Maybe more than a little, but I was in a parking lot. I wasn't going to cry. I wasn't going to let go then and there.

Or maybe I did get a little teary eyed. I think it was the hormones from the fertility drug.

"You okay?" Bill asked.

"Yeah," I said. "Disappointed, I guess."

Bill's feelings? Thoughts? Look, the thing about Bill back then was that he wore a Winnie-the-Pooh watch (I think I got it for him, but he wore it). His nickname was "Wooly Bear" from birth because he came out covered in peach-fuzz hair. I just called him "Bear." Bill was relentlessly upbeat and optimistic about just about everything, and no more so than the day we stood talking in the parking lot after hearing the bad news.

"We can always adopt!" he said.

We had talked about that. We even agreed that we could have children and adopt, too. That was Bill's idea, anyway. He was way ahead of me on this stuff.

Pause. Silence. Here it comes: Stupid Belief No. 1 (there'll be more).

"I know. But I always kind of wanted one of our own," I said, sensing that it was an idiotic thing to say.

Pause.

"We didn't *have* Chuck, and we couldn't love her any more than we do, and Chuck's a cat." This is exactly what Bill said. It's almost as if this very scenario had come up in a law class and he won the argument by proposing this position.

Chuck was our female calico cat (yes, she had a boy name and calicos are all female). Bill got Chuck from his aunt's farm in Wisconsin as a kitten. She had a little black splotch just below her nose that made her look like either Adolph Hitler or Charlie Chaplin. Bill wisely chose to name her Chuck after the latter. He took Chuck to college with him and to live in the frat house while he attended MIT. She became the Frat Cat. When he graduated, another frat member took over Chuck's feeding and care. Then when Bill went back to live at the frat house as a law student and resident advisor, Chuck was still there. By then, she had taken to hiding most of the time in the upper floors because the fraternity brothers had a full-sized gong that they would strike come meal time, drinking time, partying time, "I'm home" time, etc. Poor Chuck was shell-shocked by the time Bill returned to the frat house. So he brought her to me in New York to be my cat. We adored Chuck.

Like any couple without kids, Chuck the Cat was our "child." Idiotic since no cat means as much as a child, but that's how newlyweds think, right?

So, there in the parking lot, I paused before getting into the passenger side of the car, thinking about what Bill had just said.

I didn't have to think long.

He was right. Having a child didn't matter. This was something one of my best friends, Natalie Phillips, had also pointed out. We had worked together at the *Daily News*. Natalie was one of the smartest and best journalists I knew. She was also beautiful and warm. We were close. Around that time, she asked me to lunch, and as we sat across from each other, she slid a couple of small sheets of paper across the table for me to see. The grainy black-and-white images were from her recent ultrasound. She was pregnant at age forty-one.

I was overjoyed for her. She shared the entire pregnancy journey and the birth of her son.

I had gotten used to friends and family members beating me to the punch, as they say. It started soon after I married, but all kinds of people I knew were getting pregnant, and I had to learn to accept that I couldn't feel cheated because we weren't.

After her son was born, I told Natalie that Bill and I were looking into adoption. Knowing I could be honest with her, I shared Stupid Belief No. 2.

"I'm worried I won't love an adopted child enough," I said.

Natalie said that she made no connection between her pregnancy and her son. It was as if the two were completely disconnected events.

"My son could have been dropped off in a basket on my front porch, and I wouldn't care and it wouldn't change a thing," she assured me.

So when it seemed adoption was our only option and Bill made it clear that it was not a consolation prize, that became our focus.

We quickly researched domestic and foreign adoptions and opted for a domestic adoption. Neither of us felt we could go through the time and expense of traveling overseas to adopt a child. We hoped to be able to adopt a baby from birth.

We soon found an agency that did adoptions. The company was headquartered somewhere in the Lower 48. We filled out all the paperwork and paid a $4,000 deposit. The firm seemed to have a good track record of connecting adoptive parents with birth mothers in a fairly timely manner, about a year or so.

We felt it was money well spent. Bill could drive the crappy Subaru awhile longer, right?

But a year went by, and we heard nothing. When I finally called, the agency seemed to be scrambling for excuses and began presenting scenarios that required us to pay thousands more with no assurance of actually getting a baby. The whole thing seemed fishy, and we stopped talking to them. We kept moving forward.

During that last visit with my doctor, he had mentioned that he had done all he could do. At my age, he recommended we pursue IVF (in vitro fertilization). No one did the procedure in Alaska, but he recommended a doctor who worked with a university in Seattle.

We mulled this over and decided to do what no doubt many couples in our position do: hedge our bets, go for broke, and do it all to better assure our chances of having or getting a baby. None of our options were a sure thing. Even our own biology had already proven to not be a sure thing.

We made our appointment with the doctor in Seattle.

GO THROUGH BOTH adoption and fertility procedures? Who has the time, right? But it seems I had gotten used to doing a lot at once.

Not only did I get married, buy a house, move my grandfather, begin teaching college, work at the newspaper, and cowrite a script, but I also wrote a stage play.

Before my book was even published, Molly Smith, the founder and artistic director of Perseverance Theatre in Juneau, called me in New York and asked for the stage rights to *Johnny's Girl*.

Absolutely. I had done my college practicum under Molly and considered her a friend and mentor. I gave her the rights for nothing. She may have asked me if I wanted to do the adaptation, and I remember thinking not. I needed a break from the story, and she had plenty of talented playwrights.

While I finished up at Columbia and moved back to Alaska, Molly contacted me again. The theater had received a National Endowment for the Arts grant to adapt *Johnny's Girl* to the stage. I was thrilled. An NEA grant? Perseverance had long been recognized nationally by the NEA and other large arts funding organizations. It was a great honor.

A playwright had been chosen to do the adaptation but left the project for a new job. At that point, having worked with John Harrison, I decided to try to adapt the stage version myself.

I quickly immersed myself in theater. This had long been one of my first loves; and had it not been for worrying about being employable after graduation, I might have pursued it as a major in college. Along with my adolescent experiences doing children's theater in Anchorage, I had done some behind-the-scenes work in theater before and during college. There have been many times I've wondered if I didn't miss my calling. I saw theatrical productions whenever I could while traveling to major cities and in Anchorage.

The time felt right to do the adaptation. Since the grant was tied to a specific season, I had to get started immediately, and I did. Between lessons in human biology and fertility and everything else, I began work on the adaptation for a spring 1996 premiere. Between drafts, the theater had a professional reading where actors were hired to come in and a completed draft.

When the play was finished, I flew to Juneau and stayed for at least a month in preproduction as the play was rehearsed and mounted on the stage. I thoroughly enjoyed being back in Juneau and spending time with old friends there. I loved every minute spent watching rehearsals and taking notes for changes from actors and the play's director.

I spent time with the director, Anita Maynard Losh, at her home on North Douglas. At the time, she had young sons and a preschool daughter. I loved the feeling of Anita's home, which was full of life and kids' art. I adored her youngest, who often wandered around us as we met and talked and wrote new scenes. Anita's love of being a parent and having a family only fueled my desire to have a family of my own even more.

I was also at the theater for the technical week of checking lights and sounds and such, known in theater as "tech week." There's an old joke in theater: if you have one week to live, let it be tech week. It's the longest week of anyone's life.

Finally, I was there for opening night and the first weekend the play ran.

The local newspaper and TV news teams did stories about me, the book, and play. I felt warmly welcomed by Juneau, and the play's reception was fine. I don't recall any bad reviews. The entire experience was wonderful, and I wanted to do it again.

I would have that chance when Cyrano's Playhouse in Anchorage asked to stage the play a year later. Of course, I said yes.

This time I was less involved, as the play was already written. What was most gratifying was having my dad's old friends come to see it. Bill

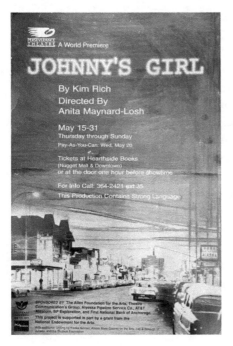

The poster for the world premiere of the stage play
Johnny's Girl *at Perseverance Theatre.*

A ticket stub for the play.

and I even brought my grandfather.

In both productions, I came to know the cast and crews. We held the opening night party in Anchorage at our house.

The review in Anchorage was memorable—and critical. I knew the play had flaws and needed some rewriting, but I found new ways of breaking down my adherence to nonfiction.

In the play, my mother appears as a ghost of sorts, a voice or visitor to the teenage me. The ending remains my favorite scene. In it, my deceased parents dance in a spotlight to the music of Henry Mancini's romantic "Moon River." Back in our home on Fireweed Lane, before I was six, before it all fell to pieces, I remember my parents playing "Moon River." The song was from *Breakfast at Tiffany's*, the first movie my parents took me to, even though the film was way beyond a young child's comprehension. I never forgot the film's orange tabby named Cat, who is rescued in an alley in the pouring rain near the end of the film. A small child remembers a kitty in the rain.

The novel *Breakfast at Tiffany's* was written by Truman Capote, who would become one of my favorite writers in grad school. He was one of the first practitioners of what would become the New Journalism, where the elements used in novels are applied to nonfiction stories, along with the placing of the journalist in the story.

The stage production of *Johnny's Girl* brought up all this and more. The production of the play once again immersed me in my past, and the final scene brought back my earliest years as a small child and how well my parents raised me then. They were together and in love, and they adored their only child.

I would be reminded of this while beginning what would become a journey to have a child. Adopt, conceive—I knew it wouldn't matter.

But that journey came to an abrupt halt in 1999, when I was diagnosed with breast cancer.

CHAPTER 16

Breast Cancer

The worst came Friday, July 30, when at nine in the morning the nurse in my obstetrician's office called with the results of a breast needle biopsy I had undergone a few days earlier.

My doctor was off on Friday, and I had begged his nurse to call as soon as she knew anything. Normally, biopsy results are given in person by the doctor, I had been told. But I was not going to wait until Monday.

The way I figured it, there was a one-in-three chance I'd get positive news. If the test was negative, I was home free. If the test was positive, my weekend was ruined. If I had no news, my weekend was ruined. I was willing to take my chances.

Two weeks earlier, I had gone in for my routine yearly mammogram. A day or so later I got a call from my doctor's nurse telling me they wanted me to come in for another mammogram. They had found calcifications and needed to take a closer look. Calcifications were usually nothing, I was assured; they were quite normal for a woman of forty-one. Milk ducts sometimes dry up, the nurse explained. Just to be safe, though, they needed to take another look; 80 percent of these turn out to be harmless. So, I went back in.

After the second mammogram, the technician placed my mammogram film up on the light box so I could see my calcifications. What I saw was a cluster of minute white spots, tiny, barely seven millimeters in diameter, looking like clumps of white sand.

"They're nothing," the technician said, smiling. "Really, nothing. They have uniform margins."

I stared at the images on the film. To me, the margins did not look uniform, and there was something about her cheery patter that felt false.

A day later, I got another call, this one telling me that the second mammogram did not reveal enough to tell doctors whether or not I had anything to worry about.

"You'll need a stereotactic needle biopsy," the hospital clerk said.

"A what?"

Now if you thought mammograms were no picnic, try this baby.

"It's where they insert a needle into your breast to pull out some of the tissue for testing."

"They do *what?*"

"Don't worry, they numb the area. You are awake for the procedure, but if you feel anxious, you will be offered something to calm you."

How much, I wondered, *and can I get it now?*

The procedure was scheduled for the following week. I was told not to worry; again, 80 percent of these procedures turned out negative.

I felt as if I were on the TV game show *Let's Make a Deal*, except in my case, I was not allowed to pick what I wanted. Someone else picked for me. I wanted the Firebird convertible that sat behind one of the curtains. But instead, I kept ending up with what was on the table—a box of Duz for dishes. I wanted to be in that 80 percent category. But I kept ending up, as I said to my husband, a "20 percenter."

By the time that Friday had rolled around, I was dying to get the biopsy results and was no longer feeling hopeful. I was more like, "What's next?"

I was sitting at my kitchen table when the phone rang. I had tried to prepare myself for whatever the outcome might be. I told myself everything would be fine. I tried to imagine how I would react to a worst-case scenario. But either way, I wouldn't know until I knew.

The nurse hemmed and hawed. I knew the news could not be good.

She tried to summarize the pathology report but decided to read it to me straight. I heard words I had never encountered before, such as "ductal carcinoma in situ" and "high grade nuclear type" and "solid and cribriform types with focal comedo necrosis," and finally, the only part that sounded remotely positive: "no invasion is seen."

"No invasion?" I asked the nurse. I could live with that; this is good, right?

More hemming and hawing. "You have what some consider a precancerous condition."

"What stage?" I asked. I had read somewhere about these things being labeled in stages.

"The report doesn't say."

"That it?"

"There's more."

She continued to read through to the end, and I was more confused than ever. I asked her to reread it, and I stopped her at every medical term to ask what it meant. My mind was whirling, and I felt a huge lump forming in the back of my throat. But I still had not heard the words I had feared. Finally, I asked point-blank: "Do I have breast cancer?"

She hesitated, then answered, "Yes."

"What stage?" I asked again.

And again, she said she didn't know. She said I would need a surgeon to interpret fully the report and discuss my treatment options.

I got off the phone and called Bill at work. With my voice cracking, I told him he better come home. The biopsy had come back positive.

After I hung up with Bill, the next thought that went through my mind was, *Am I going to die?*

THAT DAY, BILL and I began a nearly year-long journey neither of us wanted to take. All efforts to get pregnant were stopped. We went from wanting a baby and learning everything there was to learn about that to learning everything there was to know about breast cancer.

Not as much fun.

The former had proven more difficult than we had imagined, but at least one could dream about the end product—a baby! The latter came with no such happy visual. It all ended at the same miserable place: surgery, maybe some radiation, maybe some more surgery, maybe some

202 *A Normal Life*

chemotherapy.

I couldn't wait.

But first I had to confront a major obstacle—my ambivalence about talking about my diagnosis. First, I was premenopausal. I hadn't expected to have to deal with such an outcome until I was much older.

Second, I didn't want people to treat me differently. I didn't want to hear, "Does cancer run in your family?" Or worse, "Cancer doesn't run in our family." My reluctance to talk about the disease came from what I had heard growing up about my mother's mental illness from ill-informed family members: "None of that's on our side of the family!"

I figured it's human to want to feel safe from bad news. I was good at that. With my infertility, I initially had assumed I was fine because of how I had lived my life up to that point. I knew to duck when bullets fly, to wear a car safety belt, not to smoke, and so on. Despite all that, here I was struggling first with infertility and now breast cancer.

Worse, I felt shame and embarrassment, as if I had done something to bring the cancer on. As if that mattered. The most telling anecdote about the cloak of shame surrounding breast cancer occurred when I called a cousin to inquire about my aunt, my mother's sister, who had already passed away.

I had long been aware of the breast cancer my aunt had been diagnosed with thirty years earlier. But I knew very little of the kind of cancer or the stage of her illness when she was diagnosed. Now I had to know everything because I needed to find out if there was a connection between her cancer and my own.

"We're not even sure Sandy had breast cancer. She always called it 'chest cancer,'" my cousin's wife told me.

I got the name of my aunt's doctor. I called his office and within minutes learned not only the type of breast cancer my aunt had but a complete history of her reoccurrences and treatment. Yes, she had breast cancer. The year was 1969. She was forty-nine and had found a lump that was diagnosed as "infiltrating ductal carcinoma." By referring to it as "chest cancer," Sandy may have been trying to explain that the cancer had metastasized into her bone and hence was in her chest. Or maybe my aunt just couldn't say the word "breast," so no one around her used that word, either.

If I was having trouble talking about my diagnosis, no doubt my poor aunt had struggled with the subject, too. I felt different and didn't want to. I didn't want to feel unlucky or doomed. Sorry, not in my DNA.

I'm fairly certain Aunt Sandy felt as if a scarlet letter had been placed around her neck that marked her as less than the vibrant, upbeat, warm, outgoing person she always was. I would have loved to have talked to her about her experiences, but I couldn't. She had died several years earlier at age seventy-five, succumbing to liver cancer, which is where her breast cancer eventually ended up.

Knowing she lived a long life after her diagnosis gave me plenty of hope. But my life was going to shift radically. I had some hard choices to make. I knew I was going to have to take time off from teaching. I had finally gotten a teaching position as an assistant professor of writing at Alaska Pacific University. I loved teaching as much as I loved newspaper work.

Only a few months earlier, a dear friend had also been diagnosed with breast cancer. I called her first, leaving a message on her office voicemail telling her that I had "just joined the club." I left another message with my mother-in-law, a registered nurse.

I had been getting mammograms since my mid-twenties. Because of my aunt's breast cancer, my primary care doctor believed I was at a higher risk for the disease (this was before only a mother-daughter link was determined to be a factor in whether one had a predisposition to breast cancer). My doctor had me get a baseline mammogram at about age twenty-five. Then throughout my thirties, I returned yearly. By the time I turned forty, the age most women begin getting mammograms, I was all too familiar with the procedure. Yet with all that practice, so to speak, I never thought about "What if?" Not once.

During the year prior to my own diagnosis, I was surrounded by the disease. First, there was the friend I called the morning of my own diagnosis. There was another friend who had to travel away from home and undergo eight months of chemotherapy treatments. Then there was the woman from my gym who also had been diagnosed with breast cancer.

Probably like many women, every time I heard of someone else being diagnosed with breast cancer, I tried to think of why it wouldn't happen to me. I tried to think of reasons they got it and I wouldn't. One friend who was fairly busty like myself even remarked that from what she could tell, only small-breasted women got the disease. Another woman said only big-breasted women get it. Or blondes, or brunettes, or heavyset or

204 A Normal Life

skinny, or you name it. Each time I heard someone's theory of the disease, I could come up with a reason why it wasn't going to happen to me. But I knew I was living with a false sense of security.

Like any woman, I was familiar with the alarming statistics: one out of eight women will get breast cancer. What's more, 80 percent of those diagnosed with breast cancers have no known family history of the disease. But I never really thought about it until I had to. In all the years that I had gone in for mammograms, never once had I thought about what the result might be. It was in the back of my mind, but I never worried. My yearly mammograms and self-exams were pro-forma, as if going through the motions in and of itself immunized me against the disease.

Beginning that Friday morning when I got my diagnosis, it would be all I would think about for weeks and months to come.

Once Bill got home, the first order of business was to find a doctor who could see us that afternoon and fully interpret the report. The nurse I'd spoken with said the next step was for her to send a referral to a surgeon. She would make an appointment the following week and get back to me. That seemed too long to wait. Way too long.

All of my usual doctor's offices were closed or had no openings. We called any doctor who had a general practice or was a surgeon. Try reaching a doctor's office on a Friday afternoon. Or any doctor's office staff. Many doctors' offices close early or are closed all day on Fridays. Added to everything was that it was Friday in the summer in Alaska, and the salmon were running.

Bill and I took turns pleading with staffers at offices that were open. We explained we had a report indicating cancer. Everyone we spoke to was sympathetic, but little could be done. I got frustrated. Angry. I banged the phone on the table. I broke down in tears. I even screamed at one receptionist, "Do you know what I'm going through? Do you have any idea?!"

One receptionist advised me to get on the Internet and look up the National Cancer Institute website. Thank God for the Internet. I can't imagine what it must have been like in my aunt's day when she got her diagnosis. Back then, she probably relied mostly on her doctor for information. Or she might have gone to the library and labored through the time-consuming process of finding books on the subject. Me? Within minutes I had exactly what I needed. News that gave me hope and comfort. Enough so that by early that afternoon, I turned to my husband and with a mock whine in my voice declared, "I have breast cancer. I'm going to Nordstrom's!"

THE MOMENT I could make a joke was when I knew I could get through this. Between searching the National Cancer Institute website and calling its toll-free hotline, I learned that I was lucky.

I was Stage 0 out of five stages of breast cancer. In some literature, ductal carcinoma in situ is referred to as a "precancerous condition." I learned that this was a misleading label, since precancerous or not, the treatment options I faced were still formidable. Nonetheless, words like "Stage 0" and "noninvasive" (which means the cancer cells were contained within a tiny section of my left breast duct system), and "precancerous" helped me get through that shadowland I entered following my diagnosis.

By Saturday, I began calling close friends and family members who I thought should know. I found myself saying, "It's not the best news one could get, but it's not the worst."

My aunt's breast cancer is now considered a second-degree risk. But cancer seemed to run all through my family. My mother had died at age thirty-eight of throat cancer. She was a heavy cigarette smoker. While my mother's type of cancer and my breast cancer are not related, as one radio-oncologist put it, "Lots of people smoke and never develop cancer." A cousin had had a brain tumor at age thirty. He'd survived it, but not without undergoing horrendous treatments. Aunt Sandy, while remaining active following her diagnosis of breast cancer, might have lived longer otherwise. At age seventy-five, she was an avid golfer, a dedicated bowler, active in her church and community, and she still liked to go out dancing on a Saturday night. Seventy-five used to sound old to me. Not anymore.

The bottom line is, as one cancer geneticist put it, my family may have a predisposition to cancer of any kind. Given that my breast cancer had shown up at such a young age (80 percent of breast cancers occur in women over age fifty-five), I knew that I would need to treat my disease aggressively. From my research that weekend, I knew I not only wanted to cure this cancer now but to protect myself against reoccurrence and any new cancers in either breast. The tiny specks of white dots on my mammogram film were around nine years in the making. It takes that long for the cells to divide enough to be detected by mammography. I wondered: *what if I hadn't gone in for my mammogram?*

The irony about my breast cancer diagnosis is that only a few months earlier, I had written a passage about contemplating the meaning of a woman's breasts in a novel I had been working on. In the story, my thirty-year-old protagonist, Leah, works at a glamorous women's magazine in New York. One day, during an editorial meeting, she goes off on a diatribe about the magazine's fascination, and society's fascination, with women's breasts. I've had breasts since I was thirteen. Like my novel's protagonist, I was not pleased when they arrived. Mine went from nothing to a B cup overnight. Men said the dumbest things to me. I had a T-shirt I got from the Dodge family. On the front, along with the airlines logo and colors, it read: "Ski British Airways."

"I'd like to ski her slopes," an older man said one summer day as I was out walking down the sidewalk wearing it.

I was fourteen. I never wore the shirt again.

Not only have I always had boobs, but once I entered my thirties they continued to grow, much to my dismay. Soon, I went from B to a C cup. Could D be far behind? Keep in mind, I'm five foot two and petite. All I could think about was an ad I used to see in the newspapers when I was a kid about a woman whose stage name was Big Bertha. She appeared in strip clubs around Anchorage showing off her "double-barreled double Ds." My dad once cracked that Bertha could twist beer bottle caps off with her breasts. In my novel, Leah ponders: how was Bertha with pull tabs?

What did any of this mean when it came to my breast cancer diagnosis? Everything. For the first time, I had to think about something that the editors of *Playboy* used to think about a lot more than I ever had: women's breasts.

THE WEEK FOLLOWING my diagnosis became what I now call "hell week." It felt like something cadets go through upon entering a military academy. My hell week consisted of poring over countless reports, studies, and books about breast cancer. Everything I read left me feeling as if I were gasping for air. Everything reminded me of how grave this was. Throughout it all, like a mantra, all I could think was, *I can't believe this is happening.*

On Tuesday, I began my odyssey through a series of doctor's offices. The previous Friday, Bill and I had been convinced that if we could only get in to see a doctor, we would feel better. By Tuesday, after our first visit with a general surgeon, we felt worse. We discovered that the doctors could spend only a limited time with us. An hour at the most. But for every doctor we saw, we felt as if we could sit all day asking questions.

My husband and I had already read enough to make us conversant in issues such as recurrence rates, new cancers, and the side effects of the various treatment options. We developed a new vocabulary. Words like "contralateral breast" (the otherwise healthy breast) and "lumpectomy" became part of our everyday language.

By the end of that first week, we had seen five doctors: my general practitioner, then two general surgeons, a radiation oncologist, and a plastic surgeon. All told me the same thing: I was fortunate because we caught mine early. I had choices. That seemed to make my choice harder. Women with more advanced cases of the disease have no choice. They have to march hard and fast into one treatment or the other. But I had time and two choices: lumpectomy with radiation, or mastectomy with or without reconstruction.

Every night I would devour the reading material, and every night I would cry. None of it appealed to me. I'd read about the side effects from the prescribed six weeks of radiation. I could feel anything from simply being tired to feeling as if I were coming down with the flu or, worse, hepatitis A, over and over again. There was a possibility, albeit minor, that I would develop a nagging cough as the rays nipped the corner of my lungs. There was the remote possibility that I might sustain damage to my heart for the same reason. Never mind that the side effects years from now, while remote, include developing cancer in the otherwise healthy breast.

The prospect of mastectomy left me feeling equally depressed. My most vivid memory of that first week was sitting up in bed at night and reading *Dr. Susan Love's Breast Book*. I cried as I tried to imagine myself with drains—soft plastic tubes placed under the skin that drain excess fluids during the immediate postoperative recovery period.

Reconstruction seemed abhorrent. Two of the procedures involved cutting muscle and tissue from either your abdomen or back. Another, called the "tissue expander," involved using implants, but it took up to half a year or longer before the actual reconstruction would be complete, never mind the additional time to have nipples reconstructed.

I read and reread the rates of recurrence. In my case, the recurrence rate was pegged between 10 and 15 percent. Mastectomy could get me as low as 1 or 2 percent, or even lower, since my lesion was so small and my diagnosis early. But mastectomy? I would never have thought, six months earlier, that I'd even be considering such a thing. My aunt had a mastectomy decades ago. Hadn't things advanced at all?

I knew I was still in denial the day I sat in my office and tried to organize all the material I had collected into files. I could not bring myself to write the words "Breast Cancer" on the label.

In that way, I was just like my aunt. Yet, despite the moments when things got hard, I never lost my sense of humor. I suddenly began sounding like Mae West. After being asked to disrobe for the umpteenth time by yet another doctor, I turned to one nurse and exclaimed, "I'm gonna start charging you guys!"

A SHIFT IN my thinking occurred after that first week. First, I realized that I was not going to die. This much was made clear not only in the literature but by my doctors.

Secondly, things had indeed changed since my aunt's day. Back then, once diagnosed, a woman's breast cancer may very well have been too far along for a cure. Even now, advanced cases of the disease benefit from advances in chemotherapy. Further, mastectomies are not what they used to be. Plastic surgery has made many things possible in terms of reconstruction. I also realized that I could possibly be cured completely.

Another equally important realization was that I didn't like any of my options. Throughout the first couple of weeks, I would think to myself, *I don't want to do any of this.* But I knew I had to do something. I could not walk away, nor could I sit on the fence forever. My doctors were pressing me to make a decision within a month. While I had time, they said. They worry that when a woman waits too long, she's not dealing with it.

I had heard that, like picking a surgeon, deciding on a treatment option often boils down to a gut reaction. By the eighth day following my diagnosis, my gut was already leaning in one direction. It had to do with how much risk I was willing to live with.

My father was a professional gambler. I, on the other hand, have never gambled. I have been to Reno once, a long time ago, but I didn't care for the slot machines. I have never been to Las Vegas. Should I go, I will go to see the stage shows. I have never, nor would I ever, buy a lottery ticket. While my father's stock-in-trade was poker, I have never learned to play the game.

I wanted to play it as safe as I could. I wanted to get as close to zero recurrence as possible. As my husband noted to one doctor, "Kim isn't worried about this cancer; she's worried about the ones she has yet to get."

Some doctors tried to reassure me about salvage mastectomies, those mastectomies performed when the cancer returns after a lumpectomy. I did not relish the idea of being back in my doctor's office eighteen months, three years, five years, eight, ten, or even twelve years down the line.

Further, 50 percent of breast cancers that recur come back invasive, which means cancer cells may have gone onto other parts of the body, such the lungs, bone, and liver. Not one doctor could assure me that even with diligent follow-up, medical science could detect a new breast cancer before it became invasive.

As my husband pointed out, if we could put some kind of an alarm clock inside of me, one that would go off at the earliest moment a cell decided to mutate, then we'd seek a less aggressive option. But, of course, no such alarm clock exists.

I began to see what I was going through as being on a path where, at different points, I had to pass through another gate. Call them Gates of Realization. The next had to do with the very thing I'd written about in my novel only months earlier. As my husband pointed out, if we were talking about a vital organ, a piecemeal approach to surgery followed with radiation might make sense.

"It's not like we're talking about her kidneys," my husband remarked to my plastic surgeon.

Yes, I leaned toward a double mastectomy.

SOME MIGHT CONSTRUE Bill's remark as insensitive. Quite the opposite. Bill was clear that in no way could he know what it meant for me to consider having my breasts removed. One surgeon—a woman doctor, no less—actually insinuated that before I considered removing my breasts, I should ask my husband how he felt about it. I was floored.

This occurred after some friends had counseled me about the value of finding a woman surgeon for my breast cancer. The implication was that a woman doctor would be more sensitive. So much for the sisterhood. She was telling me to ask him. I found the notion of seeking out a female doctor ludicrous. What if I were facing heart surgery? What gender doctor is appropriate then?

Early on, I had heard and read all about the insensitive male medical establishment regarding breast cancer. That may have been the case in the past, but I encountered a medical community that bent over backwards to be sensitive. In fact, the only insensitive remark I encountered was from that female surgeon.

I traveled to two other cities to get second and third opinions at nationally known breast cancer centers. I'll never forget my visit at one clinic in Chicago. The male surgeon walked into the examination room. He gently squeezed my hand. Speaking softly, he said, "Kim, whatever else we talk about today, I want you to keep in mind that we have two goals here. One, to save your life, and two, to preserve the breast."

I had brought a good friend with me that day, Ginny. After the surgeon said his piece, Ginny asked, "Is there any clinical reason to keep the breast?" In other words, was there some side effect to removing a breast or two that might endanger or compromise my health?

The doctor was astounded. He gave us a ten-minute lecture on the value of a woman's breast. Like we didn't know. He talked about women who woke up from their mastectomy surgeries collapsing and screaming. He talked about his own adolescent daughter's budding puberty. All in all, he cautioned me to think very hard about my decision and its repercussions. That much I appreciated. But I was thinking about it. All the time.

That night, Ginny and I visited a couple she knew and recounted the doctor's visit. I don't know why, but "preserve the breast" sounded an awful lot like "save the rainforest" or "save the whales."

Then it dawned on me. The breast cancer folks have their fundraising all wrong. The way I figured it, all they had to do was send a bunch of scantily clad women into campus bars and fraternity houses across the land seeking donations to preserve the breast. For that matter, any bar, anywhere, and make the same plea.

At one point in the evening, I turned to the husband of the couple and apologized for monopolizing the conversation with this "preserve the breast" thing.

"Hey, I'm all for it!" he said.

NOT LONG AFTER my visit to medical centers in Chicago and San Francisco, I spent part of a Saturday afternoon watching a rerun of *Baywatch*. Why? Homework, I guess. I paid really close attention to the shapely female lifeguards' you-know-whats. I thought about something a friend had said at dinner the night before. A well-endowed woman at a table next to ours was wearing a low-cut top.

My friend turned to me and whispered, "Do you think they're real?"

And for the first time ever, I thought, *What does it matter?*

There was a time when I questioned the judgment of women who chose to get breast implants. After all, I'd always had 'em, and I couldn't figure out why anyone would want 'em. I don't know what any of this means in terms of sexuality, societal and cultural expectations, whether women are regarded as sex objects, oppressed, or any of it. All I know is that for the first time in my life, I was being forced to think about the worth of a part of my anatomy that I'd always been at odds with. Plus, since I hadn't had children yet, I did not appreciate the biggest and most important function of breasts.

"Gee, I guess the only real function of breasts is breastfeeding," I said to Bill.

Duh. But I had to think this through.

"I guess they are a really attractive part of the female anatomy," I told him a day or so later. He concurred.

Then I ran through all the ailments I didn't have. I wasn't facing the prospect of losing one of my senses, a limb, a vital organ. I hadn't been in an accident that had left me paralyzed. I wasn't facing a degenerative disease. I say this with all due respect to anyone who has faced any of the above. I believe that whatever cards we're dealt, most people try to make the best of it. I am not a pessimist. I have always considered myself an optimist, and when it came to my breast cancer, I had become a realist.

I met with a geneticist who showed me a chart that depicted the steps that lead to a cancer cell. They included genetics, aging, and environmental risk factors such as the use of birth control pills, terminated pregnancies, delaying childbirth past age thirty, or engaging in risk factors such as high-fat diets, smoking, and heavy drinking.

I knew my family's history. I knew my own environmental risk factors. I hadn't even begun to age, much less go through menopause, one of the biggest shifts in a woman's hormonal balance. Again, I was less concerned with the here and now than what was ahead.

So what did I think of my breasts? For me, they were not worth risking my health or my life for. The ones I had needed to go.

WHAT HELPED ME most in making my decision was finding other women with my diagnosis and hearing what they had done. I talked to women who chose a bilateral mastectomy with reconstruction. They sounded a little like religious converts.

"They're great! I don't have to wear a bra," said one I spoke with. "I can wear strapless dresses! They're not hanging down to my belly anymore!"

"They're outta here! I want to live," another woman told me.

I, too, wanted to live.

This is what I tried to relay to all the doctors I saw, including the female surgeon who advised me to ask my husband what he thought of my giving up my breasts. She told me what other doctors had said: this cancer, the one I had now, was curable. But none of them could promise me that this would be true should the cancer come back. And this baby was most likely coming back. The odds were not in my favor.

Not all doctors agreed with me. "You're using a sledgehammer when a flyswatter will do," said one. *Fine*, I thought. I was dealing with an angry tarantula.

Finally, the woman surgeon conceded that doctors had wrongly believed that younger woman would seek to preserve their breasts through lumpectomy, but the opposite was occurring. Younger breast cancer patients were seeking more aggressive treatment. We have more years for the cancer to come back. And maybe, just maybe, when all is said and done, some of us aren't so attached to our breasts that we're not willing to give them up entirely—or, as I say, trade them in for a new set.

Furthermore, women have different goals. I spoke with one woman who was diagnosed with breast cancer in her late thirties and who still wanted to have a child. She was told she would need either a lumpectomy with radiation or a mastectomy. She rejected both options and chose a lumpectomy without radiation. She was leery of the side effects of the radiation, and she wanted to keep her breast because she wanted to be able to breastfeed. She ultimately had her baby through in vitro fertilization, but her cancer came back two more times. She had another lumpectomy, then eventually chemotherapy was needed. I told her I didn't think I could tolerate all the surgery and the unknowns. But she was upbeat and glad that she had been able to breastfeed her daughter.

The choices a woman makes regarding her breast cancer are deeply personal. Some women approach their cancer in stages. I ran into a friend recently who had a lumpectomy, but her doctor told her she had a type of breast cancer that would be back and she would need more surgery. She told me she needed time to get used to it all. Another woman who had a lumpectomy only to have to have a salvage mastectomy three years later felt glad to have the extra time with her breast. Still another woman I knew had one breast removed, and when the cancer appeared in the other, she had it removed as well.

Some women I know—strong, beautiful, smart, and successful—have breast cancers that left them with no choice but to fight it with all modern medicine can offer. I couldn't get that upset about my diagnosis or become that self-absorbed when I had friends who were fighting for their lives.

That's what I mean by feeling lucky. My cancer was detected early. I've heard of women who blame their lifestyles. I've heard about stress being a risk factor. What stress did my plastic surgeon's nineteen-year-old breast cancer patient endure to cause hers?

I was feeling a lot of stress trying to decide what to do.

Once I made up my mind, I spent the better part of the next six weeks trying to find a reason not to go through with my decision. I never found one that worked for me. Again, I found humor helped me stay sane as my surgery date in late September approached. I imagined myself on the operating table, with my general surgeon and plastic surgeon hovering over me, and telling them, "Do your best work, boys!"

A girlfriend joked that plastic surgeons "must know what they like!"

Let's face it, we live in a culture obsessed with a woman's breasts. I know women who chose no reconstruction, which is fine. For me, I knew I'd want my body back as close to what it used to be as possible. If not better.

THE SURGERY WENT without a hitch. Prior to going under, I handed my general surgeon a CD I'd been listening to, Nat King Cole's greatest hits. I might have read somewhere that music was good for surgery patients.

"I'll play this," he said, nodding his approval of the choice.

The surgery, while long, went smoothly. They took some lymph nodes to check, just to be sure. They came back negative, as had been expected. Otherwise, I dodged a bullet: tissue from my noncancerous breast was found to have hyperplasia, a precancerous condition.

After my surgery, I felt like I had a new lease on life. My surgeons and their staffs were heroes to me. My doctors showed up in my hospital room the next morning, one as early as 7 a.m.

Several friends who worked in the hospital stopped by to check on me. My room was jammed with flowers. When I went home a couple of days later, there were so many floral displays that my living room looked like a damn funeral parlor. My phone rang constantly, making it hard to rest. Marla Williams, the friend from Seattle who chauffeured me around during my book tour, came up for a week to be my nurse. It's nice to know where you stand at a time like that.

My biggest concern was how I would feel after surgery. The first time I looked into a mirror was about five days after my surgery. I was bandaged up like a Japanese concubine and wearing a button-up cotton shirt. I looked at myself in the mirror and exclaimed, "I look like Gwyneth Paltrow!" I liked looking flat-chested for once in my adult life.

Within a week of my surgery, I was walking in my neighborhood. Within a month, I was back at the gym where I'd been doing circuit training. The manager, a young man named Jeff, spent the winter helping me recover and regain my strength. I wanted to be in the best shape possible since I was scheduled for more surgery in the spring to get breast implants put in.

I chose saline implants for my reconstruction. This involved getting the tissue expander inserted during my surgery. I called it the Reebok Air pump. One friend called it "boobs by Nike." I called the expanders my "training-wheel boobs."

Over the winter, I regularly went to my plastic surgeon's office to have the expander slowly pumped up. After the brief procedure, the nurse would place a small adhesive bandage in the shape of a red heart over the spot where the needle was inserted (I hear needles aren't needed anymore with the advent of wireless technology).

As another woman who had the expanding procedure joked, "We've gotta go through puberty all over again! We'll have to grow our hair out to hide our growing breasts."

Another friend gave me a *Playboy* magazine in a manila envelope. On the outside he'd written, "Sears & Roebuck and Company Boob Catalog, Pick a set!" That came to mind when, prior to my implant surgery, Bill and I met with my plastic surgeon to pick what size implant.

There we were—two men and myself and the female nurse—handling a series of different-sized saline implants. What did I want? The choice was between a B or C cup. The clear implants were smooth and squishy and kind of fun to play with. We took turns handing them around. I'd hold them as if weighing them or toss them from hand to hand.

Given my athletic build, the doctor recommended C. I can't pick out a pair of shoes, and I have to make this decision? I might have taken longer than the average woman. I'm bad with decisions. Always have been. Finally, I picked C.

"You thought this choice for me was hard, just you wait until I decide to have a nose job," I said to my doctor as he was going out the door.

Shortly thereafter, I had surgery to put in the implants.

Okay, so mine don't look like a "mature woman's breasts," as one doctor put it. I have a rack that looks like it belongs to a twenty-year-old. I wasn't worried about it. I had a larger, more important goal to return to after all the breast cancer business. I still wanted a child. After my implant surgery in the spring of 2000, we were told we could continue to pursue getting pregnant.

Red Dodge's clever gift to me. This is about the only moment when having breast cancer was funny.

CHAPTER 17

When You Wish Upon a Star

No story of infertility is easy to write. Ours was no different. I was thirty-nine the year we married and in the bonus round of fertility.

Forget that. No fertility worth a damn, really. Testing showed I had a blocked fallopian tube. An effort to unblock it failed. This didn't mean I could not get pregnant; it just meant my chances were halved.

I don't know what it is about me, but I'm pretty much late to most things in life. I was a little later than most of my peers in going to college, marrying, and now planning a family. And as I've said, I was fairly clueless about how and when to start.

I just never felt any urgency—until suddenly, I did.

After healing up from the unsuccessful unblocking surgery, we launched into our first in vitro fertilization (IVF). If you are afraid of needles, stop reading here. This part of the story contains lots of needles.

First, our Anchorage doctor had to refer us to the fertility clinic we would work with in Seattle. No needles yet. Then we had to fill out some paperwork. Maybe a lot of paperwork. Then we had to take a bunch of blood tests.

First my blood type was determined, and then I was screened for conditions that could affect the health of a pregnancy, including immunity to rubella (German measles), varicella (chicken pox), and a partridge in a pear tree. Both Bill and I were also tested for hepatitis B and C, HIV, syphilis, yellow fever, leprosy, and—just kidding. Yes, his sperm was tested (don't ask how), and finally other genetic tests were required. One was for Tay-Sachs disease, a rare inherited disorder that destroys nerve cells in the brain and spinal cord.

I had done testing for the genetic mutation associated with breast and ovarian cancer as part of my treatment for my breast cancer diagnosis (both were negative). At that time, I had been anxious, hoping for a negative outcome. This time I had no expectations.

My indication for such testing came from my father's side of the family. His mother's parents were of Polish-Russian, or Ashkenazi Jewish heritage—those Jews who originated in Eastern Europe as opposed to Sephardic Jews from areas around the Mediterranean Sea, including Portugal, Spain, the Middle East, and Northern Africa. World History 101.

My Tay-Sachs test came back positive.

Now, most people are devastated when they get such news. Not me. I was elated. Thrilled. A lifetime of wondering and questioning and research and a few years of attending Temple and learning some Hebrew finally confirmed in no uncertain terms that I, indeed, had a Jewish heritage. I'm fairly certain I startled the genetic counselor with my whoops and jumps of joy. Counselors are usually prepared to deal with patients suddenly plummeted into grieving. If a partner is also a carrier for the disease, one's hopes of having a child are decimated. Bill is not from a Jewish heritage, and his test results came back negative.

I had not realized until that moment how large the question of my father's Jewish background loomed in my mind. In *Johnny's Girl*, I wrote that he had Jewish roots after uncovering what I thought was enough evidence. But I had lingering doubts, since no one alive could confirm it. I knew that immigrants of the Jewish faith sometimes denied their background once in the United States, especially those from the geographic area and time frame where my great-grandparents were born. But despite a preponderance of evidence, I still wondered. The day that test came back positive, I finally had the proof I had sought.

My first action was to email the Rabbi Harry Rosenfeld, who had helped me a decade earlier when he was the rabbi at Temple Beth Shalom Congregation in Anchorage.

"Rabbi Harry!" I wrote. "I'm a Tay-Sachs carrier!!!! It's confirmed, my dad was Jewish—I'm Jewish!"

He wrote back one simple sentence: "Welcome to the tribe."

THIS WAS A bright moment in what became an otherwise difficult process. Warning: here come more needles.

Further blood testing was done to check what I call the "female reproductive tests" to measure what's known as the ovarian reserve. This is not like the National Reserve. Think of these tests as the SATs of fertility. "As women age," begins one description, "they have a decreased ability to conceive and an increased risk of miscarriage. Ovarian reserve testing tries to measure egg quality, quantity and reproductive potential."

Basically, these tests determine whether one goes to, say, Harvard and gets to move forward in the process, or to the University of... nowhere, actually. Or at least not with our preferred clinic, which had a high rate of success for couples hoping to conceive. The clinic doctors were looking to see if I was a good candidate to maximize the chances for success and a healthy pregnancy.

ALL MY TESTS came back with good results. What happened next was more needles. I began a series of injections to stimulate egg production. This allowed the doctors at the fertility clinic to take over the controls of my body's reproductive biology—in essence, my menstrual cycle. In my mind's eye, I pictured the controls of a car. Not a luxury sports car—though at about $13,000 a pop, IVF was not cheap—but maybe a practical starter sedan. Multiple eggs are desired because some eggs will not develop or fertilize after retrieval.

Ultrasounds were next performed to examine how things were going, and there were more blood tests to check hormone levels. Then, at just the right moment, which could come with little or no advance notice, we flew south to Seattle for the next phase of the procedure: the extraction of said eggs.

I still recall how excited we were to be at the clinic. I finally met the staff members I had only talked to on the phone. I was impressed at how efficient and carefully run my first appointment was. What occurred was all part of a detailed yet set procedure preparing me to have my eggs retrieved during a minor surgical procedure, for which I was awake. An ultrasound image allowed a technician to guide a hollow needle through my pelvic cavity to remove the eggs.

Did I mention I was awake for the procedure under light sedation? When I learned this, I was scared. But that wasn't the worst of it. I was told there would be some "discomfort." Indeed, there was. Some. Some that made me want to levitate off the table. Yes, it was tolerable, but not exactly anything I'd sign up for unless the end result was worth it. Trying to have a baby was more than worth it. I used to hate shots. I used to be afraid of needles. No more.

Next, the eggs and Bill's sperm were combined during insemination and stored in a laboratory to encourage fertilization. The eggs were monitored to confirm that fertilization and cell division were taking place and embryos were growing. Eggs that fertilize and look good are given a grade, like an A or F, for how many cells divide and how they generally look. As a colleague and friend from Alaska Pacific University put it, "The pressure to do well starts so young!"

A few days later, the doctor called and told us what we had. At that time, we had to decide how many embryos to transfer into my womb. I believe our limit was three or two, but no more. The clinic didn't want to create a set of quadruplets—or more—and neither did we! I don't recall what number of embryos we chose, but whatever it was, it worked.

A few weeks later, in the fall of 2000, we learned we were pregnant.

We couldn't believe our luck. We were winners in the IVF lottery! My chance of success at age forty-two was like point-zero-zero-zero-zero and more zeros.

Maybe a bit better than that. After all, I was three-quarters Italian, a group of people known for large families. At least, that's what I told myself. Plus, Bill was younger than me. Surely that must have helped. We had the right attitude, we were healthy, we paid our dues, and I'm sure I came up with a hundred other reasons to explain the good fortune.

What came next is a blur of memories. We went to a small clinic located in a little wood-sided house in East Anchorage. It was the opposite of a hospital or clinic setting. Nothing sterile or medicine-y about it. The kind of place you'd want to go to see your baby's first heartbeat.

And there it was, beat, beat, beating away. Wow. We were home free, we thought. We were ready for the next phase of this train we had boarded—the IVF Express.

Next followed another visit with my local obstetrician. The visit entailed a physical evaluation of my symptoms, which had blessedly been mild. Morning sickness? None. I seemed to be one of the lucky few who did not get morning sickness.

But when the doctor felt my lower abdomen, he made some comment about things not being as large as they should be, or big enough, or far enough along. He ordered another ultrasound from the soft and fuzzy place that I'm pretty sure had some kind of embroidery work on the wall and maybe some lace, and a small, cozy waiting room where I didn't mind waiting for that next ultrasound. Transvaginal ultrasounds were the easiest part of this whole IVF process. No pain, no discomfort, only confusion trying to make out the blurry gray-and-black-and-white imagery on the ultrasound monitor that made no sense to anyone other than the ultrasound technician.

I was alone this time. We were so confident and happy that Bill felt comfortable enough to go to Hawaii for a big case his law firm was handling there. I had survived breast cancer and two surgeries and all that worry, but we were pregnant and incredibly lucky. I was convinced we would stay lucky.

I dutifully climbed up on the examination table and thought, *Let's get this ultrasound over with!* A few seconds passed as the technician went about inserting the ultrasound probe and began getting images on the monitor—more black, white, and gray fuzzy mishmash that meant nothing to me.

What did was the silence.

She turned up the volume on the control panel. Still silence. I felt a fear like none I had ever known. I prayed that the technician just didn't have things lined up right. Where was that rhythmic *beat-beat-beat*? Where was the rapid-fire heartbeat we had heard before, fast and comforting and strong?

Silence.

Then.

"There's no heartbeat," the tech said.

"What do you mean, no heartbeat? Where is it?" I said, sitting up and trying not to sound alarmed.

She took a deep breath and pushed back from the monitor with the most God-awful look on her face. "The heartbeat is gone. The baby is gone."

I went into shock. I know that I did because all I could think to say was, "Where did it go?! Where did it go?! What do you mean, it's gone?!"

I was crying and yelling, and the technician kept saying how sorry she was and these things happen, and somehow someone else came into the room, and all I could do was yell and cry and try to breathe. I couldn't breathe.

"Is there someone you'd like us to call?"

Someone managed to get Bill on the phone in Hawaii. I don't know if I spoke to him or they did or what. All I knew was that I was moved to another room—a dark, empty office—while they called a friend to come for me.

She got there within minutes. Deborah was also a veteran of the infertility wars, an older newlywed, a career woman trying to get pregnant, just like me. She sat silently as I slowly, very slowly, got control of my runaway emotions. I just could not stop crying.

I'm not sure how long we sat in that darkened room. I remember my friend's kind, empathetic face. She knew what this meant. I knew she knew.

Eventually, she got me to the point where I could walk out of that room and into her car. By the time I got home, I felt numb. Bill's boss got him a ticket on the next flight to Anchorage. Later, he would tell me how he cried most of the way back, all six-and-half or so long hours. Nonstop, Honolulu to Anchorage.

My grief soon turned to anger. Why hadn't someone warned me this could happen? How could the technician just blurt out the words, "No heartbeat"? She seemed as surprised and shocked as I was.

I did what I always did. I immediately began researching what I learned was my first-trimester miscarriage. It is fairly common. Many women—those struggling with infertility and those not, young and old—have them all the time, although it's not something anybody talks much about.

But when Bill got home and we tried to talk about it, we struggled to describe what we were feeling. It was a death, but the death of someone we hardly knew. There would be no funeral service, no burial. No way to come to terms with what had just happened.

Bill finally found a way to describe it. "It's like the death of the future."

We spoke with the counselor at the Seattle clinic. She was extremely empathetic and told us the percentages of how often these things occur, especially with older moms-to-be like myself. She explained that as a woman ages, so do her eggs; the chances of some kind of genetic mutation or something wrong with said eggs dramatically increases. It happens with younger women, too, those who hadn't waited forever to try and start a family and who were doing everything the way they were supposed to, and then the cruelest of things occurred, causing grief and anguish that no one understood and no one could talk about, and just about everyone you knew said incredibly stupid, hurtful things. Things like, "It wasn't meant to be," or "You can try again," or "It was probably better it didn't survive."

The counselor advised us to grieve good and hard, though our friends and families advised us to move on. But a fertility counselor who had seen a lot of these understood that a death is a death, and while there was no context or experience to miscarriage, it is perhaps the most awful thing a person or a couple could go through short of losing a child.

It was a child, in one's mind, where potential names get bantered about. One starts to wonder if it's a girl or a boy, whether one's current house will work and what room could be the nursery, and without reservation, you go out and tell everyone you know you are *pregnant*. One does this the first time one is pregnant and not expecting anything to go wrong. But when things do go horribly wrong, you remember how there are those who don't tell anyone they are pregnant until they get past the critical first trimester.

The counselor told us to take at least six weeks and up to several months to grieve heavily. We couldn't try another IVF anyway for several months at the earliest. We knew this was sound advice, and we took it to heart.

We also visited a specialist who worked with older women and high-risk pregnancies. We met with her in her office after she had reviewed my records. In the end, she concluded I was just older and there would likely be more first-trimester miscarriages.

Knowing that made the next two years easier as we went through three more pregnancies and three more first-trimester miscarriages. But only two were from IVF; two were from the old-fashioned way.

Things got to the point where it all felt like one big science fair project. It wasn't that we weren't disappointed; we just steeled ourselves not to get emotionally invested until we could hear that first heartbeat again.

MEANWHILE, WE DISCOVERED a nonprofit organization in Anchorage that did nonprivate adoptions in Alaska. (Private adoptions are arranged between biological mothers and adoptive parents through the use of an attorney.) The fees were nominal, just enough to pay for the social worker assessment and legal fees. We were also required to attend a weekend-long workshop.

It felt as if there was as much paperwork involved in trying to adopt as in trying to conceive. We completed background checks, had a home visit by a social worker, and filled out a series of forms, including a lengthy and detailed questionnaire about what circumstances we would be willing to consider. We could answer "Yes," "No," or "Maybe," depending on the circumstances. The questions included: Would we wish to adopt a child of another race or ethnicity? (Yes!) A biracial baby? (Yes!) A child the product of a rape? (Maybe.) If the birth mother was a drug abuser? (Maybe). A special needs child? (Maybe). If the mother was a smoker? (Yes.) And so on.

Open adoption had become the norm in the field of adoption. The days of hiding identities and shielding birth certificates were largely over. With open adoption, the birth mother selects the parents she wants for her baby. Adoptive parents prepare a portfolio, including a photo album of their lives and a "Dear Birth Mother" letter. I jokingly referred to it as our sales brochure. The agency showed us examples of portfolios used by parents who had been selected and had already adopted with the agency. I noted prospective parents included photos of pets, their home, and their families. We did the same, including photos of gatherings at our home, the children of friends who we adored, and our cat, Chuck. I might even have thrown in photos of friends' puppies for an extra measure of cute and cuddly.

We went to the office store to find stationery for the "Dear Birth Mother" letter. I was leaning towards a corporate, tasteful look when it dawned on me: the letter wasn't a business letter. It was likely going to be read by a young woman, probably a teenager. I asked myself, *What would*

I have liked when I was a teenager? So our stationery featured a rainbow on a pastel background.

By the time the required weekend adoption workshop came up, I balked at going. I was exhausted. I just didn't feel up to jumping through any more hoops. After four pregnancies in two years, I was feeling worn out. But I knew I had to go, and from the moment the first program began, I was hooked.

The first evening involved a panel of parents who had adopted babies through the agency we were working with. These parents had their babies with them and talked about how open their adoption arrangements were. One couple met regularly with their birth mom. Another had sporadic in-person meetings, and the third kept in touch through letters and photographs.

Mostly the message was clear: the adoptive parents were over-the-moon happy.

The next day, one panel featured a group of grown adoptive children. None had been adopted during the open adoption era, so their stories were painful, and in the case of one older man, it involved an emotionally searing search for his roots.

Throughout the weekend, and later, I would learn that studies show adoptive children need the story of their birth families. The bad old days of ushering newborn infants out of the arms of their biological mothers and placing them with adoptive parents, with birth families never knowing where or how the child was, did enormous emotional damage to all involved.

Thankfully, open adoption ended all that. The workshops also emphasized that children were no longer "given up" but "placed" for adoption. Birth mothers were not choosing to abandon children; they were finding a home prepared to love and care for the child. Far from turning their backs on their babies, the act of placing a child for adoption was a selfless act, one filled with courage and sacrifice.

At the conclusion of the workshop, we felt more confident than ever that adoption was the right thing to do. The agency told us that as soon as we got our paperwork in and we were approved, we could expect to get a call soon. There was no waiting list; birth mothers simply looked through available portfolios of those prospective families that matched their situation and picked.

They weren't exaggerating. Within a few weeks of completing the paperwork, we got a call. A young woman had just given birth to a child who was the product of a rape. Were we interested in having her see our portfolio?

Bill had a few questions about what was known of the rape. Was the biological father a violent criminal? A relative? What were the circumstances? After we learned what we could, we said yes!

We allowed ourselves to get excited and even think about names. But within a day, we were told the mother had decided to keep the child. We felt a letdown, but we were optimistic about our overall chances.

Soon we got another call. A birth mother had picked us! Within a day, we met with the birth mother and her other small children. The meeting went well enough, but the circumstances were tricky. She was married, but she and her husband had separated. She had gotten pregnant from another relationship, but then she and her husband reconciled.

The birth mom wanted to have the most open of adoptions, where we would spend all holidays together, including the baby's birthday and those of its siblings. The only obstacle was that her husband detested the idea of this new baby. This was made clear. He wanted nothing to do with the child.

We left feeling uneasy about the birth mother's requirements. Agency workers had told us that finding the right birth mother was not unlike finding a romantic partner. "You know when it's right," we were told.

Nothing about this scenario seemed even remotely right. The adoptive child would no doubt feel the wrath of the husband with every get-together. What harm would this do to a child's sense of self-esteem and well-being? We spent a restless night debating the pros and cons of the scenario.

Something didn't feel right. Agency workers had told us to rely on our gut. We did. We finally concluded we would be thrilled to have the birth mother's baby placed with us. But we would have to keep the adoption fairly closed and minimize in-person contact until such time as it seemed to be a good idea.

The birth mother decided against us.

MEANWHILE, AS PART of going forward with adoption, we were required to stop efforts to get pregnant. We had put those efforts on hold. We had already discussed the possibility of one more IVF with the clinic in Seattle. But that was it; four first-trimester miscarriages in two years was enough.

We figured we'd try one more time, then go back to adoption. I'm not sure what conversations we had with the adoption agency because I was too busy getting shot up and run through the mill of reproductive medicine.

What I do remember clearly is that everything went smoothly. We arrived in Seattle and went through the so-called egg extraction and were in our hotel room when the doctor called. It was the middle of the day. He told us how many viable embryos we had in the lab, maybe two or three; I don't recall. But our choice was simple: put back in either one or two. That was it.

We had to decide then and there. For some reason, the choice seemed more ominous than before. Perhaps it's because we knew it was the last time we would try this.

Bill and I put aside the receiver and talked. We knew this call was coming, we knew this choice was coming, we knew we couldn't keep the doctor waiting.

The issue boiled down to whether or not we wanted to risk having twins. Could we handle twins? We went back and forth on this.

The TV in the room was playing *Butch Cassidy & the Sundance Kid*. It was the scene where Paul Newman and Robert Redford are cornered by the posse on a ledge high above a river below. It goes like this:

"I'll jump first," says Newman.

"Nope," says Redford.

"Then you jump first," says Newman.

"No, I said," says Redford.

"What's the matter with you?" asks Newman.

"I can't swim," yells Redford.

"Why, you crazy," says Newman, laughing. "The fall'll probably kill ya!"

I was watching this scene when we decided to go with two.

As Bill turned to tell the doctor on the phone, I watched as Butch and Sundance fell down, down, down to the river below.

About a month and a half later, we were back in Anchorage. On a

Monday, our dear friend Lynette was in town and came by for a visit.

Lynette is one of the loveliest people I know. I met her through her work as a producing director at Perseverance Theatre in Juneau. Beloved by all who know her, she comes from a large, close-knit Anchorage family with parents who had long been involved in civic and cultural affairs. In recent years, Lynette had begun devoting herself to spiritual pursuits and helping others by studying dreams and the effects of a positive attitude. She even wrote and published a book, *The 10 Be's of Positivity: 10 Steps To A More Positive Way of Living*.

Lynette is the person you want around under any circumstances, but she's especially the person you want by your side when times are tough. She is the one you want next to you when facing a difficult task or taking on a new challenge; she's the one you want in the seat next to you when the plane hits a bad patch of turbulence. She's the one you want there, at your house, spending the afternoon with you if you think, believe, worry, fear that you are about to miscarry.

I had some light bleeding and cramping and not-so-light anxiety.

Unlike Lynette, I tended to be more cynical, maybe pragmatic, and ignored the more esoteric sides of life. That's not to say I have no faith. I do. On the spectrum of spiritual beliefs, my faith falls somewhere between my Catholic baptism and introduction to the faith with my mother's family and my early teen experience with the "Jesus people" movement. I also learned of faith from my later teen exploration of Eastern religions and my adult quest to connect with my Jewish ancestors and faith. I have been known to pray, and pray I did that day, and then Lynette showed up.

We talked about her book and spiritual studies and dreams, angels and the power of positive thinking and being happy. Here's the thing. When I look back to that day, I see Lynette not so much as an earthly being—my friend—but as some kind of modern-day angel, there on a mission.

You will, too, when I tell you what happened.

THE NEXT DAY, Tuesday, I had a late-morning appointment with my new obstetrician, whose staff kindly squeezed me in after a weekend of frantic calls. The cramping and light bleeding had me panicked, and I think I called about thirty-two times. Okay, just a dozen, but I'm pretty sure my image went up on some doctor warning list: "Do not deal with this patient—she will drive you nuts!" By that Tuesday morning, I was almost surprised that my doctor's office hadn't called to tell me to find another physician.

Bill went into work then came home to pick me up for the drive to the obstetrician's office. On the drive, he gave me the news: there was a message from the adoption agency. We had been picked by a birth mother.

And there was more. *A big* more, the biggest more in the history of big mores.

The baby. A girl. Had been born *that morning* around six.

Allow me to repeat: the baby was BORN and healthy and at the hospital and was ours.

All ours.

The baby.

A healthy seven-and-a-half-pound girl.

Did you catch that? Because I'm pretty sure Bill had to repeat it twice, maybe three times or more. All I know is we both felt like driving to the hospital where the baby had been born *right then.*

We talked briefly about how we had never imagined such an adoption scenario. The Hollywood version of open adoption usually has the birth mom going through her pregnancy with the adoptive parents, who are there when the baby is born. I said I was sad to have missed that.

"Not me," said Bill. "The anxiety would have killed me, worrying about whether the mother would change her mind."

He was right. One of the staff at the adoption agency had said that more adoptions were last minute than the other way around.

"This is perfect," Bill said. "I like having the baby already here."

It was July 9, 2002.

WHEN WE GOT to our doctor's office, we announced the news. The doctor decided to do an ultrasound to check my pregnancy, which now was about the farthest thing from my mind. Bill and I, a nurse, and the doctor were all in the exam room for the ultrasound.

You could have brought in a high school marching band and I don't think it could have drowned out the sound we were all waiting for: a heartbeat of a seven-to-eight-week-old fetus. There it was—a steady, strong 90–110 beats per minute, *thump, thump, thumping* along.

A baby? Plus the baby waiting for us at the hospital? We were going to have twins!

"What's that dark spot over there?" Bill asked, pointing to a corner of the monitor screen.

"Let's take a look," my doctor said.

As he moved the wand, he said something about how it might be the cause of the bleeding I'd had. But then suddenly, like a Vegas marquee, we all saw the outline of... could it be? Then we heard it, a second heartbeat.

Another heartbeat. That made two.

And the baby at the hospital made... three. Could we actually be looking at the prospect of having three babies? Three?! Triplets?

I don't remember what I said next. I've joked over the years that I went into shock and have yet to come out. What I do remember was what Bill said: "They were meant to be together."

THE DOCTORS AT the clinic in Seattle had said getting pregnant with twins meant—and I never asked why—the pregnancy was viable.

It's a go. We are good for lift-off, Houston.

After the appointment, Bill called the adoption agency to tell them we were expecting twins but would still like to go forward with the adoption. They said they would tell the birth mom about my pregnancy and ask what she wanted to do. We didn't have to wait long. She thought about it, talked to her family, and called the agency back.

"I want her to have siblings," she said.

THE NEXT DAY, we met with Jessica, our birth mom. We went to her hospital room on the maternity ward accompanied by a staffer from the adoption agency. I took one look at her and knew she was our birth mom. I just knew it. She was sitting in a chair and smiling, with dark brown hair—like me—and wearing eyeglasses—like me.

It felt as if we were visiting an old friend in the hospital. We felt an instant connection, derived from her choice of us out of all the adoptive parent portfolios and our long wait for her. At one point, I asked what made her pick us.

"You both have higher education," she said.

You mean it wasn't the rainbow-covered letterhead of our "Dear

Birth Mother" letter or the photos of fluffy kittens? Higher education. I liked that.

Jessica had chosen a name for our daughter: Charlotte. Perfect, Bill and I said. Not only did we like it, but it seemed right that the name came from her birth mom. We gave Charlotte my mom's name as her middle name, and she became Charlotte Frances.

The following day, we brought Charlotte home from the hospital after first going over some basic baby care instructions—diapering, feeding, and so on. It's funny, but despite years of anticipating this, we never thought to practice.

The day we got Charlotte was my grandfather's ninetieth birthday. Weeks earlier, we had planned a large gathering at the facility where he lived. We had ordered a big birthday cake, balloons, party napkins, and gifts, and several friends were invited. We couldn't cancel it, so we went straight from the hospital to the nursing home.

My grandfather and other residents were already there, sitting in chairs visiting while music played in the background. We brought Charlotte up to my grandfather.

"Grandpa, we got a baby!" I told him. I'm not sure how much of the particulars he was able to absorb, as his dementia was fairly advanced.

I held Charlotte up and then placed her in his arms. "This is your great-granddaughter, Charlotte," I said.

"It's about time," he replied.

Indeed.

As our other friends arrived, they realized that we had a baby with us, and the birthday party took on a larger significance.

AFTER THE PARTY was over, we took Charlotte home. That night, since I was officially pregnant, Bill did the night feedings. I went to bed, and he slept in our family room.

Sleep came easily, though I found it hard to be away from Charlotte. At some point in the middle of the night, I heard her crying. Bill was doing his best to feed and calm her, but she kept crying. I took her and her bottle, sat in a rocking chair we had bought in anticipation of parenthood, and slowly began to rock her. She stopped crying almost immediately. I figured it might have been that I looked like her birth mom, or that I sang to her, or that I was just better at it, or she was more tired. But she took her bottle and eventually fell asleep. I continued to rock her for a long time before I started to fall asleep myself. I gave her back to Bill and went to bed.

I awoke early with a start. I felt like a little kid on Christmas morning. I jumped out of bed and rushed to see the baby. Our baby. Charlotte.

I paused in the doorway. Bill was in a deep sleep with Charlotte curled up next to him on the couch. I stood there for a while just staring, almost in disbelief. We had a baby. She was ours.

While there was a ten-day waiting period during which Jessica could change her mind, I knew she wouldn't. I just knew.

After that first night, we all slept together in our king-sized bed. We'd put Charlotte in the middle to fall asleep before later transferring her to a bassinette next to the bed. For nights on end, there'd be Bill and me, with Charlotte asleep between us, going over books on baby care and infant development. We'd both read, then stop to share something we'd just learned.

One night Bill looked at me and said, "Do you think she'll ever know what she means to us?"

WE FELT CONFIDENT we could handle three babies once the twins came. We had read that by six months old, Charlotte could hold her own bottle. This developmental milestone seemed huge to us.

My pregnancy advanced pretty normally. I won't say we didn't worry and wonder at all how we were going to handle it all once the twins arrived. We made plans to hire help initially, as we had been told to, so that the babies would always have someone to hold them. Bill's family had a condo nearby and were there to help out, too. Many of my friends promised to help, and family members planned visits for after the twins were born.

As any new parent knows, those early days with a new baby are unlike any prior experience. At one month, we got together with Jessica. I struggled to find the words to describe how in love I felt with Charlotte. The adoption staff, who were there, just smiled as I babbled on and on about how I felt—a love like no other. I could not stand to be away from Charlotte; I just wanted to hold her and look at her and play with her. I wasn't even deterred—not too much, anyway—when I realized all three babies would be in diapers for up to three years.

On the right is a picture of me with five-month-old Charlotte on Christmas Morning, 2002. We got Charlotte a fur parka much like the same parka my parents had gotten me for my first Christmas (shown above). Both parkas were from the same furrier, David Green Master Furrier.

Three years?! I thought when I learned this. I thought about it for a moment. Okay. I didn't care. I didn't care that my once neat and tidy house looked like a hurricane had blown through it in the immediate days, weeks, and months following Charlotte's birth. I didn't care.

As my pregnancy progressed, people would often stop and stare at Charlotte and me. Some said things like, "Is that your baby? And you're pregnant?!" I'd explain the story, and I'd hear a lot of, "You're going to have your hands full!" No matter how many times I tried to explain the confluence of events that led us to having three babies almost at once people still got the story wrong. "They adopted, *then* they got pregnant with twins," they'd tell others. This affirmed the belief that all anyone with infertility had to do was relax and let nature take its course. I gave up trying to explain that often those who want children work both options. Sometimes people's reactions seemed to say the joke was on us, as if we'd only known. Now we were stuck with three. Poor us.

Hardly.

But you know that. This is a happy ending.

On February 5, 2003, six months after Charlotte was born, the twins were delivered by Caesarean section at thirty-six weeks into my pregnancy. We named them Kristan Jane and Mary Shannan, names we took from both sides of our respective families.

The girls sit atop our kitchen counter in Anchorage. From left to right: Kristan, Mary, and Charlotte.
(Photo taken by professional photographer Janna Maile, of Photo Arts by Janna)

I can tell you there is no difference between the love for an adopted child and a biological one. I can tell you that the love for each is so overwhelming and so powerful that I cannot adequately describe it.

What happened to us felt like nothing short of a miracle. An editor friend at the *Anchorage Daily News* said of our good baby fortune, "It's as if your love is so strong it drew three babies into your lives."

I always liked that. I won't say it wasn't nuts at times or hard at others. Three babies, practically triplets? Of course it was hard. But it was happy. I was happy. Deliriously happy. I never wanted to be apart from any of them, and I wrote and taught and did whatever it was I could do when they napped.

MORE THAN A decade has passed. My daughters are now teenagers. The twins are thirteen, and Charlotte is fourteen. For six months out of each year, all three are the same age, though Charlotte is one year ahead in school. To me, they are perfect. Athletic, smart, fun, warm, friendly, outgoing, adventurous, beautiful, and, for now, not too into boys. Well, not as much as I fear.

I think a lot about what I was like at their age, what I dreamed about, hoped for, and mostly what I did. My entire parenting perspective has shifted from taking care of little ones to preparing them for the world they will enter on their own in just a few short years. Like many parents, I rarely feel up to the task. It seems the more experience I gain as a parent, the less I seem to know.

I do know this. There are two times children most need their parents: the first three years and during adolescence. I don't know exactly where I got that idea, but it makes sense. Children go through the greatest number of changes and growth during both of these phases of their lives.

Raising toddlers was easy and fun. I could dress them in matching outfits, take them to Toys 'R' Us for entertainment, or to a petting zoo, or even into the backyard with Big Wheels. Everything was okay. I was the best parent, or so they thought. Plus, because I worked at home, I could nap with them. Sleep. Something that has been mostly in short supply since their birth.

But now that they're older, parenting is much, much harder. Like most moms, I embarrass my girls. They laugh at my music. They gag when I dance. They cringe when I talk to their friends. They look at each other knowingly when I try to lecture them, as in, "Mom, you are so stupid!"

In other words, everything is as it should be.

Family life isn't always easy. My life, my marriage, my relationships have had their challenges. We have battled a variety of demons on many fronts.

But as I think about the years ahead, I find myself looking back on my own past. How did I get to become the mom who allows everyone to hang out at our house? (I've always loved parties.) I love to dance. (My mom was an exotic dancer when she was pregnant with me.) I still decorate the house for every holiday (I am creative), and I teach them to question their assumptions about everything (I am a journalist). I love music and athletics (both of which have accompanied me through many adventures).

Then it dawned on me. I needed to tell my daughters my story—or as much as I'm willing to reveal—and try to save them from some but never all of my own mistakes. If that's not possible, at least I could offer some insights into why I am who I am.

I learned about love the hard way. I am the product of two flawed but ultimately loving people. My childhood was a series of misadventures

Easter Sunday, 2017. The girls are on our backyard deck, built around a giant live oak tree, at our home in Lafayette, Louisiana. From left to right: Kristan, Mary, and Charlotte. (Photo by Karley Nugent)

and near misses, of struggle and self-reliance and sometimes even danger. From an orphaned child to a wandering teen to an established writer, somehow I had the good fortune to start with love and find loving people along my way. After all that, I was finally given three little girls to give me the most love I have ever known.

The feeling of wanting to belong, of wanting to recapture the love lost when my parents died, went away with the birth of my three daughters. I finally knew where I belonged—with them.

Our lives are filled with all the chaos and drama, laughter and sweetness that comes with that package. Squeezed into the daily instructions in how to behave, how to dress, how to treat others, I'm trying to make them understand how I became their mother.

How I found my normal life.

Acknowledgments

This book would not have been possible without the dedication of everyone at Graphic Arts Books/Alaska Northwest Books. Not only have they kept *Johnny's Girl* in print all these years, they enthusiastically embraced *A Normal Life*.

I want to thank Douglas Pfeiffer, who before retiring always offered his support for my work. I also want to thank Mark Ouimet for his important commitment to this project.

I also wish to acknowledge the hard work and calming influence of Jennifer Newens, publishing director at Graphic Arts Books. Editor Olivia Ngai's talent and critical eye for details made all things seem possible. Finally, I cannot thank Rachel Lopez Metzger enough for her gorgeous design and artwork on this book.

Nobody worked harder than Carol Sturgulewski, my editor on the book. I've always admired Carol's work from our days as reporters at competing newspapers. I enjoyed her company more over the years as fellow writers at book conferences. Despite experiencing different childhoods in Alaska, Carol understood everything I was trying to say in this book because she, too, had either lived it or experienced or instinctively knew it.

Her commitment to detail and prose was and is as valuable to me as her friendship and camaraderie.

I also wish to thank Karley Nugent and John Baker for their contributions to this book.

This book picks up where *Johnny's Girl* leaves off. The list of others who helped me survive and get through the initial years after my father's murder is long. Despite the dark side of the latter experience, I learned that the world is an equally bright place, full of good people.

I wrote this book in part for my generation, those of us who came of age in the 1970s. To my friends and classmates. If my memories here are exactly yours, bear with—but what's in my heart remains the same. I love you all.

I may have lost my family to tragedies, but I gained so much more from the generosity of a handful of families in Alaska and Arizona who opened their doors to me as a teenager and throughout my life.

I also want to thank my father's friends who stood by in case I needed them but knew that I was determined to find my own life. To my mother's family, thanks for believing me when I said I was "fine," thus allowing me to thrive on my own terms.

With the State of Alaska, which took custody of me as an orphan, lawyer Robert Wagstaff, and others, I was able to build a bridge between my childhood and adulthood in safety and security.

I WILL ALSO be grateful to the Anchorage Daily News, now the Alaska Dispatch News, for all the wonderful years I had working there. I still think it was the greatest job I'll ever have and I miss all of you and the newsroom every single day.

This book is also testament to my high school teachers at East High and Steller Secondary Alternative and, later, the University of Alaska, which both stood by me and challenged me. Thank you for your support and for failing me when I deserved it, which only made me work harder.

My teachers were true heroes.

This includes my mentors and professors at the Writing Division at the School of the Arts at Columbia University in the City of New

York. There I met lifelong friends and colleagues and saw many dreams come true. No experience means more to me than my time in the writing program and the friends I met there.

My film career began with writer and director with John Kent Harrison, who taught me screenwriting and many life lessons.

Dave Hunsaker has never failed to support me and my work, who along with his wife, Annie Calkins, have always welcomed me into their home.

Finally, this book is for Mike Wise, my longtime film agent. Mike stuck by me for years, always making time to meet when I was in Los Angeles. When I told Mike I wanted to be a mom and feared he'd think I'd stop working, he simply said, "Doubt it."

I'll always miss Mike's sense of humor and how he insisted on having lunch with my girls when they were babies and older.

Finally, I owe the greatest amount of gratitude to my oldest daughter's courageous, wise, and wonderful birth family. No words can ever adequately convey the love I feel for all of you and the depth of our connection. The circumstances that brought all of us together—my husband, Bill, and the twins, Kristan and Mary, and Charlotte—is nothing short of a miracle.

We are family.

CPSIA information can be obtained
at www.ICGtesting.com
Printed in the USA
BVHW07s2036250518
517462BV00004B/6/P